KEY CONCEPTS IN SECOND LANGUAGE ACQUISITION

Palgrave Key Concepts

Palgrave Key Concepts provide an accessible and comprehensive range of subject glossaries at undergraduate level. They are the ideal companion to a standard textbook making them invaluable reading to students throughout their course of study and especially useful as a revision aid.

Key Concepts in Accounting and Finance
Key Concepts in Bilingualism
Key Concepts in Business and Management Research Methods
Key Concepts in Business Practice
Key Concepts in Criminology and Criminal Justice
Key Concepts in Cultural Studies
Key Concepts in Drama and Performance (second edition)
Key Concepts in e-Commerce
Key Concepts in Human Resource Management
Key Concepts in Information and Communication Technology
Key Concepts in Innovation
Key Concepts in International Business
Key Concepts in Language and Linguistics (second edition)
Key Concepts in Law (second edition)
Key Concepts in Leisure
Key Concepts in Management
Key Concepts in Marketing
Key Concepts in Operations Management
Key Concepts in Philosophy
Key Concepts in Politics
Key Concepts in Public Relations
Key Concepts in Psychology
Key Concepts in Second Language Acquisition
Key Concepts in Social Research Methods
Key Concepts in Sociology
Key Concepts in Strategic Management
Key Concepts in Tourism

Palgrave Key Concepts: Literature
General Editor: Martin Coyle

Key Concepts in Contemporary Literature
Key Concepts in Creative Writing
Key Concepts in Crime Fiction
Key Concepts in Medieval Literature
Key Concepts in Modernist Literature
Key Concepts in Postcolonial Literature
Key Concepts in Renaissance Literature
Key Concepts in Romantic Literature
Key Concepts in Victorian Literature
Literary Terms and Criticism (third edition)

Further titles are in preparation
www.palgravekeyconcepts.com

Palgrave Key Concepts
Series Standing Order
ISBN 1–4039–3210–7
(*outside North America only*)

You can receive future titles in this series as they are published by placing a standing order. Please contact your bookseller or, in the case of difficulty, write to us at the address below with your name and address, the title of the series and the ISBN quoted above.

Customer Services Department, Macmillan Distribution Ltd
Houndmills, Basingstoke, Hampshire RG21 6XS, England, UK

Key Concepts in Second Language Acquisition

Shawn Loewen and Hayo Reinders

First published 2011 by
PALGRAVE MACMILLAN

Palgrave Macmillan in the UK is an imprint of Macmillan Publishers Limited, registered in England, company number 785998, of Houndmills, Basingstoke, Hampshire RG21 6XS.

Palgrave Macmillan in the US is a division of St Martin's Press LLC, 175 Fifth Avenue, New York, NY 10010.

Palgrave Macmillan is the global academic imprint of the above companies and has companies and representatives throughout the world.

Palgrave® and Macmillan® are registered trademarks in the United States, the United Kingdom, Europe and other countries.

ISBN 978–0–230–23018–7

This book is printed on paper suitable for recycling and made from fully managed and sustained forest sources. Logging, pulping and manufacturing processes are expected to conform to the environmental regulations of the country of origin.

A catalogue record for this book is available from the British Library.

A catalog record for this book is available from the Library of Congress.

10 9 8 7 6 5 4 3 2 1
20 19 18 17 16 15 14 13 12 11

Printed and bound in Great Britain by
CPI Antony Rowe, Chippenham and Eastbourne

Shawn Loewen:

To Pamela Loewen: for your tremendous love, support and sacrifice
To Austin, Patrick and Winona Loewen: for reminding me that life goes on

Hayo Reinders:

To Youn Soo Kim: Little Flying ...
And to all you SLA-geeks out there

Contents

List of Illustrations

Figures

Tables

List of Abbreviations

ESL   English as a second language
L1   first language
L2   second language
SLA   second language acquisition
UG   universal grammar

Acknowledgements

We would like to thank Min Young Cho, Erin Sutton and Solène Inceoglu for their valuable help in preparing this book. We would also like to thank the anonymous reviewers for their suggestions and insightful comments. In addition, we would like to acknowledge several reference books that were invaluable in preparing the entries in this book and which we would recommend for more in-depth discussion of the field of Second Language Acquisition. Two books in particular are Gass and Selinker's (2008, third edition) *Second Language Acquisition* and Ellis's (2008) *The Study of Second Language Acquisition.*

SHAWN LOEWEN
HAYO REINDERS

The authors and publishers wish to thank the following for permission to use copyright material: Cambridge University Press for Table 3, from Mackey, A., Input, interaction and second language development: an empirical study of question formation in ESL, in *Studies in Second Language Acquisition*, Vol. 21, p. 567, © Cambridge University Press 1999, and for Figure 8, from VanPatten, B. and Caldierno, T., Explicit Instruction and Input Processing, in *Studies in Second Language Acquisition*, Vol. 15. © Cambridge University Press 1993; Elsevier Limited and Copyright Clearance Center for Figure 1 from Lim, J., 'Method sections of management research articles: a pedagogically motivated qualitative study', in *English for Specific Purposes*, Vol. 25, © Elsevier 2006; Elsevier Limited for Figure 4, from Ellis, R., A theory of instructed second language acquisition, in Ellis, N.C. (ed.): *Implicit and Explicit Learning of Languages*, © San Diego, Academic Press 1994; Stephen Krashen for Figures 1 and 6, from Krashen, S., *Principles and Practice in Second Language Acquisition*, © Pergamon Press 1982; The MIT Press for Figure 5, from Levelt, Willem J.M., *Speaking: From Intention to Articulation*, Figure 1.1, page 9, © Massachusetts Institute of Technology 1989; Oxford University Press and Copyright Clearance Center for Figure 3, from Mohamed, N., 'Consciousness-raising tasks: a learner perspective, in *ELT Journal* Vol. 58, p. 236, © Oxford University Press 2004; Wiley-Blackwell for Figure 9, from MacIntyre, P, Clément, R, Dörnyei, Z. and Noels, K., 'Conceptualizing willingness to communicate in a L2: A situational model of L2 confidence and affiliation', in *Modern Language Journal*, Vol. 82, © Wiley Blackwell 1998; Every effort has been made to trace all the copyright-holders, but if any have been inadvertently overlooked the authors and publishers will be pleased to make the necessary arrangements at the first opportunity.

Introduction

What is second language acquisition and why do we need a key concept book about it? The study of second language acquisition (SLA) has become an area of academic study in its own right over the last several decades. It is housed, so to speak, within the larger discipline of applied linguistics, which in turn can be viewed as a specialized area of linguistics. However, while linguistics is primarily concerned with describing language and explaining first language acquisition, applied linguistics is more concerned with the practical applications of language in society. One of those practical applications is how people go about learning a language other than their first one. While it is possible that much of the early research into second language learning was primarily concerned with pedagogical applications, over the decades SLA research has not focused only on classroom applications, but it has also begun to try to explain the processes of SLA without necessarily considering the implications for classroom teaching. This formalization of SLA as an academic discipline has coincided (perhaps not accidentally) with the growth of the second language industry. While people have been learning second languages throughout history, there are now considerable economic resources expended to teach additional languages throughout the world. This economic reality has further increased the number of people who are concerned with teaching second languages and studying the science of SLA. Thus, the need for a book that provides a basic entry into the world of SLA.

Before getting into the details of SLA, it is important to consider its parameters. We would like to do that by considering each of the terms in turn. Although the official name of the discipline is 'second' language acquisition, it is generally acknowledged that this term refers to any language that a person learns after his or her first language. There is general agreement that people begin learning their first language, without much difficulty, from birth. In contexts where only one language is spoken, there is very little controversy over what is a first language. ('First language' has also been referred to as 'mother tongue', 'native language', 'primary language', etc.) However, the situation is more complex in multilingual settings where a child might grow up learning two languages simultaneously. Additionally some people may learn one language at birth but then become dominant in a different language. The general consensus, though, is that in most contexts it is clear what a person's first language is. Therefore, the next language that is learned, if any at all, is considered the second language. However, people are not limited to learning just a second language, they may learn a third, fourth or potentially greater number of languages. Sometimes these are called third or fourth languages (and there are studies of trilingual acquisition or multilingual acquisition), but often they are also called 'second' languages as well. Sometimes the term 'additional language acquisition' is used to avoid referring to any order of acquisition after the first language. However, such terminology has not gained popularity, and the field has been and continues to be called 'second language acquisition', even though SLA researchers acknowledge that the term applies to more than just the chronological second language.

The next term to consider is 'language'. Again, at first glance this term seems straightforward, as every person speaks a language and most individuals can name several of the world's major languages. However, when we look more closely, we find that the definition of 'language' is somewhat more problematic. The field of linguistics includes the study of grammar (morphology/syntax), vocabulary (lexis/semantics) and pronunciation (phonology), but more recently other areas have been added, such as pragmatics, which investigates how people use language to accomplish various things, such as making requests, apologizing, etc. In addition, pragmatics is concerned with how people express politeness and how different styles of language can be used in different social contexts. Another aspect of language has been called discourse, and this area is concerned with how language is used to structure texts, such as stories or expository essays, that are longer than a sentence. Clearly, the definition of language and its use is not clearly defined. This is even more so if we take into account language variation. If we take English as an example, it might seem fairly straightforward if we say someone is learning English as a second language. However, there are different types of English (these are often called dialects), some of which are regional. For instances, learners may want to learn British English or American English, depending on where they live. There are also different varieties of English in Canada, Australia, New Zealand, India, etc. In most cases, one variety of English is normally understood by speakers of other varieties, but there are abundant opportunities for misunderstanding. Just ask any speaker of British English who has asked for a rubber (eraser) in America, or an American speaker who has referred to their fanny pack (bum bag) in New Zealand.

In addition to regional variation in a language, there is also social variation, and sometimes there are social judgements that are attached to these varieties. So for example, a 'standard language' refers to a variety of language that is viewed as a socially prestigious form of that language. However, linguistics views non-standard varieties of languages to be just as valid and systematic, linguistically, as standard varieties; nevertheless, linguists recognize that non-standard varieties may be viewed as socially inferior by the wider society. In spite of societal values, learners of a second language may wish to learn a non-standard variety of a language, if that is the primary language that is spoken in their social context. Finally, there are political distinctions that are made in regard to what is considered a language. Languages such as Norwegian, Swedish and Danish, or Hindi and Urdu, or Serbian and Croatian are largely mutually intelligible, but they have been determined to be 'languages' for political or cultural reasons. In contrast, languages such as Mandarin, Cantonese and Hakka are all referred to as Chinese, even though they are not mutually intelligible. As can be seen from the above discussion, the term 'language' in SLA is more complex than one might first think.

Finally we come to the term 'acquisition'. What does it mean to acquire a language? First, we might want to make a distinction between being able to use a second language for communication or being able to describe the rules for that language. Some SLA researchers have referred to this distinction as the difference between acquisition and learning; however, this distinction is not universally agreed on in SLA. Another issue to consider is how much of the language is needed to say that acquisition has taken place. It is generally agreed that the majority of second language learners do not achieve native-like proficiency in their second language.

But what level of mastery is necessary to say that a language has been acquired? There is no agreement regarding this question, and indeed some SLA researchers prefer the term 'development' rather than 'acquisition'.

This book, then, provides an opportunity to consider these issues as we present some of the most important concepts in the study of SLA. The scope of the book includes important terms and ideas related to SLA; however, it is important to specify the decisions that we have made regarding which terms to include or exclude. Any terms that are unique to SLA are obviously included. Terms and theories from other disciplines, such as education or linguistics, have also been included if they have been influential in SLA (e.g. Sociocultural Theory or Universal Grammar), and we give their definitions as they are used within the field of SLA. In some cases, a term might have a (slightly) different meaning in other fields. We have also included terms that relate to SLA research practices.

On the other hand, we have excluded terms that are primarily sociolinguistic or linguistic in nature and that do not relate directly to L2 learning. We also do not include grammar explanations, nor terms that are only related to teaching methodologies. Although we have tried to be principled in our selection of terms, in some cases judgements were made based on our own experiences as SLA researchers. As a result, there may be terms that were omitted that others feel should have been included. In contrast, there may also be terms that are included that others feel are peripheral. Nevertheless, in the end we feel that we have presented comprehensive coverage of the key concepts in SLA.

Several other comments about the structure of the book are in order. We realize that a book such as this one can provide only an introduction to the most important concepts in the field. Therefore, we have included numerous references to published work in the various entries for readers who wish to find out more information. There are several criteria that were used in choosing these references. In many cases, the number of published studies on a specific topic is overwhelming; therefore, one or two representative articles were chosen. These articles were sometimes chosen because they have been very influential in shaping thinking about the topic under consideration, sometimes because they represent the latest research on a specific topic. Another factor that was considered was the availability of the references. We tried to pick articles from the top SLA journals, such as *Language Learning*, *Studies in Second Language Acquisition*, *The Modern Language Journal*, *TESOL Quarterly* and *Language Teaching Research*, because they represent the best work that is being done in SLA. In addition, these are journals that are commonly available in university libraries, and can therefore most likely be accessed by readers who are interested in following up on a topic. Finally, we also chose some references that are relatively old or not easily accessible, but that represent some of the most influential thinking on that topic. Often these are works that may have first proposed the topic under consideration. Thus, though these are works that are less likely to be accessed easily, we felt that readers should nevertheless be aware of them.

There are often pairs or groups of words that are related but have separate entries. Examples include: implicit and explicit knowledge, implicit and explicit instruction, positive and negative evidence, multiple types of learning strategies and multiple types of motivation. In these cases, we have cross-referenced the related topics, but we have listed key references under only one of the entries in order to avoid duplication. For example, a reference that investigates both implicit and explicit knowledge will be placed under just one of the entries. Thus, it is important for readers to follow the cross-references for a fuller understanding of the topic. We have not included entries for specific researchers and theorists in the field of SLA; however, we have mentioned individuals who are associated with specific concepts mentioned in the book.

It is our hope that you will find this book helpful, whether as a student, a teacher or a researcher (or more likely, all three!). SLA is a dynamic and fascinating field and we hope that by giving you a clear understanding of its key concepts, you will more fully be able to enjoy contributing to its development.

Academic language

In SLA, researchers and teachers often refer to different types of language. There are several different ways of categorizing language, including the frequency with which words are used and the contexts in which they occur. Academic language is the type of language that occurs more frequently in higher education settings. Although academic language occurs in most languages used in higher education, the use of English has received the most extensive investigation in SLA, given the international role of English in education.

One area in which academic language differs from other types of language is in its vocabulary. Although academic words are not confined to academic contexts, they do occur more frequently in educational lectures and textbooks than they do in general usage. The interest in academic vocabulary is due to the fact that many L2 learners are studying the target language in order to go to university. Therefore, if L2 learners can identify and learn the words that are commonly used in academic contexts, they will be able to focus their attention on vocabulary that will help them the most in their studies. There are several published lists of academic English vocabulary, such as the Academic Word List and the University Word List, which contain approximately 800 academic words that have been found to occur frequently in most academic texts, regardless of their specific field. An example of the first 15 words from Coxhead's (2000) Academic Word List are shown below:

abandon	abstract	academy	access	accommodate
accompany	accumulate	accurate	achieve	acknowledge
acquire	adapt	adequate	adjacent	adjust

In addition to vocabulary, there are also specific types of grammatical structures that are used more frequently in academic contexts. For example, Lim (2006) investigated the methodology sections of management research articles and found several identifiable patterns. One such pattern was the use of SPO, standing for Subject (nominative noun phrase relating to items in the instrument), Predicator (procedural verb relating to measurement) and Object (variable to be measured). Examples of this pattern are shown in Table 1.

Academic language is often taught in institutions of higher education as a specific area. Although the focus of such courses is often on non-native speakers, it has been found that native speakers may also have difficulty with academic language.

See also **genre and vocabulary.**

Coxhead, A. (2000) 'A new academic word list', *TESOL Quarterly*, 34, 213–38.
Lim, J. (2006) 'Method sections of management research articles: a pedagogically motivated qualitative study', *English for Specific Purposes*, 25, 282–309.

Table 1 Instances of SPO structure

S	P	O
Two items in this survey	measured	satisfaction with the appraisal review
Five items	assessed	the extent to which an employee has a tendency to make excuses for absences
Each item	identified	a task (for instance, conducting meetings, changing the work process, determining overall business strategy)

Source: Lim (2006: 293).

Acceptability judgement task

Acceptability judgement tasks involve either L1 or L2 speakers evaluating the extent to which a specific segment of either written or oral language matches the rules of the target language. Areas of language that have been investigated include grammar, pragmatics and, to a lesser extent, vocabulary. One of the purposes of having L2 learners make acceptability judgements is to investigate how closely their knowledge of the L2 is similar to that of L1 speakers. Conversely, L1 speakers are asked to make acceptability judgements in order to establish a baseline of the ways in which the target language is used by its native speakers. There are several options in the design of acceptability judgement tasks. One option involves participants making dichotomous decisions by judging whether sentences are either acceptable or unacceptable. Alternatively, participants may be asked to rate each sentence on a continuum from more acceptable to less acceptable. Finally, another option is for participants to rank several sentences in the order of their acceptability. When it comes to investigating grammar, acceptability judgement tasks have been proposed as an alternative to **grammaticality judgement tests** because it is argued that grammaticality refers to an inherent characteristic of the sentence, while acceptability refers to the L1 or L2 speaker's perception of the sentence. In practice, however, 'grammaticality judgement' is the more commonly used term.

Here is an example of an acceptability judgement test that incorporates two design features to investigate learners' knowledge of **pragmatics** (Takimoto, 2009). Learners must evaluate the characteristics of the context that is provided for them, and then rate how well the first sentence conveys the appropriate level of politeness in making their request. Learners must then rank the following two sentences as either more or less acceptable than the first one.

Read each of the situations. After each situation you will be presented with three possible responses. Score the first possible response on an 11-point scale and score subsequent responses with a proportionally higher or lower number in accordance with the response's degree of acceptability.

You overslept and missed the final exam for Professor Jackson's course. You are not so familiar with Professor Jackson and you know that he has to hand in students' grades in a few days and does not like to offer students a make-up exam. However, you need to pass the final exam to graduate and you have decided to go and ask Professor Jackson to give you a make-up exam. What would you ask him?

(a) *I was wondering if it would be possible for me to have a make-up exam.*
not appropriate at all 0—1—2—3—4—5—6—7—8—9—10 completely appropriate
(b) *I want you to give me a make-up exam.*
not appropriate at all 0—1—2—3—4—5—6—7—8—9—10 completely appropriate
(c) *Could you possibly give me a make-up exam?*
not appropriate at all 0—1—2—3—4—5—6—7—8—9—10 completely appropriate

Sorace, A. (1996) "The use of acceptability judgments in second language acquisition research", in W. Ritchie and T. Bhatia (eds) *Handbook of Second Language Acquisition* (San Diego, CA: Academic Press).
Takimoto, M. (2009) 'The effects of input-based tasks on the development of learners' pragmatic proficiency', *Applied Linguistics*, 30, 1–25.

Accessibility hierarchy

Structures within a language can be more or less difficult and often these structures are learned in a specific order. Such structures can be said to form a hierarchy or **implicational scale** from easiest to most difficult. Research into the order in which grammatical structures are learned has examined several different structures in comparison to each other (e.g. **the morpheme order studies**) as well as the **developmental sequences** within a single structure (such as English negation or wh-questions). One structure that has received considerable attention in SLA research is relative clauses, and as a result an accessibility hierarchy has been proposed for the various types of relative clauses. It is argued that relative clauses increase in difficulty, depending on the role of the relative clause in the sentence. Subject relative clauses, such as the one in Table 2, are the easiest, while object of comparative relative clauses are the most difficult. Not all languages have all types of relative clauses; however, researchers have found that a language will contain all of the clauses that are easier than the most difficult relative clause in the language. For example, if the most difficult relative clause in a language is the indirect object relative clause, then that language will also have direct object and subject relative clauses. When learning an L2, learners first acquire relative clauses at the beginning of the hierarchy and then progress through it. Research

Table 2   English relativization types

Type	Example
Subject (SU)	The student [who passed the test]
Direct Object (DO)	The student [who you saw this morning]
Indirect Object (IO)	The student [who I loaned the book to]
Object of Preposition (OP)	The student [who I had lunch with]
Genitive (GEN)	The student [whose essay was eaten by a dog]
Object of Comparative (OCOMP)	The student [who I am smarter than]

A

comprehend. However, authentic language may also be too advanced or difficult for learners; consequently, input in the L2 classroom may need to be modified in some way, especially for lower proficiency learners.

See also **modified input.**

Crossley, S., Louwerse, M., McCarthy, P. and McNamara, D. (2007) 'A linguistic analysis of simplified and authentic texts', *The Modern Language Journal*, 91, 15–30.
Kondo-Brown, K. (2006) 'How do English L1 learners of advanced Japanese infer unknown kanji words in authentic texts?', *Language Learning*, 56, 109–153.

Automaticity/automatic processing

The ability to retrieve items from long-term memory during language processing without any or with only a very small delay. Automaticity can be developed through practice in language production, such as during interactional speech, or in receptive language use, such as when reading a text. Automaticity frees up the limited capacity in **working memory**, which can then be allocated to other tasks.

A distinction is made between **controlled** and automatic processing. An example from everyday life is learning to drive a car. Initially, a beginning driver has to pay attention to every aspect of handling the car, such as changing gears and steering (controlled processing), but eventually he or she does not have to think about these (automatic processing) and instead can pay more attention to such things as the road and traffic conditions. A similar distinction can be made in language acquisition. Initially, words need to be retrieved individually and grammar rules applied consciously, but eventually part or all of these operations are executed without conscious effort.

See also **declarative knowledge, procedural knowledge, skill-acquisition theory.**

DeKeyser, R.M. and Robinson, P. (2001) 'Automaticity and automatization', in P. Robinson (ed.) *Cognition and Second Language Instruction* (Cambridge: Cambridge University Press), 125–51.

Autonomous induction theory

This theory was proposed by Susanne Carroll in the early 2000s, and it is an argument that learning is promoted when learners are unable to parse (comprehend) the incoming linguistic **input**. Thus, if learners understand everything that they hear, no learning takes place. It is only when there is a failure to understand something that learners have the opportunity to make an adjustment in their parsing system. As a result of non-understanding, learners may induce properties of the language from the input and then make generalizations about those exemplars. In this way, learners' mental representations of the grammar system are changed.

Carroll, S. (2001) *Input and Evidence: The Raw Material of Second Language Acquisition* (Amsterdam: John Benjamins).
Selinker, L., Kim, D. and Bandi-Rao, S. (2004) 'Linguistic structure with processing in second language research: is a 'unified theory' possible?', *Second Language Research*, 20, 77–94.

Autonomy

See **learner autonomy**.

Avoidance

Learners may choose not to use certain L2 structures if those structures are difficult or problematic to them. Instead they may use language that is simpler and easier for them to produce. Avoidance may therefore result in language that is more **accurate** or **fluent**, but the language may be less **complex** or advanced. Factors that may influence avoidance include the difficulty or complexity of the structure and the degree of difference between the L1 and the L2 structures.

See also **communication strategy**.

Liao, Y. and Fukuya, Y. (2004) 'Avoidance of phrasal verbs: the case of Chinese learners of English', *Language Learning*, 54, 193–226.

Awareness

The conscious orientation of our cognitive resources. When we are aware of something, we pay conscious attention to it. Some researchers, in particular Schmidt (1995), argue that in order to learn language we have to be aware of it. This has come to be known as the **noticing hypothesis**. In contrast to awareness, it is possible to attend to stimuli without consciously attending to it. In fact, we are often unaware of the vast majority of stimuli that is around us, and much is left unprocessed. For example, we may read a book but be unaware of the sounds coming from the street outside. In other words, we **detect** the information, but do not pay it conscious **attention**. Still, we are able to react to such sounds, for example, if someone calls our name or if we hear an ambulance.

The essentialness of awareness in the noticing hypothesis has been criticized by some (see Truscott, 1998), and indeed some experiments have shown that learning can and does take place without awareness. As a result, Schmidt has since softened the noticing hypothesis somewhat and has argued that awareness may not be necessary for L2 acquisition, but it certainly facilitates it. Additionally, he argues that the amount of learning that takes place without awareness is minimal.

A

See also **noticing**.

Hama, M. and Leow, R. (2010) 'Learning without awareness revisited', *Studies in Second Language Acquisition*, 32, 465–91.
Schmidt, R. (1995) *Attention and Awareness in Foreign Language Learning* (Honolulu, HI: University of Hawaii).
Truscott, J. (1998) 'Noticing in second language acquisition: a critical review', *Second Language Research*, 14, 103–35.

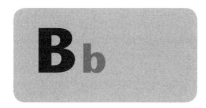

Backsliding

A term that refers to learners producing language that is at a lower **developmental stage**, even though they have progressed to a higher stage. The regression may occur because learners have not fully internalized the current developmental stage. Therefore, when they are required to produce language in a situation that taxes their interlanguage system, they may revert back to a stage that is fully internalized. Backsliding is viewed somewhat negatively as a temporary regression to a lower developmental stage. As such it contrasts with the concept of **u-shaped development** which proposes that learners pass through ungrammatical stages as they develop their interlanguage.

Basic interpersonal communication skills (BICS)

Jim Cummins introduced this term to refer to the type of language that enables learners to function socially in an L2. For example, a learner with BICS can buy a bus ticket, go grocery shopping, interact with friends – all in the L2. BICS proficiency may be developed in as little as a year of intense study or immersion in the L2. However, BICS contrasts with **Cognitive academic language proficiency (CALP)** which is language that is used for academic purposes and is more linguistically and cognitively complex. The development of CALP takes considerably longer than BICS.

Cummins, J. (1980) 'The cross-lingual dimensions of language proficiency: implications for bilingual education and the optimal age issue', *TESOL Quarterly*, 14, 175–87.
Cummins, J. (2003) 'BICS and CALP: origins and rationale for the distinction', in C. B. Paulston and G. R. Tucker (eds) *Sociolinguistics: The Essential Readings* (London: Blackwell), 322–8.

Basic variety

An early stage of L2 acquisition that is characterized by the production of language that is generally devoid of morphological features. For example, verbs are not inflected for tense, person or number, but instead occur in either their base or non-finite form.

Behaviourism

A theory of learning. Behaviourism holds that mental process cannot be measured directly, rather they can only be inferred from a person's behaviour. Behaviourism sees learning as involving conditioning or the development of a relationship between a stimulus and a response. Education involves the creation and strengthening of these relationships and the speeding up of the connections to the point where they become automatized. This process is called the formation of **habits**. Positive reinforcement was believed to encourage specific actions, while negative reinforcement discouraged them. In addition to habit formation, the process of language learning involves imitation, which involves taking another's speech and incorporating into one's own production, and analogizing, which is taking one's own linguistic knowledge and applying it to other situations.

In language teaching, behaviourist principles have translated into the use of drill practice where specific patterns of language use (for example greeting exchanges) are practised repetitively until they are memorized and automatized. Behaviourism exercised considerable influence on language teaching methodologies beginning in the 1950s. The **audiolingual** method, for example, was partly based on behaviourist principles and involved extensive practice and repetition. In the 1960s the influence of behaviourism decreased, especially with the formulation of the ideas of Noam Chomsky, who claimed that language learning draws on **innate** knowledge and does not result simply from the formation of habits developed through language practice and use.

See also **nativism, universal grammar.**

BICS

See **basic interpersonal communication skills**

Bi-directional transfer

See **transfer**

Bilingual education

Bilingual education refers to the provision of academic instruction in more than one language. There are several types of bilingual education. One type involves minority language children getting academic instruction entirely, or primarily, in their own language rather than in the language of the wider society. This type of instruction may be offered throughout their schooling or for only a limited time. Another type of bilingual education involves withdrawing minority language students from regular classes for specific instruction in the L2. Additionally, the goals of bilingual education may vary, depending on whether the goal is to provide temporary language assistance as children transition from the L1 or the L2, or to maintain education in the L1. The issue of bilingual education can be a politically controversial topic, particularly in countries with (a) large immigrant populations, (b) indigenous minority groups and/or (c) multiple national languages.

García, O. and Baker, C. (2007) *Bilingual Education: An Introductory Reader* (Clevedon: Multilingual Matters).

Johnson, D. (2010) 'The relationship between applied linguistic research and language policy for bilingual education', *Applied Linguistics*, 31, 72 93.

B

Bilingual syntax measure (BSM)

A research instrument which was designed to use pictures to elicit specific grammatical structures from learners. The BSM is particularly useful for research on the language development of pre-literate children or adults. The BSM was the main instrument used in the **morpheme studies**.

Bilingualism

Although technically the term refers to knowledge of two languages, it is sometimes used to refer to additional languages as well. Furthermore, the term has been used to encompass multiple aspects regarding the knowledge of two (or more) languages. Most typically, people think of bilingualism as an end-state condition in which a person has equal knowledge of and proficiency in two languages. However, on the continuum from monolingualism to bilingualism there are numerous possible stages. In fact, Gass and Selinker (2008) list and define 37 types of bilingualism. Some of the more common terms include 'balanced bilingualism', which refers to the condition we have just described in which a speaker has equal proficiency in both languages. This definition contrasts with 'dominant bilingual', which refers to someone who is more proficient in one language and/or uses that language more frequently. 'Additive bilingualism' occurs when learners add an additional language without losing the first one; in contrast, 'subtractive bilingualism' occurs when the second language replaces the first one. Bilingualism may also be simultaneous, for example when a child grows up hearing and using two languages at the same time. This type of bilingualism has also been called 'early bilingualism'. In contrast, 'sequential bilingualism' occurs when a language is learned after another has already been so; it has also been called 'late bilingualism'.

Research has found several advantages for bilingualism, apart from the obvious ones of being able to talk to more people in more contexts. Bilingualism has been found to alter cognitive functioning so that bilinguals tend to be better at tasks that require selective attention. It has attracted an incredible amount of research interest, and it is often considered a distinct, although related, field from SLA.

Baker, C. (2006) *Foundations of Bilingual Education and Bilingualism*, 4th edn (Clevedon: Multilingual Matters).

Bhatia, T.K. and Ritchie, W. (2005) *Handbook of Bilingualism* (Oxford: Blackwell).

Gass, S. and Selinker, L. (2008) *Second Language Acquisition: An Introductory Course*, 3rd edn (New York: Routledge).

B

Bottom-up processing

A type of cognitive activity that involves learners in the process of recognizing and decoding the individual components of language in order to comprehend a sentence or utterance. Thus, learners start with the basic units of language and combine them to make meaning. An example of this approach is English phonics reading instruction in which beginning readers are taught the sound rules of individual letters and groups of letters. Then, as learners read and identify each letter, they combine them into words. For instance, one such rule would be that when *a* is followed by a consonant and an *e*, as in *cake*, the *a* is long and the *e* is silent. In a similar fashion, each word is decoded and combined to make sense of the sentence. There is some controversy regarding the effectiveness of bottom-up processing because it is acknowledged that proficient readers do not necessarily process each letter in a word, but instead recognize the word as a whole. Bottom-up processing contrasts with **top-down** processing.

Holmes, V. (2009) 'Bottom-up processing and reading comprehension in experienced adult readers', *Journal of Research in Reading*, 32, 309–26.

Breadth of knowledge

This term is used primarily in **vocabulary** acquisition to refer to the size of a learner's vocabulary. It is concerned with the number of words that a learner knows, either productively or receptively. As such, the term contrasts with **depth of knowledge**, which refers to how much learners know about specific words. Some researchers argue that knowledge of the 3,000 most common words in a language will enable a learner to study in that language with relative ease. There are several tests that measure vocabulary size. One of the best-known tests of English vocabulary is the Vocabulary Levels Test (see www.er.uqam.ca/nobel/r21270/levels/), which tests learners on a representative sample of words from the 1,000, 2,000, 3,000, 5,000 and 10,000 most frequently occurring English words. It also has a component that tests **academic** vocabulary.

Wesche, M. and Paribakht, T. (1996) 'Assessing second language vocabulary knowledge: depth versus breadth', *The Canadian Modern Language Review/La Revue canadienne des langues vivantes*, 53, 13–40.

B

CA

See **conversation analysis.**

CAH

See **contrastive analysis hypothesis.**

CALL

See **computer-assisted language learning.**

Caretaker talk

Some L1 studies have found that the carers who interact with young children modify their speech, through simplification, elaboration, slower production, etc. These modifications it is argued are used to help with language learning. However, other studies have found that not all cultural groups use caretaker talk, and thus the necessity of such **modified input** for language learning is questionable. Caretaker talk is similar to **foreigner talk** for L2 learners, and there is a similar debate as to how helpful it is for L2 learning.

See also **language socialization, modified input.**

Case study

In SLA research, a case study involves investigating the L2 learning of one or two individuals. An advantage of a case study is that it is generally more detailed than **quasi-experimental** research and it is often **longitudinal** (i.e. it follows the learner over a certain length of time, for example from a few weeks to over a year). As such, case studies can provide rich and in-depth descriptions of L2 learning. However, a disadvantage is that case studies provide information about only a small number of individuals and are not normally generalizable to other contexts. In addition, it can be difficult to get learners to commit to extended periods of observation. An example of a well-known SLA case study is Schmidt's (1983) three-year study of Wes, a Japanese learner of English, who developed high levels of communicative ability but did not develop correspondingly high levels of linguistic accuracy.

Duff, P. (2007) *Case Studies in Applied Linguistics* (New York: Routledge).
Schmidt, R. (1983) 'Interaction, acculturation and the acquisition of communication competence', in M. Wolfson and E. Judd (eds) *Sociolinguistics and Second Language Acquisition* (Rowley, MA: Newbury House).

CBI

See **content-based instruction.**

Central executive system

See **working memory.**

Chunk/chunking

A chunk is a group of words that are commonly used together as a semantic unit. Learners may acquire chunks without processing the specific syntactic properties of the individual components of the chunk. Chunks are useful in the initial stages of learning because an entire phrase may be learned, remembered and used without reference to the individual words that make up the chunk. The use of chunks in L2 production can lead to increased fluency, since learners can access the entire chunk rather than having to access each word by itself and then string the words together. According to some theories, such as the **frequency hypothesis**, acquiring a second language predominantly involves the learning, storage and increasingly automatized retrieval of such chunks, rather than individual words. Chunks can also be called **formulaic sequences** or multiword units. An example of a chunk is 'Idunno', where the learner knows the overall meaning of the phrase, but does not know the syntactic details of the three words 'I don't know'.

Although discussions of chunks usually relate to spoken language, chunks also play a role in writing, where the use of formulaic expressions can have communicative purposes ('It is with regret that we inform you that ...'), but they can also reflect the use of unanalysed sequences, such as the example above. In addition to language production, chunks also play a part in understanding. There is evidence that learners store new lexical sequences as semantically related chunks, rather than as individual items, and rely on them in the process of sense-making. Chunks are used to explain frequency effects in SLA.

See also **usage-based theories.**

Lindstromberg, S. and Boers, F. (2008) 'The mnemonic effect of noticing alliteration in lexical chunks', *Applied Linguistics*, 29, 200–22.

Taguchi, N. (2007) 'Chunk learning and the development of spoken discourse in a Japanese as a foreign language classroom', *Language Teaching Research*, 11, 433–57.

Clarification request

An utterance that tries to elicit from a speaker a revised production that is either linguistically more accurate or semantically more transparent. Clarification requests are a common type of **corrective feedback** because they indicate that there is a problem with the preceding utterance. Clarification requests are argued to be beneficial for learning because they require learners to produce the correct forms themselves, in contrast to other types of feedback that provide the correct form for the learner. As a result, learners must engage in deeper cognitive processing in order to come up with the correct form. However, clarification requests do not normally contain an explicit indication that the linguistic form of the utterance is incorrect. It is also possible that a clarification request might be directed at the semantic content of the utterance, rather than at the linguistic error. Therefore, clarification requests are considered a more implicit type of corrective feedback. An example of a clarification request is shown below.

Student: *Est-que, est-ce que je peux fait une carte sur le … pour mon petit frère sur le computer?* [Error-multiple]
Teacher: *Pardon?* [Feedback-clarification]
(Lyster and Ranta, 1997: 47)

Other examples of clarification requests include *Could you repeat that? Excuse me? What do you mean?*

> *See also* **negotiation of meaning**.

> Lyster, R. and Ranta, L. (1997) 'Corrective feedback and learner uptake: negotiation of form in language in communicative classrooms', *Studies in Second Language Acquisition*, 20, 37–66.

CLIL

> *See* **content and language integrated learning**.

Cloze test

A test in which learners are given a sentence or a passage of text with certain words removed. Learners are then asked to supply the missing words. Cloze tests may be used as a measure of general language proficiency. In such cases, words are left out systematically (for example, every seventh word). Cloze tests can also target specific linguistic forms, such as articles. In the example below, learners were required to provide words to fill in the numbered blanks.

The industrialized countries between them possess 78% of all existing wealth. This means that the (1) ___ countries, which are usually called the 'Third World', have about 22% of (2) ___ wealth, even though their population is about 76% of the world's total. (3) ___ rich industrialized countries give aid to poorer Third World countries. However, this (4) ___ sometimes does more harm than good. This is because many Western aid (5) ___ are importing Western technology into the poorer countries. This has brought (6) ___ two problems.

Answers 1. other 2. the 3. Many 4. aid 5. organizations 6. about
(Kobayashi, 2002: 584)

> Kobayashi, M. (2002) 'Cloze tests revisited: exploring item characteristics with special attention to scoring methods', *The Modern Language Journal*, 86, 571–86.

CMC

> *See* **computer mediated communication**.

Code-switching

The act of changing from one language (code) to another. This switch may happen with each language being used relatively separately, for example with one sentence in one language and the next sentence in a different language. However, the use of multiple languages can also occur within the same sentence. Code-switching may be as minimal as the insertion of one word of another language into a sentence, or it may consist of sentences with various clauses in the two languages. The use of two languages in the same sentence is sometimes called code-mixing. In some cases such mixed use of languages is viewed negatively by society because it does not keep the language 'pure'. However, from a linguistic point of view, code-switching is simply a neutral, naturally occurring phenomenon.

In the example below, the teacher switches from English to Turkish when the initial question in English does not elicit a response from the student.

Teacher-initiated code-switching dealing with a lack of response in the L2 (Üstünel and Seedhouse, 2005: 313)

```
 1  T: okay (.) hh on Tuesday night?
 2  (0.5)
 3  on New Year's night?
 4  (1.0)
 5  on Tuesday (.) last Tuesday?
 6  (2.0)
 7  → Salı günü? [tr: on Tuesday]
 8  S4: (0.5)
 9  er-
10  T: =Yılbaşı gecesi?
    [tr: on New Year's Eve]
11  S4: I (2.0) study (0.5) English
```

Üstünel, E. and Seedhouse, P. (2005) 'Why that, in that language, right now? Code-switching and pedagogical focus', *International Review of Applied Linguistics*, 15, 302–25.

Van der Meij, H. and Zhao, X. (2010) 'Codeswitching in English courses in Chinese universities', *The Modern Language Journal*, 94, 396–411.

Cognate

Cognates are words that have a similar structure and meaning in the L1 and in the L2. Cognate words are generally easier to learn because of their similarities, as shown in the examples below. However, there are also false cognates which can hinder learning. For example, English L1 learners of Spanish often assume that the Spanish word 'embarazada' is a cognate for 'embarrassed. However, they are truly embarrassed when they say 'estoy embarazada' and find out that it means 'I am pregnant' rather than 'I am embarrassed'.

Another way in which cognates can facilitate L2 learning is by freeing up cognitive resources, so that learners can concentrate on learning other things. Below is a list of cognate and non-cognate words for Italian, English and German.

Cognates

Italian	English	German
Piramide	Pyramid	Die Pyramide
Stadio	Stadium	Das Stadion
Bomba	Bomb	Die Bombe
Pistola	Pistol	Die Pistole
Giraffa	Giraffe	Die Giraffe
Scorpione	Scorpion	Der Skorpion
Trattore	Tractor	Der Traktor
Triangolo	Triangle	Die Triangel
Violino	Violin	Die Violine
Delfino	Dolphin	Der Delphin

Non-cognates

Italian	English	German
Pozzo	Well	Der Brunnen
Spada	Sword	Das Schwert
Freccia	Arrow	Der Pfeil
Pavone	Peacock	Der Pfau
Struzzo	Ostrich	Der Strauß
Zattera	Raft	Das Floß
Sommergibile	Submarine	Das Unterseeboot
Tamburo	Drum	Die Trommel
Gambero	Crayfish	Der Krebs
Squalo	Shark	Der Hai

(Tonzar et al., 2009: 644–5)

Tonzar, C., Lotto, L. and Job, R. (2009) 'L2 vocabulary acquisition in children', *Language Learning* 59, 623–46.

Cognition

The ability for thinking and processing information. Cognition is a general term to refer to the mental activities and processes that humans engage in.

See also **cognitive theories.**

Cognitive academic language proficiency (CALP)

This is the ability that learners need in order to comprehend academic language which is often more complex and more abstract than everyday language. As such it contrasts with **basic interpersonal communication skills (BICS)**, and it takes longer to develop. Therefore, even if learners can function well in an L2 environment, it does not ensure that they will have the language skills necessary for more cognitively demanding functions. One characteristic of CALP is the ability to refer to abstract concepts, such as democracy or economics, and to events that are distant in time and/or place, such as historical events or future plans. Such types of concepts and ideas are more difficult for learners than are concrete notions, such as animals and physical objects, and topics that are present in the current context, such as describing the room that they are in.

See also **academic language.**

Cognitive comparison

When learners encounter input, they compare it with their own **interlanguage** system. In this way learners can either confirm or restructure their interlanguage system. If the comparison shows that the input and the interlanguage system are similar, the learners' knowledge is confirmed. However, if the learners notice discrepancies between the input and their interlanguage, they may change their interlanguage system to align more closely with the input.

See also **noticing-the-gap.**

Cognitive linguistics

A branch of linguistics that is concerned with the relationship between language and mental processes. As such, the discipline is concerned with how language is used to organize, process and convey information. Cognitive linguistics, **psycholinguistics**, and **cognitive theories** of SLA are all interested in similar phenomena; however, they approach the issues with somewhat different perspectives, influenced by their academic traditions.

Cognitive learning strategy

A type of learning strategy that involves the direct use of one's mental abilities. Examples of cognitive learning strategies include saying or writing new L2 words several times, trying to find patterns in the L2, and practising the sounds of the L2.

See also **learning strategy.**

Cognitive theories

Cognitive theories of learning are concerned with the mental properties that are involved in the learning process. As such, cognitive theories are not unique to SLA, but have come to SLA from psychology and education. Cognitive theories of SLA propose that learning a second language involves the use of general learning skills, and, therefore, L2 learning occurs in a similar manner as any other types of learning, such as learning multiplication tables or learning to ride a bike. Consequently, cognitive SLA theories do not believe that humans possess a special **innate** language learning mechanism, such as is proposed by linguistic theories like **universal grammar**. In SLA, cognitive theories are interested in how L2 learners acquire, as well as use, the language. Thus, research has investigated factors, such as **individual differences**, which may influence the learning process. Additionally, researchers are interested in how L2 knowledge is stored and processed in the brain.

One approach used to investigate this issue is **information processing**, which draws on a computer metaphor to explain how information enters the cognitive system and is transformed within it. Another cognitive theory is **skill acquisition theory**, which prioritizes practice as a mechanism for learning.

> Robinson, P. (2001) *Cognition and Second Language Instruction* (Cambridge: Cambridge University Press).

Collaborative dialogue

Talk in which the learner and their interlocutor are involved in co-constructing the discourse. Collaborative dialogue is of particular interest in **sociocultural theory** which views learning as a social process. In collaborative dialogues learners can help each other to produce language that may be more advanced than either person could produce on their own. L2 learning can occur as learners' jointly use language and reflect on its use. In the example below the learners reflect on their use of grammar and vocabulary as together they produce more accurate language than they initially uttered.

1 Kathy: Et brosse les cheveux.
   (and brushes her hair.)
2 Doug: Et les dents.
   (and her teeth.)
3 Kathy: Non, non, pendant qu'elle brosse les dents et ...
   (No, no, while she brushes her teeth and ...)
4 Doug: Elle se brosse ... elle SE brosse.
   (She brushes ... she brushes [emphasizes the reflexive pronoun].)
5 Kathy: Pendant qu'elle se brosse les dents et peigne les cheveux.
   (While she brushes her teeth and combs her hair.)
6 Doug: Ya!
7 Kathy: Pendant qu'elle ... se brosse ... les cheveux, I mean, no, pendant qu'elle se PEIGNE les cheveux.
   (While she ... brushes ... her hair, I mean, no while she COMBS her hair.)
8 Doug: Ya !
9 Kathy: Et se brosse ...
   (and brushes ...)
10 Doug: Les dents.
   (her teeth.)
11 Kathy: Pendant qu'elle SE peigne les cheveus et SE brosse les dents.
   (While she combs her hair and brushes her teeth [emphasizes the reflexive pronouns].)
   (Swain, 2000: 110–11)

Swain, M and Lapkin, S (1998) 'Interaction and second language learning: two adolescent French immersion students working together', *The Modern Language Journal*, 83, 320–38.

Swain, M. (2000) 'The output hypothesis and beyond: mediating acquisition through collaborative dialogue', in J. Lantolf (ed.) *Sociocultural Theory and Second Language Learning* (Oxford: Oxford University Press), 97–114.

Collocation

A collocation is a group of words that often occur together. For example, in English one 'plays tennis' but 'goes skiing'. There are often no fixed rules for collocations and they are often one of the last components of **vocabulary** that L2 learners learn.

Durrant, P. and Schmitt, N. (2010). 'Adult learners' retention of collocations from exposure', *Second Language Research*, 26, 163–88.

Webb, S. and Kagimoto, E. (2009) 'The effects of vocabulary learning on collocation and meaning', *TESOL Quarterly*, 43, 55–77.

Common European Framework of Reference

The Common European Framework of Reference for Languages: Learning, Teaching, Assessment (CEFR) is a set of descriptors of what language learners are able to do at different levels of proficiency. The CEFR includes global descriptors as well as descriptors for the four skills (i.e. listening, speaking, reading and writing) and subskills (e.g. listening as a member of a live audience). There are three main levels of proficiency, each with sublevels: (A) basic speaker (A1 breakthrough or beginner, A2 waystage or elementary), (B) independent speaker (B1 threshold or pre-intermediate, B2 vantage or intermediate), (C) proficient speaker (C1 effective operational proficiency or upper intermediate, C2 mastery or advanced). The Framework was designed by the Council of Europe and is increasingly used for the validation of language examinations. Its intended purpose is to facilitate the comparison of achievement on different assessment scales (e.g. **IELTS**, **TOEFL**), as well as between achievement in school systems in different countries. Related to this, the Framework aims to make it easier for schools, teachers, employers and learners themselves to understand the characteristics of learners' proficiency levels and what these levels mean in terms of practical ability in using the language.

Little, D. (2007) 'The Common European Framework of Reference for Languages: perspectives on the making of supranational language education policy', *The Modern Language Journal*, 91, 645–85.

www.coe.int/t/dg4/linguistic/cadre_en.asp.

Communication strategy

Methods learners use to help convey their intended meanings in situations where they may have difficulty doing so due to insufficient linguistic abilities. Some commonly used communication strategies include circumlocution, direct translation from the L1, sticking to familiar topics, and switching languages. It should be noted that such communication strategies differ from **learning strategies** in that the latter are used to help with learning, while communication strategies may or may not help with learning. Instead, communication strategies assist learners in expressing their thoughts and ideas. In order for communication strategies to be used, there are several factors that must be present. First learners must be aware that there is a problem, either in their own ability to express their intended meaning or in their ability to comprehend what someone else says or writes. In addition, learners must consciously make choices about what communication strategies they are going to use. However, it is not always clear that they can be distinguished from general language use. Examples of communication strategies are:

- Code switching: use of an L1/L3 word and its L1/L3 pronunciation to replace an L2 concept; e.g. réclame for advertisement.
- All-purpose word: use of a general word in place of a more specific one; e.g. stuff.
- Word coinage: use of L2 rules to create a word that does not actually exist in the L2; e.g. whobody for anybody who.
- Approximation: use of a synonym or superordinate to replace a related concept; e.g. colors instead of paint.
- Circumlocution: use of an illustration or description of the characteristics of an item or an action; e.g. change place for living for moving.

(Rossiter, 2005)

Rossiter, M. (2005) 'Developmental sequences of L2 communication strategies', *Applied Language Learning*, 15, 55–66.

Communicative competence

A term used to refer to a learner's ability to use language. The term, popularized in SLA by Canale and Swain (1980) refers to learners' language knowledge that includes more than just grammatical **accuracy** or an idealized **competence** in the language. Communicative competence is seen as being composed of several different components:

(a) Linguistic competence refers to learners' knowledge of the lexical, syntactic, morphological and phonological aspects of the language.

(b) Sociolinguistic competence refers to learners' ability to use language appropriately in various social contexts. For example, knowledge of when it is suitable to use formal and familiar second person pronouns (such as *du* and *Sie* in German or *tú* and *usted* in Spanish) demonstrates sociolinguistic competence.

(c) Discourse competence consists of learners' knowledge of coherence and cohesiveness in L2 written and spoken production. As such, it refers to learners' linguistic ability beyond the sentence level, for instance by being able to write a cohesive paragraph or tell an extended narrative.

(d) Strategic competence refers to learners' capacity to deal with communication difficulties. Learners may not have the linguistic resources that they need to express their intended meanings, or they may have difficulty in understanding others' language production. Learners' ability to navigate such difficulties by using **communication strategies** is an illustration of strategic competence.

C

Communicative competence has become an important construct in language **assessment** because teachers and researchers often want to know more about learners' knowledge of language beyond just their linguistic competence. Tests of communicative competence are especially important in assessing the effects of communicative language teaching which aims to develop learners who can use the L2 for communicative purposes.

Canale, M. and Swain, M. (1980) 'Theoretical bases of communicative approaches to second language teaching and testing', *Applied Linguistics*, 1, 1–47.

Savignon, S. (1998). 'Communicative competence: theory and classroom practice', 2nd edn (New York: McGraw-Hill).

Communicative language teaching (CLT)

The beginnings of communicative language teaching are associated with Stephen Krashen who, in the late 1970s and early 1980s, proposed that learning discrete grammar rules was not helpful for L2 acquisition. Instead he suggested that learners needed to communicate in the L2. As such, the role of L2 teaching and the L2 classroom was to provide an 'acquisition rich' environment, which basically meant that learners were exposed to large amounts of L2 input. CLT became popular in the 1980s and 1990s, particularly in North American and European contexts, in response to some disillusionment with traditional grammar instruction which often resulted in learners with considerable grammatical knowledge, but with little ability to use the L2 to communicate. For example, learners might know how to conjugate verbs, but not how to ask for directions on the street. In its strong form, CLT excludes a role for explicit attention to grammar. However, after several research studies of L2 learning in CLT contexts, it became clear that, while learners did achieve high levels of fluency in the L2, they did not always achieve correspondingly high levels of accuracy. Thus, there has been an acknowledgement that some attention to grammar within a CLT context can be beneficial for learners.

See also **task-based language teaching.**

Savignon, S. and Wang, C. (2003). 'Communicative language teaching in EFL contexts: learner attitudes and perceptions', *International Review of Applied Linguistics*, 41, 223–49.

Communicative orientation in language teaching (COLT)

The COLT is a coding checklist that can be used to assess various aspects of classroom instruction to determine how communicative it is. The COLT includes categories such as who is in control of the topic of discussion in the class, the configuration of the interaction (whether whole class, teacher to student, or student to student), and the content of the interaction. The COLT also covers the skills that are being used in the class – reading, writing, speaking, listening – as well as the resources that are being drawn upon, such as the textbook. The COLT has been used in a number of research studies into classroom interaction.

Fröhlich, M., Spada, N. and Allen, P. (1985) 'Differences in the communicative orientation of L2 classrooms', *TESOL Quarterly*, 19, 27–57.

Spada, N. and Fröhlich, M. (1995) *COLT Communicative Orientation of Language Teaching Observation Scheme: Coding Conventions and Applications* (Sydney: Macquarie University).

Comparative fallacy

In considering the grammaticality of learners' L2 production, it is argued that it is unfair to compare L2 learners' language to that of **native speakers** because even though learners' language may not be target-like, it still consists of a systematic set of rules, often referred to as **interlanguage**. In addition, the production of non-target-like utterances may indeed reflect linguistic advances as learners progress through natural **developmental stages** that consist of both target-like and non-target-like forms. Rather than comparing learners to native speakers, it is suggested that learner language be considered in its own right.

See also **u-shaped development.**

Lakshmanan, U. and Selinker, L. (2001) 'Analysing interlanguage: how do we know what learners know?', *Second Language Research*, 17, 393–420.

Lardiere, D. (2003) 'Revisiting the comparative fallacy: a reply to Lakshmanan and Selinker, 2001', *Second Language Research*, 19, 129–43.

Compensation learning strategy

A type of **learning strategy** that is used to help learners make up for limited L2 knowledge. Examples of compensation strategies include making guesses to understand unfamiliar L2 words, using gestures to convey unknown words during an L2 conversation, and using other words or phrases with a similar meaning to an unknown L2 word.

See also **communication strategy.**

Competence

This term was first used in theoretical linguistics, particularly in **universal grammar**, to refer to the underlying, abstract, linguistic knowledge that first language speakers possess. It is the idealized system of language inside the speaker's head, and it allows native speakers to recognize implicitly which sentences are possible in their language and which ones are not. Competence is often contrasted with **performance**, which refers to the actual production of the language. A speaker's performance may not match his or her competence, given slips of the tongue and other performance errors; however, such flaws in native speaker production are not the result of faulty competence. Universal grammar researchers have traditionally been interested only in competence because it represents the idealized system of language. However, competence cannot be measured directly; it can only be measured indirectly through performance. Just as L1 speakers have competence in their L1, it is also argued that L2 learners possess competence in their L2; however, L2 competence may be less stable and more varied. Finally, some researchers reject the competence/performance distinction, arguing that learners' ability to use the language constitutes their competence and that there is no underlying, idealized system.

See also **interlanguage.**

C

Rothman, J. (2007) 'Sometimes they use it, sometimes they don't: an epistemological discussion of L2 morphological production and its use as a competence measurement', *Applied Linguistics*, 28, 609–14.

Competition model

The competition model proposes that various cues or signals are used to interpret and understand language. Cues may consist of morphological, syntactic and lexical markers. For example, *yesterday* and *verb + ed* are both cues for past tense in English. The types of cues that are used vary in different languages. Additionally, the importance of specific cues for interpreting a sentence may vary. When learners are learning an L2, they may rely on L1 cues which may not possess the same strength in the L2. For example, learners use cues to determine the subject in a sentence. In English, the cue of word order is a very strong predictor of the subject, with the subject almost always coming before the verb. Thus in the example, *The man bites the dog*, it is the man that is doing the biting. However, in *The dog bites the man*, it is the dog that is doing the biting. We know that these two sentences are interpreted differently in English because of the fact that the noun before the verb is almost always the subject. However, other languages rely on different cues to mark the subject. Languages that are more highly inflected than English often rely on morphological markers to help identify the subject. In such languages, there is much more flexibility in the location of the subject within the sentence. Thus, English L1 learners of such languages may rely on the wrong cues in determining the subject of a sentence because they are relying on L1 cues that are not as strong in the L2. Other types of cues include animacy and semantic cues.

See also **connectionism.**

MacWhinney, B. (2002) 'The competition model: the input, the context, and the brain', in P. Robinson (ed.) *Cognition and Second Language Instruction* (New York: Cambridge University Press).

Su, I. (2004) 'The effects of discourse processing with regard to syntactic and semantic cues: a competition model study', *Applied Psycholinguistics*, 25, 587–601.

Complexity

(a)   Complexity refers to language production that expresses multiple ideas within a sentence by using subordination. In this sense it is one way to measure a language learner's ability in the second language in addition to **fluency** and **accuracy**. For example, a learner may be able to speak confidently and without mistakes when talking about everyday topics, but may be unable to express complex ideas. Tests that measure only fluency or accuracy would be unable to detect a learner's ability to produce complex language. Measuring complexity often involves calculating the ratio of independent and dependent clauses. The more dependent clauses a learner produces, the more complex his or her language is considered to be. Thus, the two independent clauses in example A would be less complex than the one independent and one dependent clause in example B.

A: *The book is on the table. The book is blue.*
B: *The book that is on the table is blue.*

Other measures of complexity include:

- the number of turns per minute (i.e. in a conversation);
- the number of idea units (e.g. topics);
- the use and frequency of advanced language functions, such as
- hypothesizing;
- the number of **C-units, T-units** and **AS-units;**
- the number of different verb forms used;
- the lexical **type–token** ratio;
- the number of different word families;
- the ratio of structural words to content words.

Learners' ability to produce complex (as well as accurate and fluent) language has received considerable attention within **task-based language learning** studies of pretask planning, and there is evidence to suggest that giving learners planning time results in the production of more complex language.

Ellis, R. and Yuan, F. (2004) 'The effects of planning on fluency, complexity, and accuracy in second language narrative writing', *Studies in Second Language Acquisition*, 26, 59–84.

Housen, A. and Kuiken, F. (2009) 'Complexity, accuracy, and fluency in second language acquisition', *Applied Linguistics*, 30, 461–73.

(b)   Complexity is a measure of the degree to which an activity involving language requires greater amounts of mental effort and attention. Complexity can be varied by task designers, for example by asking learners to pay attention to more than one feature in a task.

Kuiken, F. and Vedder, I. (2008) 'Cognitive task complexity and written output in Italian and French as a foreign language', *Journal of Second Language Writing*, 17, 48–60.

Comprehensible input

This construct was particularly important to Krashen's **monitor model** of SLA. He proposed that language acquisition proceeded when learners were exposed to language that was just slightly beyond their current proficiency level. However, only if the majority of the input was comprehensible to the learners would they be able to figure out or acquire the forms/structures that were unknown to them. He called this type of input $i + 1$. On the other hand, if learners are only exposed to language that is already known to them, no acquisition can take place.

Krashen's conception of $i + 1$ and its role for L2 acquisition has been challenged as being unfalsifiable and as being necessary but not sufficient for language learning. Nevertheless, most other approaches to SLA agree that learners need to be able to understand most or all of the input that they are exposed to in order for learning to be possible.

Comprehensible output hypothesis

In 1985, Merrill Swain suggested that not only did learners need comprehensible input for L2 learning, but they also needed to produce comprehensible output. She based this hypothesis on her observation of the French immersion programmes in Canada in which English L1 elementary school students study in French. She, and other researchers, found that, in spite of years of L2 input, learners often were not able to use accurately some common grammatical structures. Additionally, she noted that these learners did not have many opportunities to produce the language. Therefore, she argued that the learners would benefit from producing the language. When learners actually had to produce the language, they would have to think about what grammatical structures would encode the meanings they were trying to convey. This attention to grammatical features is unlike what can happen with input in which learners can rely primarily on semantic cues to understand an utterance. If learners are pushed to produce language that is comprehensible, they will then have to process the language syntactically rather than just semantically. In this way, Swain suggested that output is also a crucial part of the L2 learning process, something that had not been promoted until this point.

Swain also proposes several functions for output. First, it can have a noticing/triggering function in that, as learners are trying to produce output, they may realize that they do not have the linguistic resources to produce the correct form. As such, learners may **notice the gap** between their own interlanguage system and the target language system. Another function of output is hypothesis testing. When producing output, learners can try out new forms and gauge the kind of reaction they get from their interlocutors. If learners try out a new form, and the conversation continues as normal, they can assume that the linguistic structure has been used correctly. If, however, the communication breaks down or if the learners receive corrective feedback, then they might realize that their hypothesis was incorrect and that it needs to be modified. The final function of output is a metalinguistic (reflective) one. As learners produce language, they are able think about what they hear and to reflect on it.

Swain, M. (1985) 'Communicative competence: some roles of comprehensible input and comprehensible output in its development', in S. Gass and C. Madden (eds) *Input in Second Language Acquisition* (Rowley, MA: Newbury House), 235–53.

Swain, M. (2005) 'The output hypothesis: theory and research', in E. Hinkel (ed.) *Handbook of Research in Second Language Teaching and Learning* (Mahwah, NJ: Lawrence Erlbaum), 471–83.

Comprehension check

A discourse move that involves a speaker in confirming that an interlocutor has understood the meaning of his or her previous utterance. Comprehension checks may result in the provision of modified input if the interlocutor has not understood the previous meaning. Comprehension checks are a component of interactionist approaches to L2 learning. In the following example, the first learner is checking to make sure that the second learner understands the words that he is using.

Learner A: *Draw a tree big tree on the left. You understand on the left? You know the left?*
Learner B: *Yep, the left.*
(Mackey et al., 2007: 304)

Mackey, A., Kanganas, A.P. and Oliver, R. (2007) 'Task familiarity and international feedback in child ESL classrooms', *TESOL Quarterly*, 41, 285–312.

Computational model

This approach to L2 learning, adopted from cognitive psychology, takes an **information processing** perspective on language acquisition. It is concerned with the cognitive processes that occur inside the learner's head. In this model, acquisition is proposed to occur by learners processing language input and incorporating it into their interlanguage systems. In other words, language must enter the cognitive system through mechanisms such as **attention** and **working memory**. The input is then processed and stored in long-term memory, where it is available for output. The computational model draws upon a computer-processing metaphor of language acquisition.

Eysenck, M. (2001) *Principles of Cognitive Psychology*, 2nd edn (Hove: Psychology Press).

Computer-assisted language learning (CALL)

The study of the role of technology in language learning and teaching. The issues investigated in CALL research include the use of technology in face-to-face L2 classrooms, the nature of online L2 instruction, the use of computers and technology for interaction, among others. CALL studies have increasingly contributed to our understanding of second language acquisition processes. An example is the area of **computer-mediated communication** or CMC, which investigates online interaction (between learners, learners and teachers, or learners and native speakers, such as is common in tandem learning) and its opportunities for negotiation of meaning, focus on form and other characteristics of interaction said to contribute to second language acquisition. Another area is that of the role of technology in providing learners with feedback, especially an area of CALL called Intelligent CALL (iCALL) or parser-based CALL, which aims to provide learners with specific and detailed feedback in relation to their errors and their previous learning.

Besides its use for teaching purposes, CALL programs are also increasingly used to facilitate SLA research and data collection. Furthermore, this area of inquiry has its own journal, the *Computer Assisted Language Learning Journal* (see www.tandf.co.uk/journals/titles/09588221.asp).

Chapelle, C. (2009) 'The relationship between second language acquisition theory and computer-assisted language learning', *The Modern Language Journal*, 93, 741–53.
Jamieson, J. and Chapelle, C. (2010) 'Evaluating CALL use across multiple contexts', *System*, 38, 357–69.

Computer-mediated communication (CMC)

Computer-mediated communication is a term used to describe online interaction between learners, learners and teachers, or learners and native speakers. Studies of CMC started with the arrival of online communication tools such as email and instant messaging and added a social perspective to the research done on technology-enhanced learning by describing the unique social, affective and linguistic characteristics of online communication. Another important strand of CMC research has attempted to apply SLA theories and methodologies, for example by investigating **focus on form** and **negotiation of meaning** in online interaction. Initially, studies of CMC were concerned with the characteristics of L2 learner language in online environments; however, research has expanded to investigate how online interaction can contribute to L2 development. In this way CMC is probably the area of **computer-assisted language learning** that has made the greatest contribution to SLA as a field. At a practical level CMC is said to make an important contribution to L2 learning by allowing access to the target language community and opportunities for practice.

See also **tandem learning**.

Peterson, M. (2009) 'Learner interaction in synchronous CMC: a sociocultural perspective', *Computer Assisted Language Learning*, 22, 303–21.
Warschauer, M. (2000) *Network-Based Language Teaching* (Cambridge: Cambridge University Press).

Confirmation check

A confirmation check is a discourse move that involves a speaker verifying the meaning of a previous utterance. Confirmation checks are an important component of **negotiation of meaning**, and are an example of a **communication strategy**. For instance, in line 4 of the example below, Learner B is making sure that he or she understands Learner A's instructions in doing an interactive task. In addition to checking understanding, confirmation checks may serve as a type of indirect **corrective feedback** when a teacher provides a confirmation check after a learner's incorrect utterance, even though the teacher has understood the meaning of the utterance.

1. Learner A: Now draw some ducks in a pond.
2. Learner B: Yeh.
3. Learner A: Draw now.
4. Learner B: Now? All the time you tell me now what to draw?
5. Learner A: Yeh I have the picture and you need to draw it. No looking.
6. Learner B: Oh, I draw ducks then all over here.

(Mackey et al. 2007: 303)

Mackey, A., Kanganas, A.P. and Oliver, R. (2007) 'Task familiarity and international feedback in child ESL classrooms', *TESOL Quarterly*, 41, 285–312.

Connectionism

Connectionism is a general theory of learning that is not specifically limited to language learning; however, in SLA, connectionism refers to a group of models of language processing and learning that are **usage-based**. Learning in connectionism is not based on innate language learning mechanisms, as it is in UG accounts. Rather, learning occurs as learners are exposed to input over and over again. Each time a specific linguistic item is encountered in the input, it is reinforced in the learner's cognitive system. Thus, the connection between that word and the rest of the interlanguage system is strengthened. Furthermore, learners are able to extract patterns of language use (what might be called 'rules' in other approaches) based on the input. Learners' interlanguage is distributed across a network of interconnected, simple processing units. In this model, language is not stored discretely or symbolically (i.e. in rules), but resides in a network of connections between numerous simple processing units (similar to the way in which neural networks operate in the brain). Repeated encounters with a stimulus affect the strength between these connections. As an example, seeing the words *by the way* written together will strengthen the relationship between them and facilitate retrieval the next time these words are encountered (i.e. *by the* ... will trigger *way*). In this way, connectionism attempts to explain not only how knowledge is stored but also how it is learned. Experiments have had some success in showing that a computer program based on a connectionist model can acquire morphemes, in a similar fashion as do language learners.

See also **emergentism.**

Ellis, N. (2002) 'Frequency effects in language processing: a review with implications for theories of implicit and explicit language acquisition', *Studies in Second Language Acquisition*, 27, 305–52.

Ellis, N. and Larsen-Freeman, D. (2009) 'Constructing a second language: analyses and computational simulations of the emergence of linguistic constructions from usage', *Language Learning*, 59, 90–125.

Elman, J.L. (1999) 'The emergence of language: a conspiracy theory', in B. MacWhinney (ed.) *Emergence of Language* (Hillsdale, NJ: Lawrence Erlbaum).

Consciousness

The state of being aware of something. Arguably, L2 learning cannot occur without some degree of consciousness; however, the precise role of consciousness in L2 acquisition has been debated. In general, constructs such as **noticing**, **awareness**, and **attention** have been used more frequently than consciousness in SLA theory and research.

Ellis, N.C. (1995) 'Consciousness in second language acquisition: a review of field studies and laboratory experiments', *Language Awareness*, 4, 123–46.

Consciousness-raising task (CR task)

These are **tasks** that involve inductively drawing learners' attention to characteristics of the target language. As such, they do not aim to enable learners to produce the target form; instead, the goal is for learners to become aware of specific L2 characteristics so that they can notice them in the input. An example of a CR task would be to provide learners with a group of sentences that contain examples of a specific rule. Learners would induce the rule by looking at the sentences and then writing out the rule after they have identified it. An example of a consciousness-raising task is shown in Figure 3.

Fotos, S. (1994) 'Integrating grammar instruction and communicative language use through grammar consciousness-raising tasks', *TESOL Quarterly*, 28, 323–51.

Mohamed, N. (2004) 'Consciousness raising task: a learner perspective', *ELT Journal*, 58, 228–37.

C

Indirect Task for Relative Clauses: task sheet for student A

STUDENT A

A Look at the table below. The relative clauses are in italics, the prepositions are underlined and the relative pronouns are in bold.

B You need to work with your partner to complete the table. Ask your partner to read out his/her sentences. Listen carefully, then write them down in the appropriate column in your table.

C Talk about the sentences. Why are the sentences in the second column incorrect?

Complete the rules in the final column by filling in the blanks.

	Correct	Incorrect	Explanation of incorrect sentences
1	The place _to_ **which** _you will want to go_ is Singapore. The place **which** _you will want to go to_ is Singapore. The man _at_ **whom** _I shouted_ is deaf The man **whom** _I shouted at_ is deaf.		Don't use prepositions both at the _____ and at the _____ of the clause.
2		The girl _to_ **who** _we gave the message_ is not here. The house _in_ **that** _we live_ is pink.	Don't use prepositions at the _____ of the clause.
3	These are the books **which** _I told you about._ The man **who** _you were talking to_ is my uncle.		Don't use personal pronouns at the _____ of the clause.

D Now write down a sentence of your own for each of these rules.

1 _____

2 _____

3 _____

Source: Mohamed (2004).

Figure 3 Consciousness-raising task

Content and language integrated learning (CLIL)

In CLIL, the target language can be used to teach subject matter, or the subject matter can inform the content of the language instruction, for example by including technical terms or text types common in that field. The rationale behind CLIL is that the teaching of language separate from the purposes of using it is not helpful in preparing learners for academic study. According to proponents of CLIL, the differences in language use and domain-specific conventions between different subject fields are such that learners need to acquire the language and the subject matter simultaneously. CLIL is similar to **content-based instruction**; however, CLIL is a term more frequently used in the European context than in North America.

Dalton-Puffer, C., Nikula, T. and Smit, U. (2007) *Language Use and Language Learning in CLIL Classrooms* (Amsterdam: John Benjamins).

Ruiz De Zarobe, Y. and Jimenez Catalan, R. (2009) *Content and Language Integrated Learning: Evidence from Research in Europe* (Clevedon: Multilingual Matters).

Content-based instruction (CBI)

CBI is a type of meaning-focused instruction in which academic subjects, such as science, mathematics and history, are taught in the target language. The goal of CBI is primarily the learning of this academic content; however, L2 learning is often a secondary goal. CBI is related to but distinct from **content and language integrated learning** (CLIL), in that there is less of an emphasis on language learning in CBI; however, the two terms can also refer to very similar types of instruction, with CBI being more commonly used in the Americas, and CLIL more in Europe.

Lyster, R. (2007) *Learning and Teaching Languages through Content: A Counterbalanced Approach* (Amsterdam: John Benjamins).

Rodgers, D. (2006) 'Developing content and form: encouraging evidence from Italian content-based instruction', *The Modern Language Journal*, 90, 373–86.

Context

This term may apply either to the surrounding linguistic environment or to the situation in which an utterance is produced. Both types of contexts may help learners in understanding L2 input. For example, in a context in which the topic of conversation is about money, the learner may better understand that the word *bank* refers to a financial institution. In contrast, when the context is a computer-related discussion, the word *bank* is most likely to refer to a memory bank.

Contextualization cues

Information from the surrounding **context** that helps learners understand language.

See also **competition model.**

Contrastive analysis

The comparative study of two or more languages to identify similarities and differences between their grammatical, phonological, lexical and pragmatic systems. In the 1960s contrastive analysis served as a basis for the **contrastive analysis hypothesis** which claimed that the greater the differences between structures in the L1 and L2, the more difficult the acquisition of the L2.

C

Contrastive analysis hypothesis (CAH)

The hypothesis that L2 acquisition consists of a transfer of L1 habits to the L2. In the 1960s contrastive analysis was used to explain why some languages or elements of a language were more difficult for specific L1 speakers to acquire than others. Such information had a direct effect on L2 pedagogy. It was thought that L2 acquisition involved the gradual learning of the differences between the L1 and L2. The greater the differences between structures in the L1 and L2, the more difficult the acquisition of the target language was thought to be. Furthermore, structures in the L1 that were similar to structures in the L2 were more easily transferable by learners. These ideas came to be known as the **contrastive analysis hypothesis (CAH)**. The strong form of the CAH claimed that difficulties in L2 learning could be predicted by differences between the L1 and L2. However, researchers discovered that the difficulties that learners had with certain structures (as evidenced by learners' errors) were not always predicted by differences between the L1 and target language. A weak version of the CAH suggested that contrastive analysis could be useful in explaining some of the linguistic errors that were actually produced by learners. Later empirical research showed that differences between the L1 and L2 do not necessarily produce difficulties for learners, and researchers identified certain **developmental stages** that learners, regardless of their L1s, go through in acquiring the target languages, during which their interlanguage differs from the target language norm.

As an example, Zobl (1980) studied the learning of direct object pronouns in French and English by L1 speakers of those languages. In English, the direct object pronoun always follows the verb.

I see her.
But in French, the direct object pronoun comes before the verb.
Je la vois.
I her see.
I see her.
The contrastive analysis hypothesis would predict that French L1 learners of English would put the direct object before the verb as they do in their L1.
*I her see.
The CAH would also predict the English L1 learners of French would put the direct object after the verb.
*Je vois la.
I see her.

While the latter is a common error made by English L1 learners of French, the former error is almost never made by French L1 learners of English. Thus, a difficulty predicted by the CAH is not supported by learners' actual production of the target language.

In addition, it was found to be difficult to compare languages as they need to be described along the same theoretical lines in order to have a point of comparison. As a result of these difficulties, use of contrastive analysis has declined; however, it is acknowledged that the characteristics of a learner's first language can influence the learning of a second language, and this has been referred to as

cross-linguistic influence. Nevertheless, current thinking on L2 learning is that both L1 influences and developmental factors must be taken into account in order to explain L2 learning.

See also **contrastive analysis.**

Lado, R. (1957) *Linguistics across Cultures* (Ann Arbor: University of Michigan Press).
Zobl, H. (1980) 'The formal and developmental selectivity of L1 influence on L2 acquisition', *Language Learning*, 30, 43–57.

Controlled processing

This type of language processing contrasts with automatic processing. Controlled processing requires explicit and direct effort on the learner's part, and it occurs with language that is less familiar to the learner. Learning, then, proceeds from controlled to automatic processing.

See also **skill acquisition theory.**

Conversation analysis (CA)

A type of analysis that examines talk. CA is concerned with how interactional participants use language to do things and to make sense of the interaction. CA is especially interested in turn taking and the repair of communication problems in interaction. CA also highly discourages the use of externally imposed categories to make sense of the data. For example, in looking at classroom interaction, the researcher should not be concerned with labels such as teacher/student or male/female. Rather the researcher should look at if, and how, those roles may be realized in the discourse. CA did not begin by examining L2 interaction; however, it has become a popular method for analysing L2 interaction.

Mori, J. (2007) 'Border crossings? Exploring the intersection of second language acquisition, conversation analysis, and foreign language pedagogy', *The Modern Language Journal*, 91, 849–62.
Richards, K. and Seedhouse, P. (2005) *Applying Conversation Analysis* (Basingstoke: Palgrave Macmillan).

Corpus/corpora

The collection of a body of language, typically of written material, though collections of oral data are becoming common. An example of a corpus is the British National Corpus which consists of 100 million words from a variety of documents, such as newspapers, books and interviews (see www.natcorp.ox.ac.uk/). Corpora from both first language and second language speakers (so-called learner language corpora) are possible and they are increasingly becoming available for languages other than English (the Modern Chinese Language Corpus, for example, contains over 700 million characters, dating back to 1919).

Corpus analysis

The process of investigating the linguistic usage in large samples of language use. Corpus analysis can provide information about how native speakers actually use a language. For instance they can empirically document the most frequent words and expressions in the corpus. Such information can then be useful for L2 instruction. In addition, analysis of learner corpora can provide insight into how learners use and learn the language. Corpus analysis is used for research but also by teachers for the purposes of selecting samples of the target language. In addition, some teachers train students in the use of a corpus, especially for support in writing.

The software used to analyse a corpus is called a concordancer. Common concordancers in language research include *Wordsmith* and *MonoConc.*

One study (Fan 2009) – involving a corpus analysis that investigated ESL student use of collocations in writing – found several patterns. One specific example involves *look*. The data revealed that as many as 12 instances of *looked like*, three instances of *looked as if* and one case of *look as if* were used. Corpus data are often presented in the manner below with the immediate surrounding linguistic context:

. . . *looked as if he had a cut down the . . .*
. . . *looked as if it had been broken.*
. . . *a pendant that looked like a ring*
. . . *a pendant on it that looked like a round ring . . .*

Bowker, L. and Pearson, J. (2002) *Working with Specialized Language: A Practical Guide to Using Corpora* (London: Routledge).
Fan, M. (2009) 'An exploratory study of collocational use by ESL students: a task based approach', *System*, 37, 110–23.

Corpus linguistics

The study of language with the use of **corpora**. Corpus linguistics can provide information into how language is actually used, based on the spoken and/or written texts that are used. Information can be gained about the frequency of word occurrence in a corpus, as well as the **collocations** in which specific words occur. Corpus linguistics has primarily investigated L1 language corpora; however, L2 corpora have also been examined. Insights from corpus linguistics have informed aspects of SLA research and pedagogy.

Ellis, N.C., Simpson-Vlach, R. and Maynard, C. (2008) 'Formulaic language in native and second language speakers: psycholinguistics, corpus linguistics, and TESOL', *TESOL Quarterly*, 42, 375–96.

Corrective feedback

Corrective feedback occurs in response to learners' production errors. As such, it provides **negative evidence** to learners about what is not possible in the target language. The usefulness of corrective feedback for L2 learning has been debated in SLA. Some argue that corrective feedback may be embarrassing for learners and that it does not affect learners' interlanguage system. Other researchers argue that corrective feedback, particularly during **communicative language teaching**, can help learners notice the difference between their own L2 production and the correct target language form. Corrective feedback can occur in several different ways, with several broad distinctions made regarding their characteristics. One dimension, related to the **noticing hypothesis**, concerns the explicitness of corrective feedback. Some researchers argue that more implicit types of feedback are beneficial, while other researchers counter that more explicit types are needed for acquisition to occur. Another contrast in types of feedback is whether the feedback is input-providing, with the teacher providing the correct form, or output-prompting, with the teacher encouraging the learner to self-correct the error. Opponents of input-providing feedback suggest that learners may simple mimic the correction without mentally processing it, while output-prompting feedback involves learners in deeper mental processing as they search for the correct form. Three of the most common forms are recast, elicitation or metalinguistic feedback. Recasts, which reformulate the incorrect utterance, tend to be more implicit, but they provide the correct form for the learners. Elicitations provide an opportunity for learners to self-correct, and thus are argued to be better for L2 learning. Metalinguistic feedback is more explicit, which may interrupt the communicative flow, but this type makes the error more noticeable. Studies that have compared different types of feedback have produced varying results. In general, corrective feedback appears to be beneficial and it would seem that more explicit feedback options may be somewhat more effective.

Li, S. (2010) 'The effectiveness of corrective feedback in SLA: a meta-analysis', *Language Learning*, 60, 309–65.

Lyster, R. and Saito, K. (2010) 'Oral feedback in classroom SLA', *Studies in Second Language Acquisition*, 32, 265–302.

Cotext
The immediately surrounding linguistic environment in which a word or grammatical feature occurs.

Covert error
See **error.**

CR task
See **consciousness raising task.**

Creole
A language that develops as a result of extended contact between speakers of several different languages. Speakers may first develop a pidgin that combines the grammar and vocabulary of two or more languages. When that language is passed on to their children as a first language it becomes a creole. An example is French Creole in Haiti.

Siegel, J. (2008) *The Emergence of Pidgin and Creole Languages* (Oxford: Oxford University Press).

Critical pedagogy

Critical pedagogy is a philosophy that is concerned with the power structures in society and how they are maintained or resisted. Critical pedagogy in SLA seeks to point out underlying assumptions about language use that reinforce unequal power relationships and to provide learners with the means to change these situations. An example of critical pedagogy in action is in the area of sexist language. Critical pedagogy would be concerned with identifying sexist language and rectifying its occurrence in society.

Crookes, G. (2010) 'The practicality and relevance of second language critical pedagogy', *Language Teaching*, 43, 333–48.

Norton, B. and Toohey, K. (2004) *Critical Pedagogies and Language Learning* (Cambridge: Cambridge University Press).

Critical period hypothesis

The debate about the effects of age on L2 development has resulted in the formation of the critical period hypothesis which states there is a specific age beyond which it is very difficult, if not impossible, for a person to achieve native-speaker-like status in a second language. Simply put, the argument is that if someone begins to learn an L2 before this critical age, they can achieve native speaker proficiency, but if they begin after the critical period, they cannot. It is suggested that the onset of puberty coincides with the critical age. Thus by the age of around 13, an individual's ability for L2 learning changes. However, some argue that the age of 13 may be a cut off point for grammar learning, but that a cut off point for native-like pronunciation may be as early as six or seven. Some researchers suggest that 'critical period' is too narrow, implying a specific cut off point. They argue instead that a 'sensitive period' may be a better description, allowing for a wider range of ages. Finally, some researchers reject a critical period at all.

Some argue that L2 learners can never acquire native proficiency, while others argue that the age of starting to learn a language is not the critical factor. Rather it is the amount of time and the intensity of the learning that is important.

Birdsong, D. (1999) *Second Language Acquisition and the Critical Period Hypothesis* (Mahwah, NJ: Lawrence Erlbaum).

DeKeyser, R. and Larson-Hall, J. (2005) 'What does the critical period really mean?', in J. Kroll and A. de Groot (eds) *Handbook of Bilingualism: Psycholinguistic Approaches* (Oxford: Oxford University Press), 88–108.

Cross-linguistic influence

This refers to the influence of the L1 on the L2. Although a strong form of the **contrastive analysis hypothesis**, which stated that differences between the L1 and L2 could predict learner difficulties, has been rejected, it is still acknowledged that a learner's L1 can influence their L2 learning. However, rather than a simplistic view of **transfer**, current research is more concerned with the different ways in which the L1 can influence L2 learning and when such influence might occur. This transfer may have a positive effect in that it helps in L2 learning. For example, the presence of similar sounds in the L1 and L2 can be helpful for L2 learning, as can be the presence of **cognates** in the L2. Negative transfer involves the presence of L1 characteristics that hinder the development of the L2. It may be in the form of 'false friends' – words that look similar in both languages but have different meanings. It may also take the form of transferring incorrect grammatical or phonological properties. Finally, it should be noted that the L2 can also have an influence on the L1.

Arabski, J. (2006) *Cross-linguistic Influences in the Second Language Lexicon* (Clevedon: Multilingual Matters).

Kellerman, E. and Sharwood Smith, M. (1986) *Cross-linguistic Influence in Second Language Acquisition* (Elmsford, NY: Pergamon).

Cross-sectional research

A type of research that attempts to look at language development by collecting a one-off sample of data from a large number of learners of different proficiency levels rather than by following learners over a period of time. Thus, differences in language ability among beginning, intermediate and advanced learners are argued to be representative of language development. Cross-sectional research is relatively common in SLA because it is easier to collect data from multiple learners at one point in time, rather than to follow learners over a longer period of time to measure their development, as is done in **longitudinal research**.

Caprin, C. and Guasti, M. (2009) 'The acquisition of morphosyntax in Italian: a cross-sectional study', *Applied Psycholinguistics*, 30, 23–52.

Jansen, L. (2008) 'Acquisition of German word order in tutored learners: a cross-sectional study in a wider theoretical context', *Language Learning*, 58, 185–231.

C-unit

C-unit is the commonly used abbreviation for a communication unit. A c-unit is similar to the **t-unit**, in that it consists of an independent clause and all of its associated dependent clauses, but a c-unit also includes non-clausal structures, such as one or two word utterances like *yes* or *okay*, which have communicative value.

See also **AS-unit.**

Curriculum

The course of study that is employed by a school or in a class. In SLA, there is debate about the balance between the linguistic and communicative components of a curriculum. Some advocate an entirely meaning-focused curriculum where the focus is on activities that facilitate communication; others advocate a curriculum that focuses on a series of linguistic structures. It is also possible to have curricula that contain elements of both approaches.

See also **communicative language teaching.**

C

Data

(a) This term can refer to the information that learners receive in order to develop their L2 knowledge. This may include information about linguistic rules, as well as the actual language that they are exposed to. A more common way of expressing this concept is **input**.

(b) In terms of SLA research, 'data' refers to information gathered for the purposes of increasing our understanding of SLA. Data can consist of many different things: learners' written and oral production, test scores, grammaticality judgements, beliefs and attitudes, introspective comments and reaction times.

Declarative L2 knowledge

A type of knowledge that is open to conscious reflection and that can be verbalized by learners. Not specific to language learning, declarative knowledge consists of facts and knowledge that people possess, for instance 2 + 2 = 4 or the capital of Italy is Rome. In reference to L2 learning, such verbalizable knowledge consists of facts or rules that learners know about the L2. Such knowledge can consist of **metalinguistic** terminology (e.g. subjects and verbs have to agree in English) or it can consist of non-technical terms (e.g. when talking about the present, add -s to English verbs followed by *he* or *she*). However expressed, the learners are aware of what they know about the language. For example, L2 learners of Mandarin Chinese might know that Chinese is a tonal language and that the tones are necessary for word production. However, this does not mean that learners necessarily know how to use these tones when speaking or listening to the language. Declarative knowledge is similar to **explicit L2 knowledge** and contrasts with **procedural knowledge**. The acquisition of declarative knowledge is the starting point of learning for **skill acquisition theories**, with declarative knowledge becoming proceduralized with practice. However, one of the controversies in SLA is whether or not declarative knowledge can become proceduralized. Some researchers argue that it is distinct from proceduralized knowledge and that it cannot be converted. Others, particularly those associated with skill-building theories, see it as becoming more and more proceduralized through practice.

See also **interface hypothesis.**

Deductive instruction

Deductive instruction involves teaching explicit rules about the L2. Learners are aware of what they are being taught, and they are expected to be able to apply the rules that they are taught. Deductive instruction is often associated with **grammar translation** methods of L2 instruction. It is generally accepted that deductive instruction can result in learners having **explicit** or **declarative knowledge** about the L2; however, it is less clear if deductive instruction can result in **implicit** or **proceduralized** L2 knowledge that learners can use for spontaneous language production.

Erlam, R. (2003) 'The effects of deductive and inductive instruction on the acquisition of direct object pronouns in French as a second language', *The Modern Language Journal*, 87, 242–60.

Takimoto, M. (2008) 'The effects of deductive and inductive instruction on the development of language learners' pragmatic competence', *The Modern Language Journal*, 92, 369–86.

Depth of knowledge

A term, primarily associated with vocabulary learning, that describes the amount of information that a learner knows about a specific word. Learners may only know the basic form and meaning of a word, or they may have a deeper knowledge of the word, such as its derivational forms, its collocations or its connotations. For instance, learners may know the basic meaning of *break* as 'to cause something to go into pieces', but a deeper knowledge would also include knowing other aspects of the word, such as its use in expressions like *take a break* and *break up*.

Haastrup, K. and Henriksen, B. (2000) 'Vocabulary acquisition: acquiring depth of knowledge through network building', *International Journal of Applied Linguistics*, 10, 221–40.

Nassaji, H. (2006) 'The relationship between depth of vocabulary knowledge and L2 learners' lexical inferencing strategy use and success', *The Modern Language Journal*, 90, 387–401.

Depth of processing theory

Depth of processing theory claims that the way information is processed will to a large extent determine learning, with more elaborate forms of processing leading to more learning. Originally proposed by Craik and Lockhart in 1972, depth of processing theory suggests that what one remembers is affected by the number of times that a stimulus is encountered and by the quality of those encounters. Furthermore, input that is attended to in greater detail and enriched by its environment is more likely to be remembered. These statements would imply that conscious attention to language input and deliberate activities involving that input could help with acquisition. In practice, however, it has been found to be difficult to apply the theory, partly because it is difficult to measure to what depth information has been processed. Even when it is possible to estimate depth of processing based on external factors such as number of encounters with a linguistic feature, it is not always clear how to interpret such data, as what may be shallow processing for a learner in one situation may be deep and meaningful processing in another, depending on the type of retrieval the learner expects to have to perform. In addition, research has shown improved learning can occur without a change in processing depth (for example through task repetition). Another problem is that the tests used to measure learning are often biased towards deep processing.

An example of the use of depth of processing to make claims about L2 learning comes from studies of **corrective feedback**. It is argued that getting students to

D

self-correct after they have made an error, as in Example 1, rather than having them repeat a correction provided by the teacher, as in Example 2, leads to deeper processing.

Example 1
S: *yesterday I go to town*
T: *yesterday you what?*
S: *I went to town*

Example 2
S: *yesterday I go to town*
T: *yesterday you went to town?*
S: *yes, I went to town*

Craik, F.I. and Lockhart, R. (1972) 'Levels of processing: a framework for memory research', *Journal of Verbal Learning and Verbal Behavior*, 11, 671–83.
Craik, F.I. and Tulving, E. (1975) 'Depth of processing and the retention of words in episodic memory', *Journal of Experimental Psychology: General*, 104, 268–94.

Detection

The cognitive registration of input in working memory. Detection can take place without **awareness** and is the first, and prerequisite, stage in the processing of information. Not all information that is detected is processed, and most information decays quickly, unless it is attended to.

See also **attention, awareness.**

Simard, D. and Wong, W. (2001) 'Alertness, orientation, and detection: the conceptualization of attentional functions in SLA', *Studies in Second Language Acquisition*, 23, 103–24.

Development

A way of thinking about L2 learning that emphasizes the process rather than the end product. Rather than looking only at accurate use of the target language and acquisition as evidence of learning, researchers can also look at how learners develop their interlanguage systems. Research has shown that learners do not go immediately from non-target-like use to target-like use. Instead, learners go through **developmental sequences**, some of which do not conform to the target language norms. Nevertheless, the progression through developmental sequences, even the non-target-like ones, can be viewed as a positive indication of learning. Thus, development can still be a measure of L2 learning progress, even though the final stage of target-like use has not been reached.

See also **U-shaped development.**

Developmental error

This refers to the type of error that is to be expected as learners progress in learning an L2. Additionally, developmental errors contrast with transfer errors, which are due to specific L1 influences. An example of a developmental error occurs in the learning of the L2 English past tense. Learners first acquire irregular forms. Then they learn the regular past tense rule of adding -ed to verbs. Consequently, learners may **overgeneralize** the rule to irregular contexts before they fully acquire regular and irregular past tense. Thus, the production of *eated* could be considered a developmental error. These types of errors are also seen regardless of a learner's L1.

See also **U-shaped development.**

Developmental readiness

The learner's potential to acquire a particular linguistic item. A learner is considered developmentally ready to acquire a given structure when he or she is at the required stage of the **developmental sequence** of the structure. In this view, the acquisition of grammatical structures proceeds in a fixed order and learners can only advance to the next stage after they have acquired the earlier stages. For example, there have been six stages identified in the developmental sequence of the acquisition of English question forms, and learners progress through these stages. Research into developmental readiness suggests that it is important to take into account learners' developmental readiness in curriculum development, syllabus design and classroom instruction to ensure there is a match between the **input** provided and the learners' readiness to acquire it. An example of the investigation of developmental readiness comes from Mackey and Philp (1998) who found that only learners who were developmentally ready were able to benefit from corrective feedback on their errors in the production of English question forms.

See also **developmental sequence.**

Mackey, A. and Philp, J. (1998) 'Conversational interaction and second language development: recasts, responses, and red herrings?', *The Modern Language Journal*, 82, 338–56.

Developmental sequence

The acquisition of certain individual **morphemes** has been shown to proceed through a fixed series of stages. Thus, a learner will produce a series of different forms as he or she progresses towards accurate use of the morpheme. Sequences of development have been found for English morphemes such as question formation, past tense and negation. An example of the developmental sequence for English irregular past tense is the following. (1) It is used accurately at first (e.g. *he went*) because learners learn the forms as individual lexical items. (2) As learners understand the rules that apply to the formation of English regular past tense, they apply this rule to all verbs they encounter; in other words, they **overgeneralize** and produce incorrect forms like *he goed*. (3) Eventually, learners are able to distinguish between regular and irregular verbs, and they will again use the correct irregular forms, such as *he went*. This progression is referred to as **u-shaped development.** Another sequence of development for English question formation is shown in Table 3. Instruction has been shown to help speed up the learner's progress through these

D

Table 3 Stages of English question development

Stage	Description of stage	Examples
2	SVO Canonical word order with question intonation	*It's a monster?* *Your cat is black?* *You have a cat?* *I draw a house here?*
3	Fronting: *Wh*/*Do*/Q-word Direct questions with main verbs and some form of fronting	*Where the cats are?* *What the cat doing in your picture?* *Do you have an animal?* *Does in this picture there is a cat?*

4	Pseudo Inversion: Y/N, Copula
	In yes/no questions an auxiliary or
	   modal is in sentence-initial position.
	In *wh*-questions the copula and the
	   subject change positions.
		(Y/N) *Have you got a dog?*
		(Y/N) *Have you drawn the cat?*
		(Cop) *Where, is the cat in your*
		   picture?

5	Do/Aux-second
	Q-word → Aux/modal → subj (main
	   verb, etc.)
	Auxiliary verbs and modals are placed
	   in second position to *wh*-questions
	   (and Q-words) and before subject
	   (applies only in main clauses/direct
	   questions).
		Why (Q) *have* (Aux) *you* (subj) *left*
		   home?
		What do you have?
		Where does your cat sit?
		What have you got in your picture?

6	Cancel Inv, Neg Q; Tag Q
	(Canc Inv) *Can you see what the time is?*
	Cancel Inv: *Wh*-question inversions are
	   not present in relative clauses.
	Neg Q: A negated form of *do*/Aux is
	   placed before the subject.
	Tag Q: An Aux verb and pronoun are
	   attached to end of main clause.
		(Canc Inv) *Can you tell me where*
		   the cat is?
		(Neg Q) *Doesn't your cat look*
		black?
		(Neg Q) *Haven't you seen a dog?*
		(Tag Q) *It's on the wall, isn't it?*

Source: Mackey (1999: 567).

D

sequences, but instruction does not appear to alter their order nor allow learners to skip a stage. In addition, it is important to note that developmental sequence is used to refer to the order of progression within a single morpheme, such as question formation or past tense. Developmental order and **order of acquisition** are terms that are used to refer to the order in which multiple morphemes (such as past tense, articles and plural -*s*) are learned in relation to each other.

Mackey, A. (1999) 'Input, interaction and second language development: an empirical study of question formation in ESL', *Studies in Second Language Acquisition*, 21, 557–87.

Pienemann, M., Johnston, M. and Brindley, G. (1988) 'An acquisition-based procedure for second language assessment', *Studies in Second Language Acquisition*, 10, 217–43.

Developmental stage

See **developmental sequence.**

Dictogloss

A type of classroom activity in which learners take notes while listening to a short L2 passage. Learners are subsequently asked to reconstruct the passage. The primary aim of the activity is for learners to notice gaps in their L2 grammar and vocabulary knowledge as they work on the reconstruction. Often a dictogloss is performed with learners working in pairs or groups, with the goal of having them help each other in reconstructing the passage. Dictogloss has been used in a number of research studies investigating learners' collaborative interaction.

Wajnryb, R. (1990) *Grammar Dictation* (Oxford: Oxford University Press).

Difficulty

The extent to which language or an activity involving language is challenging for the learner. Difficulty is thus a subjective term as different aspects of the language and different activities may be more or less difficult for each individual learner. Difficulty can also be variable for a learner over time, either because the learner improves or because of the context in which the language is used. For example, a stressful situation such as public speaking may raise **anxiety**, and in turn make language production more difficult than in a pair-work activity in class. In this way, difficulty relates to both ability and **affect**. Difficulty could be said to be the subjective experience of **complexity**.

Ellis, R. (2008) 'Investigating grammatical difficulty in second language learning: implications for second language acquisition research and language testing', *International Journal of Applied Linguistics*, 18, 4–22.

Discourse

A term used to refer to linguistic production that is comprised of multiple sentences or **utterances** that are related to each other in some way. Discourse may refer to paragraphs or other extended written texts. Oral discourse can be produced by a single speaker, for example as story or narrative, or it may be produced by multiple speakers, such as a conversation or debate.

Discourse analysis

(a)   A type of analysis that examines the ways in which language is used in interaction. This type of discourse analysis attempts to describe systematically the talk that occurs in a specific context. Specifically, discourse analysis is often concerned with how specific **speech acts**, such as requests, invitations, complaints, etc., are performed in different contexts. Discourse analysis may investigate typical native speaker patterns for specific speech acts and compare L2 learners' performance of the speech acts. Another way in which discourse analysis has been used is in the

D

study of L2 classroom interaction, with researchers describing and categorizing, for example, the types of questions that are asked or the types of corrective feedback that are provided. As such, discourse analysis is a tool that has been used extensively in **interactionist** approaches to SLA.

(b)   A type of analysis that examines how language is used to form larger segments of discourse, such as sentences, paragraphs and whole texts. This type of discourse analysis is concerned with concepts like 'cohesion', which examines how specific words, such as pronouns, are used to link portions of the text together. For example, in the sentences *I saw Mary. She was in the story.* the pronoun *she* refers to *Mary*. In addition, discourse analysis is interested in discourse markers which bring coherence to the text by showing the relationships among the meanings expressed in the text. Thus, discourse markers such as *but*, *however* and *nevertheless* can be used to indicate a contrast between two propositions.

Cole, K. and Zuengler, J. (2008) *The Research Process in Classroom Discourse Analysis: Current Perspectives* (New York: Erlbaum).

Schiffrin, D., Tannen, D. and Hamilton, H. (2003) *The Handbook of Discourse Analysis* (Malden, MA: Blackwell).

Discourse completion task (DCT)

A data collection instrument that is often used in research on **pragmatics**. Learners are provided with a scenario in which they must use language to perform some type of action, such as making a request or declining an invitation. Sometimes learners are also provided with an initial utterance to get them started. Then learners are asked to write (or less often, speak) what they would say in the specific context to accomplish the purpose stated in the task. In this way, learners' ability to use pragmatics appropriately can be measured. An example of a DCT is:

You need to borrow a pen from your classmate. What would you say?

You need to ask your teacher for an extension on your homework assignment. What would you say?

One of the benefits of DCTs is that they allow a researcher to collect data on speech acts for which it might otherwise be difficult to obtain authentic data. However, a disadvantage is that learners may supply what they think they should say, which may differ from what they would say in the actual situation.

Byon, A. (2006) 'Developing KFL students' pragmatic awareness of Korean speech acts: the use of discourse completion tasks', *Language Awareness*, 15, 244–63.

Discourse hypothesis

This hypothesis states that L2 learners will systematically distinguish between foreground information and background information when telling narratives. Foreground information is that which moves the storyline forward, while background information provides additional context and information. Learners use different morphosyntactic forms to express different types of information. This hypothesis is part of a **functionalist approach** to language learning.

Bardovi-Harlig, K. (1998) 'Narrative structure and lexical aspect: conspiring factors in second language acquisition of tense-aspect morphology', *Studies in Second Language Acquisition*, 20, 471–508.

Disrupted turn adjacency

A phenomenon in **computer-mediated communication** whereby chat messages that appear adjacent to each other on a computer screen are not pragmatically relevant to each other. This lack of adjacency can be a result of delays between message production and message appearance on the screen. In the example below, L1's question is followed immediately by L2's question, rather than by the answer to the question. Such disrupted turns differ from face-to-face interaction, and they can lead to **communication breakdown** and **negotiation of meaning**, which can play a role in second language acquisition.

Example:
L1: Hi ☺
L2: Hi there!
L1: So what did you do yesterday?
L2: So what's up?
L1: Nothing special … just chilling out
L2: I went to see the latest Harry Potter movie

Domain

A specific context of language use. Language use may be different across domains. For example, the language that is used in the classroom may be different from the language that is used in the courtroom or on the street.

Dual-mechanism model

See **dual-mode model**.

Dual-mode model

This model proposes that learners' knowledge of language is comprised of two distinct types. One type of knowledge is rule-based and the other is item-based. The rule-based system is made up of rules about the language that can be applied in many instances. For example, the rule of regular plural formation in English states that an -s is added to the end of singular nouns. This knowledge of the rule is then applied when learners want to express plurality. In contrast, item-based knowledge consists of individual, memorized, lexical items. Examples of item-based knowledge associated with English plural formation would be *children*, *mice* and *oxen*. These plural forms cannot be generated by applying rule-based knowledge. Instead, they must be memorized and recalled as individual items.

D

Skehan, P. (1998) *A Cognitive Approach to Language Learning* (Oxford: Oxford University Press).

Dynamic assessment

An assessment procedure that has its origins in Vygotsky's **zone of proximal development** and that integrates assessment with instruction. The assessment involves interaction between the assessor and the learner, during which the assessor offers help to the learner with task completion. Dynamic assessment is intended to gauge a learner's potential to draw on available resources and help. It is thought that a learner's ability to make use of such assistance gives a good indication of his or her ability to complete the task independently in the future. In this way dynamic assessment is a measure of a learner's ability to learn, not a static measure of the outcome of the learning process. The score on a dynamic assessment may be expressed as the difference between the initial performance and the final performance, or the score on the final performance only. Additional measures include learners' ability to transfer what they have learned to other situations and their ability to complete the task independently.

Poehner, M.E. and Lantolf, J.P. (2005) 'Dynamic assessment in the language classroom', *Language Teaching Research*, 9, 233–65.

D

EAP

See **English for academic purposes.**

Elaboration

See **modified input.**

Elicited imitation test

This is a testing instrument that is used primarily in L2 research. It consists of presenting learners with input, generally in the form of oral sentences. After hearing a sentence, learners must respond to its semantic meaning in some way (e.g. by indicating whether the sentence is a true statement or not) and then repeat/reconstruct the sentence. The intention of the test is to measure learners' **implicit L2 knowledge**. If learners have implicit knowledge of the linguistic structures in the sentences, then they will be able to reconstruct them accurately. However, if they only possess **explicit knowledge** or have no knowledge of the structures, then they will not be able to reconstruct the sentences accurately because they will not have sufficient time to draw on their explicit knowledge.

Erlam, R. (2006) 'Elicited imitation as a measure of L2 implicit knowledge: an empirical validation study', *Applied Linguistics*, 27, 464–91.

English for academic purposes (EAP)

EAP is a commonly used abbreviation for the term English for academic purposes. EAP refers to courses taught to those in or entering higher education that focus on **academic language**. EAP is a form of **English for specific purposes** (**ESP**) that aims to prepare learners for using the language in a specific **domain**. The field of EAP has its own journal, the *Journal of English for Academic Purposes*.

James, M. (2006) 'Transfer of learning from a university content-based EAP course', *TESOL Quarterly*, 40, 783–806.

McCarter, S. and Jakes, P. (2009) *Uncovering EAP. How to Teach Academic Writing and Reading* (Oxford: Macmillan Education).

Emergentism

A theory of SLA that proposes that patterns in L2 knowledge emerge as a result of exposure to the target language. Emergentism sees language as a complex, dynamic system that develops in sometimes unsystematic and surprising ways. It sees language learning as similar to other, general, types of learning, and it does not see a role for a unique language learning component of the brain.

See also **connectionism, usage-based theories.**

Behrens, H. (2009) 'Usage-based and emergentist approaches to language acquisition', *Linguistics*, 47, 383–411.
MacWhinney, B. (2006) 'Emergentism: use often and with care', *Applied Linguistics*, 27, 729–40.

English for specific purposes (ESP)

ESP refers to the types of English that are used in specific **domains** or contexts. In addition, ESP often involves the teaching of those characteristics of English to learners who are a part of (or who plan to be a part of) that particular context. In order to know what to teach, researchers generally conduct an analysis of authentic language use in the target domain. For example, Janet Holmes and Maria Stubbe have conducted a large scale study of language in the workplace. Other studies have looked at the language that is used by doctors and nurses, business people and engineers. Furthermore, the field of **English for academic purposes** (EAP) may be considered a subcategory of ESP because it focuses on academic domains of language use. Once the types of language used in those contexts have been identified, those features can then be taught to L2 learners. In many instances, lexical items will comprise a large part of the language that is primarily found in a specific context; however, some speech acts and grammatical structures may also be more common in a specific domain than in other contexts. For example, a hospital may have a number of English L2 speaking nurses; consequently, it may have someone to offer a course on the vocabulary and speech acts that are frequently used in this context. The goal of ESP instruction is to help learners to function in their immediate context or to prepare them for a context. The journal *English for Specific Purposes* presents research specifically in this area.

Basturkmen, H. (2010) *Developing Courses in English for Specific Purposes* (Basingstoke: Palgrave Macmillan).
Holmes, J. and Stubbe, M. (2003) *Power and Politeness in the Workplace: A Sociolinguistic Analysis of Talk at Work* (London: Pearson).

Enhanced input

See **input enhancement.**

Enriched input

Input that has been manipulated in some way to increase the possibility of learners paying attention to a particular feature in the input. By artificially increasing the saliency of the target structure, it is thought that learners will notice and thus acquire the structure more easily. Examples of this manipulation include glossing, bolding, underlining or increasing the frequency of the target feature (also called **input flooding**). Enriched input is a form of **input enhancement** and is used as a type of **form-focused instruction**.

Sharwood Smith, M. (1993) 'Input enhancement in instructed SLA: theoretical bases', *Studies in Second Language Acquisition*, 15, 165–79.

Episodic memory

A memory store of specific events, or the recollections of specific events contained therein. It is distinct from **semantic memory**. Episodic memory has been investigated in relation to how language is stored in and retrieved from the brain.

Schrauf, R., Pavlenko, A. and Dewaele, J. (2003) 'Bilingual episodic memory: an introduction', *International Journal of Bilingualism*, 7, 221–33.

Error

A systematic divergence in the learner's L2 production from the target language. In the early behaviourist days of SLA, errors were viewed negatively because it was believed that if the learner was allowed to continue making them, they would become a learned **habit**. However, as **error analysis** gained popularity in the 1970s and 1980s, errors came to be viewed as evidence of learning/development, as learners tried systematically to incorporate L2 rules into their interlanguage systems. Errors differ from **mistakes** in that the latter are not systematic. Mistakes may be the result of time pressure or simple slips of the tongue, and consequently learners can correct them quite easily. A distinction can be made between overt errors, which can be detected by inspecting the sentence or utterance in which it occurs, and covert errors, which only become apparent when a larger stretch of discourse is considered. Another distinction that is made is between global errors and local errors. Local errors occur within the context of one or two words, for example *He eated yesterday*. Global errors occur within a larger context, such as an entire sentence or utterance, or even with an extended piece of discourse such as a paragraph. For example, *Mary is a very nice girl, and I really like him*.

Lennon, P. (1991) 'Error: some problems of definition, identification and distinction', *Applied Linguistics*, 12, 180–95.

Error analysis

The study of learner errors in the production of L2 speech and writing. (Errors in comprehension are less commonly investigated as they are difficult to detect.) Error analysis consists of the identification, description and explanation of errors. Error analysis was popular in the 1970s and was often used to show the effects of the L1 on the L2, as emphasized by the **contrastive analysis hypothesis**. The underlying thinking was that errors in L2 learning were caused by differences between the L1 and L2. In practice, however, many error analysis studies showed that learners produce errors that cannot be attributed to the L1; rather, the errors reflect different **developmental sequences** that learners go through in developing target language competency. In fact, error analysis identified two types of errors: interlingual and intralingual. Interlingual errors are those that can be attributed to L1 influence. Intralingual errors are those that cannot be explained by the L1 and instead are seen as being developmental in nature. Thus, intralingual errors would presumably be made by all learners of the target language, regardless of their L1s.

E

This acknowledgement of developmental errors contributed to **interlanguage** theory and **nativist** theories, which suggest that L2 learning is not merely a process of **habit** formation.

Error analysis is limited in scope because it focuses on what learners do wrong and not on what they do right. It also does not take into account learners' avoidance in producing difficult grammatical structures. Additionally, it is also sometimes difficult to determine what the error is or what caused the error. As a result, the use of error analysis has declined from the late 1970s, although it is still used as a tool for measuring linguistic **accuracy**.

Corder, P. (1967) 'The significance of learners' errors', *International Review of Applied Linguistics*, 5, 161–70.
Corder, P. (1981) *Error Analysis in Interlanguage* (Oxford: Oxford University Press).

Error correction

The provision of a target-like linguistic form in response to a learner's production of a non-target-like form. This term is often used interchangeably with **corrective feedback**.

ESP

See **English for specific purposes.**

Ethnography

A type of **qualitative research** in which researchers immerse themselves in the context under consideration in order to gain a better understanding of that context. For example, a researcher may observe an L2 classroom over a length of time, and then describe important aspects of the classroom environment. Ethnographers often do not begin a research project with preconceived research questions that they seek to answer; instead, they may have a more general focus. In addition, ethnographers want to present an insider's perspective in their analysis that presents the participants' views and perceptions of the context under investigation.

Han, H. (2009) 'Institutionalized inclusion: a case study on support for immigrants in English learning', *TESOL Quarterly*, 43, 643–68.
Rivers, W. (2001) 'Autonomy at all costs: an ethnography of metacognitive self-assessment and self-management among experienced language learners', *The Modern Language Journal*, 85, 279–90.

E

Exemplar

The occurrence of a specific linguistic item or structure in the input, which serves as an example of what is possible in the L2.

See also **exemplar-based learning.**

Exemplar-based learning

A type of learning in which learners use newly encountered instances of words or syntactic structures to build their interlanguage system. The more exemplars or instances of the linguistic item that are encountered, the stronger the particular structure in the learner's system becomes. Exemplar-based learning theories of SLA propose that language learning occurs in a similar fashion to other, non-linguistic, types of learning; consequently it differs from theories of L2 learning, such as **universal grammar**, that propose a role in the learning process for an underlying system of abstract grammar.

See also **connectionism, emergentism.**

Explicit corrective feedback

A response to a learner's error that directly draws attention to the error in some way. Explicit correction may involve **metalinguistic** feedback, but it does not have to. One of the proposed benefits of explicit correction is that it makes the errors more salient, and it can also help pinpoint the nature of the error for the learner. However, explicit correction can also be disruptive to the flow of interaction and potentially embarrassing for the learner. In the example below, the provision of a metalinguistic description of the error helps to identify the error as well as draw considerable attention to it.

Learner: *He kiss her*
Researcher: *Kiss – you need past tense.*
Learner: *He kissed*
(Ellis et al., 2006: 353)

See also **implicit corrective feedback.**

Ellis, R., Loewen, S. and Erlam, R. (2006) 'Implicit and explicit feedback and the acquisition of L2 grammar', *Studies in Second Language Acquisition*, 28, 339–68.
Kang, H. (2009) 'The relative efficacy of explicit and implicit feedback in the learning of a less-commonly-taught foreign language', *International Review of Applied Linguistics*, 47, 303–24.

Explicit instruction

Language teaching that draws attention to language items and language rules in a clear manner and with the express purpose of teaching those linguistic items and rules. Oftentimes, explicit instruction involves the overt presentation of rules of the L2. Learners are expected to learn the L2 rules and then to apply them in their L2 production. This approach is **deductive**, and it is exemplified in the **grammar-translation** method and the **PPP** (present, practice, produce) approach. It is also possible for explicit instruction to be inductive, with learners directed to work out a language rule on their own from a dataset of language that contains examples of the target rule. Although the presentation of the rule is 'discovered' by the student rather than presented by the teacher, the goal of the activity is still to draw attention to the target language. An example of an inductive approach to explicit instruction is the use of **consciousness-raising tasks**. Explicit instruction generally results in **explicit knowledge** about the L2, and, as a result, explicit instruction has been criticized for producing learners who know many language rules, but may not be competent in using the L2 for communication.

E

See also **implicit instruction.**

Macaro, E. and Masterman, L. (2006) 'Does intensive explicit grammar instruction make all the difference?', *Language Teaching Research*, 10, 297–327.

Tode, T. (2007) 'Durability problems with explicit instruction in an EFL context: the learning of the English copula be before and after the introduction of the auxiliary be', *Language Teaching Research*, 11, 11–30.

Explicit knowledge

Explicit knowledge is knowledge that is consciously available to learners. Often learners are able to verbalize their knowledge, although they may not do so in **metalinguistic** terms. (Some argue that it may be possible to have conscious knowledge without being able to verbalize that knowledge.) An example of explicit knowledge is when learners are able to explain why they choose to say *When I saw him yesterday he had already bought the suit* instead of *When I saw him yesterday he already bought the suit*, although they may not use the terms 'past perfect' and 'past simple'.

Explicit knowledge is distinct from **implicit knowledge** which does not involve a conscious representation of the knowledge, and thus does not allow learners to verbalize that knowledge. In the example above, learners might use the correct tense by drawing on their implicit knowledge, but they would not be able to explain why or under what circumstances they should choose one tense over the other.

The distinction between implicit and explicit knowledge lies at the heart of several SLA theories. Krashen, for example, argues that explicit knowledge ('learned knowledge') cannot become implicit knowledge ('acquired knowledge'). This is known as the **non-interface position.** Others have argued that explicit knowledge can become implicit knowledge and that in addition explicit knowledge can be drawn on during language learning and language use. In the latter view, explicit knowledge can help learners to **notice** aspects of the language which can then be analysed. It can also help learners to identify and solve problems that occur in their use of the language. Explicit knowledge in the form of metalinguistic knowledge can also play a facilitative role by allowing learners to talk about language with others more easily.

Ellis, N.C. (2005) 'At the interface: dynamic interactions of explicit and implicit language knowledge', *Studies in Second Language Acquisition*, 27, 305–52.

Ellis, R. (2004) 'The definition and measurement of L2 explicit knowledge', *Language Learning*, 54, 227–75.

Explicit learning

Learning that occurs with awareness of the L2 feature that is being learned and with an intention to learn that feature. Explicit learning often results in **explicit knowledge**; however, it is arguably possible for explicit learning to contribute to **implicit knowledge**. The role of explicit learning in SLA is controversial because researchers do not agree on the role of explicit knowledge in L2 learning. Those who view implicit and explicit knowledge as separate entities which do not influence each other see only a limited role for explicit learning. However, researchers who believe that explicit knowledge can help in the development of implicit knowledge propose a greater role for explicit learning.

See also **implicit learning, interface hypothesis.**

Explicit memory

Recollections that can be consciously retrieved. The explicit memory is where explicit knowledge about the L2 is stored, and this knowledge can be accessed by learners. However, the retrieval of information from explicit memory is not automatized, and therefore learners are generally not able to draw on it during real-time communication.

Bird, S. and Williams, J. (2002) 'The effect of bimodal input on implicit and explicit memory: an investigation into the benefits of within-language subtitling', *Applied Psycholinguistics*, 23, 509–33.

Exposure

The amount, duration and type of **input** that learners experience. Researchers agree that learners cannot acquire the target language without exposure; however, the precise role of exposure to input is debated. For example, **nativist theories**, drawing on the **poverty of the stimulus** argument, propose that even limited exposure can be used by learners' **innate** language learning system. However, **connectionist theories** argue that frequency of exposure plays a much greater role in L2 learning. Another issue in SLA is the age at which learners are first exposed to the target language, as well as the length of time that learners are exposed to the L2.

See also **critical period hypothesis.**

Paradis, J. (2010) 'Bilingual children's acquisition of English verb morphology: effects of language exposure, structure complexity, and task type', *Language Learning*, 60, 651–80.

Extrinsic motivation

A motivational orientation to language learning that comes from a source external to the learner. Examples of extrinsic motivation include studying a language in order to complete a school requirement or to get a job promotion. Extrinsic motivation is similar to **instrumental motivation**; however, even though instrumental motivation may be directed towards achieving an externally imposed goal (such as passing a class), it is still viewed as coming from within the learner. In practice, however, such distinctions may not be meaningful or measurable.

See also **intrinsic motivation.**

Noels, K. (2001) 'Learning Spanish as a second language: learners' orientations and perceptions of their teachers' communication style', *Language Learning*, 51, 107–44.
Vandergrift, L. (2005) 'Relationships among motivation orientations, metacognitive awareness and proficiency in L2 listening', *Applied Linguistics*, 26, 70–89.

E

Extroversion/introversion

An **individual learner difference** that relates to how sociable and outgoing a person is. Although extroversion and introversion are often presented as a dichotomy, it is perhaps better to conceptualize them as being at either end of a continuum. Personality characteristics such as extroversion/introversion have been measured with test instruments such as the Eysenck Personality Questionnaire and the Myers Briggs Type Indicator. Extroversion may influence L2 learning because extroverts are more likely to seek out opportunities for interaction with other speakers of the L2. In contrast, introverts may have fewer opportunities for interaction, due to their personality type. Some research indicates that extroverts may indeed be more fluent in using the language; however, it has also suggested that introverts tend to be more accurate in their language use.

Dewaele, J. (2005) 'Investigating the psychological and emotional dimensions in instructed language learning: obstacles and possibilities', *The Modern Language Journal*, 89, 367–80.

E

Facilitation

A type of **transfer** in which characteristics of the L1 help in the learning of the L2. Such help may occur in various linguistic areas, such as grammar, vocabulary and pronunciation. An example of facilitation would involve the ease with which English learners of Spanish have in learning to mark plurality since both languages use -s as a plural marker. Another example is the help that **cognates** provide in learning L2 vocabulary.

FFE

See **focus on form episode**.

FFI

See **form-focused instruction**.

Field dependence/independence

An individual cognitive difference that refers to the ability of people's visual perception to recognize objects that are embedded within larger contexts. Thus, field dependent individuals are more holistic in their perceptions and are less able to distinguish specific elements within a larger context. In contrast, field independent individuals are more analytic and are able to ignore the larger visual field in order to find specific objects within it. One way to measure field dependence is by using the Embedded Figures Test in which participants have to find a simple geometric object within a more complex figure. Although the effects of field dependence/independence on L2 learning are debated, it is argued that field independent learners may be better at analysing the components of the L2, while field dependent learners may be better at taking in the whole context of the L2 situation.

See also **individual differences**.

Chapelle, C. and Green, P. (1992) 'Field independence/dependence in second language acquisition research', Language Learning, 42, 47–83.
Johnson, J., Prior, S. and Artuso, M. (2000) 'Field dependence as a factor in second language communicative production', Language Learning, 50, 529–67.

First language (L1)

(a) The initial language that a person learns as a child. This language may also be referred to as a **native language** or **mother tongue**.

(b) The language that an individual is most proficient in. Often an individual's most proficient language is the one that they first learned as a child; however, in some cases, a person may be more proficient or more comfortable in using a language that they learned subsequent to their initial childhood language.

First language acquisition

The study of how children acquire their native language. Research into first language acquisition has been influential in the study of SLA, with many issues of language acquisition being first identified in L1 acquisition and then investigated in L2 acquisition. In addition, theories of L1 acquisition, such as **universal grammar**, have had a profound impact on SLA. Nevertheless, there are clear differences between first and second language acquisition. The most notable difference is the level of ultimate attainment that learners achieve. First language learners always achieve full proficiency (barring some types of cognitive impairment). On the other hand, the majority of L2 learners do not attain similar levels of proficiency.

See also **morpheme studies.**

Clark, E. (2009) *First Language Acquisition*, 2nd edn (Cambridge: Cambridge University Press).

Lust, B. and Foley, C. (2004) *First Language Acquisition: The Essential Readings* (Malden, MA: Blackwell).

Fluency

A measure of learners' ability to produce language (usually used to refer to spoken, but sometimes also written, language) at a speed similar to that of native speakers. Common measures of fluency investigate temporal variables, such as the rate of speech (words per minute); the number and length of pauses; the length of run (average number of syllables between two pauses); and hesitation variables, such as false starts, repetitions and self-corrections. Fluency is often measured together with **accuracy** and **complexity** to provide an overall picture of L2 learners' **proficiency**.

Rossiter, M., Derwing, T., Manimtim, L. and Thomson, R. (2010) 'Oral fluency: the neglected component in the communicative language classroom', *The Canadian Modern Language Review/La Revue canadienne des langues vivantes*, 66, 583–606.

Trofimovich, P. and Baker, W. (2006) 'Learning second language suprasegmentals: effect of L2 experience on prosody and fluency characteristics of L2 speech', *Studies in Second Language Acquisition*, 28, 1–30.

Focus on form

Focus on form is a term that has been used in a variety of ways in SLA. The term was introduced by Michael Long in the early 1990s to refer to brief and spontaneous attention to language items during otherwise meaning-oriented L2 classroom activities. As such, it contrasted with **focus on forms** and **focus on meaning**. It was proposed as a type of **negotiation of meaning** that could help draw learners' attention to language items that were hindering communication. Subsequently, however, focus on form has come to refer to attention to language items that are

F

used inaccurately, even if the inaccurate use does not impede communication. Furthermore, focus on form is now often viewed as containing a pre-emptive element as well. Ellis (2001) refers to this distinction with the terms 'planned focus on form' and 'incidental focus on form'. Incidental focus on form is in keeping with Long's original definition, in that it occurs spontaneously in response to learners' errors. However, planned focus on form occurs when teachers (or researchers) decide to target specific errors that learners make. For instance, a teacher might wish to focus on past tense errors that learners make during a communicative task. Often focus on form takes the shape of **corrective feedback** in response to learners' errors; however, other types of attention-drawing instruction methods, such as **input flood** and **input enhancement**, have also been classified as types of focus on form. In addition, students may also initiate questions about language items during meaning-focused activities. Research into focus on form has mushroomed in recent years because it is considered a helpful way to emphasize both **accuracy** and **fluency** in the classroom. However, much of the research has not investigated focus on form in general, but rather it has investigated different focus on form options, such as corrective feedback or input enhancement.

Doughty, C. and Williams, J. (eds) (1998) *Focus on Form in Classroom Second Language Acquisition* (Cambridge: Cambridge University Press).

Ellis, R. (2001) 'Investigating form-focused instruction', in R. Ellis (ed.) *Form-focused Instruction and Second Language Learning* (Malden, MA: Blackwell), 1–46.

Long, M. (1991) 'Focus on form: a design feature in language teaching methodology', in K. de Bot, R. Ginsberg and C. Kramsch (eds) *Foreign Language Research in Cross-cultural Perspective* (Amsterdam: John Benjamins).

Focus on form episode (FFE)

All of the **discourse** that constitutes uninterrupted attention to a single linguistic item during a communicative activity. An FFE may begin when a learner **error** is highlighted in some way, when a question about a linguistic item is raised or when the teacher advises learners to pay attention to a specific linguistic item. The FFE ends when the discourse returns to the original topic of communication or when attention turns to a different linguistic item. As such, an FFE is an attempt to operationalize the construct of focus on form.

F

FFE example:
In this FFE, the student is talking about his army experiences. The FFE is triggered by the student's incorrect preposition use in line 3, which the teacher corrects in line 4. The student repetition of the correct form in line 5 ends the FFE, since the topic of conversation shifts back to the original topic in line 6.

1 S: *when I was soldier I used to wear the balaclava*
2 T: *and why did you wear it S for protection from the cold or for another reason*
3 S: *just wind uh protection to wind and cold*
4 T: *protection from*
5 S: *uh from wind and cold*
6 T: *right (·) okay not for a disguise*
Loewen and Philp (2006: 543)

Ellis, R., Basturkmen, H. and Loewen, S. (2001) 'Learner uptake in communicative ESL lessons', *Language Learning*, 51, 281–318.

Loewen, S. and Philp, J. (2006) 'Recasts in the adult L2 classroom: characteristics, explicitness and effectiveness', *Modern Language Journal*, 90, 536–56.

Focus on forms

A term used by Michael Long to refer to L2 instructional activities that have as their primary goal the teaching of specific aspects of the language, generally by presenting discrete grammatical rules in a systematic manner. Critics of focus on forms instruction argue that the presentation of language rules in this manner does not contribute to L2 learning because it does not necessarily coincide with the **natural order** of acquisition that learners engage in. In addition, learning grammar rules may not help learners to communicate successfully when they must produce language in real time. However, it has been recently acknowledged that some types of language structures, such as those that are not very **salient** in the L2, may need some type of focus on forms instruction for students' to notice them. Focus on forms instruction contrasts with **focus on form** and **meaning-focused instruction**.

Laufer, B. (2006) 'Comparing focus on form and focus on forms in second-language vocabulary learning', *The Canadian Modern Language Review/La Revue canadienne des langues vivantes*, 63, 149–66.

Foreign language

In common usage, a foreign language is a language that is not one's first language. More specifically, it is a language that is not spoken as a majority or official language in a country.

Foreign language learning

The study of an additional language in a context where that language is not the dominant language of society and the learners do not have any familial or social ties to the language. For example, if an L1 speaker of English is studying Japanese in the United States, they are in a foreign language learning context. Conversely, if an L1 speaker of Japanese is studying English in Japan, they are also engaged in foreign language learning. This term contrasts with **second language learning** and **heritage language learning**. One important distinction between foreign and second language learning contexts is based on the amount of exposure that learners have to the target language outside of the classroom. Typically, learners have very little such exposure in foreign language learning contexts. In contrast, heritage language learners may have some exposure to the target language and its culture because they have family ties to the language. However, the amount of exposure in heritage language learning may vary greatly. In spite of the differences in the amount of exposure between foreign and second language contexts, there is little clear evidence to suggest that the cognitive processes involved in L2 learning are qualitatively different in the two learning contexts.

Foreigner talk

A type of language that is sometimes used by native speakers to communicate with L2 learners. Foreigner talk is characterized by modifications such as the use of simpler vocabulary, a slower speech rate, increased volume, repetition and sometimes even ungrammatical utterances. While foreigner talk may be helpful for immediate communication, its benefits for L2 learning are debated because it does not generally provide target-like **input** for learners.

Example: These two utterances illustrate the differences in language that was used during a communicative task involving native speaker to native speaker interaction and native speaker to non-native speaker interaction respectively.

1. Native speaker to native speaker: *There's a bird, like it's coming out of the chimney of the broken house.*
2. Native speaker to non-native speaker: *Bird. The bird, did you find the bird? Put in the broken house. That was broken. At the top. The broken house. That was broken. On top-on top (=at the very top) of the broken house.*

(Ravid et al., 2003: 84)

See also **caretaker talk, modified input.**

Ravid, D., Olshtain, E. and Ze'elon, R. (2003) 'Gradeschoolers' linguistic and pragmatic speech adaptation to native and non-native interlocution', *Journal of Pragmatics*, 35, 71–99.

Formal approaches to SLA

Theories of L2 learning that draw upon linguistic theories, that is to say formal descriptions of language. **Universal grammar** is an example of a formal approach that is used widely in SLA theory and research. Another example is lexical functional grammar, a systematic description of the relationship between components in a sentence used specifically to underpin Pienemann's **processability theory**.

Form-focused instruction (FFI)

A range of instructional methods that direct learners' attention to language items. As such, FFI contrasts with **meaning-focused instruction**. One of the main issues in FFI is the amount of attention that is given to language items. Consequently, FFI is generally divided into two main categories: **focus on forms** and **focus on form**. The former consists of instruction that is primarily oriented towards language items, with explicit instructional methods such as **grammar translation** and **PPP** being examples of such overt attention. In contrast, focus on form consists of instructional methods that have less of an emphasis on language items and that incorporate such attention to language within a larger, primary focus on communication. Examples of this type of instruction include **input flood** and **input enhancement** in which learners are given texts that incorporate numerous exemplars of a specific linguistic structure. Other types of instruction include communicative tasks in which **corrective feedback** is given in response to **errors** in learners' production. Thus, in these types of activities, there is a primary focus on meaning, but there is also deliberate, albeit generally brief, attention to language form.

F

The role of FFI in instructed SLA is controversial. Communicative language teaching approaches argue that FFI should have a limited role, if any, since it views language acquisition as a process that is not greatly influenced by overt instruction. In contrast, some theorists argue that overt and extensive attention to language form is essential in the classroom. However, the predominant view is that FFI can be beneficial for learners, and that there should be a balance between meaning-focused and form-focused instruction. However, the question still remains as to what types of FFI are most beneficial for L2 learners.

Ellis, R. (2001) 'Investigating form-focused instruction', In R. Ellis (ed.) *Form-focused Instruction and Second Language Learning* (Malden, MA: Blackwell), 1–46.

Nassaji, H. and Fotos, S. (2011) *Teaching Grammar in Second Language Classrooms: Integrating Form-focused Instruction in Communicative Context* (New York: Routledge).

Form-function analysis

This process involves identifying the specific functions that a language form can perform. At the broadest level, an example of such form-function mapping could be seen in the suffix -*s* in English which can indicate plurality (*dogs*), possession (the dog's bone) or third person present tense (*The dog likes the bone*). Consequently, one form has three different functions. However, more specifically in SLA, form-function analysis is often used to investigate the variation that occurs in learners' **interlanguage** use of specific morphosyntactic features. Because L2 learners' interlanguage differs from L1 speakers' linguistic system, researchers can use a form-function analysis to investigate the ways in which learners use specific forms for specific functions. For example, several studies have examined how L2 learners of English use the article system. L1 speakers of English use articles to express a combination of two functions: (1) articles are used to indicate information that is assumed to be either known or unknown to the listener, and (2) articles are used to express specific or generic reference. The details of this form-function mapping are shown in Table 4. Studies of L2 learners' use of articles have shown patterns that may not conform to L1 speakers' use of the article system; nevertheless, learners consistently use specific forms to express specific functions. Furthermore, the learners' use of such forms can evolve over time as it becomes more target-like. The benefit of form-function analysis is that it enables researchers to identify such systematic use when it might otherwise be obscured by an analysis that simply compares learners' production to target language norms.

F

Table 4   Noun phrase types

	– Hearer Knowledge	**+ Hearer Knowledge**
– Specific Referent	a or Ø article *I'm looking for a good book.*	the, a or Ø article *Elephants are large animals.* *The elephant is a large animal.* *An elephant is a large animal.*
+ Specific Referent	a or Ø article *He has a nice cat.*	the *The dog in the picture is cute.*

Tarone, E. and Parrish, B. (1988) 'Task-related variation in interlanguage: the case of articles', *Language Learning*, 38, 21–44.

Form-meaning mapping

The relationship between specific language items and the meanings that they express. Arguably, L2 learning is a process of attaching meaning to specific language items. For instance, beginning learners of English soon come to realize that the -*s* in *cats* and *dogs* indicates plurality. Thus, they have made the connection between (or mapped) the form and the meaning. While this process can happen with grammatical forms, it also happens with lexical items as learners make connections between specific words and their meanings. In form-meaning mapping, learners tend to start off with a **one-to-one principle**, in which they assign one, and only one, meaning to a specific form. However, as a learner's **interlanguage** system develops, he or she realizes that one form may have multiple meanings. For example, *bank* refers to both a financial institution as well as the border of a river. Conversely, one meaning may be expressed by multiple forms. For instance, the sentences *I'm flying to Chicago tomorrow* and *I fly to Chicago tomorrow* both express future time; however, they use different verb forms to do so. **Interactionist** theories of SLA claim that the ideal conditions for the occurrence of form-meaning mapping are contexts where attention can be given to both form and meaning at the same time, and where the overall meaning is relatively clear to the learner. Thus, in communicative activities in which the learners are expressing their own ideas, they can focus briefly on linguistic items that they may need to help them express themselves accurately. This bringing together of meaning and form at a time of communicative need is argued to be ideal for form-meaning mapping.

Jiang, N. (2002) 'Form-meaning mapping in vocabulary acquisition in a second language', *Studies in Second Language Acquisition*, 24, 617–37.
VanPatten, B., Williams, J., Rott, S. and Overstreet, M. (2004) *Form-meaning Connections in Second Language Acquisition* (New York: Routledge).

Formulaic sequence

A series of two or more words that often occur together. These may also be referred to as **chunks**. Formulaic sequences may consist of readily identifiable units such as 'I don't know' or 'how are you'. These types of formulaic sequences can be useful for learners because they can help to facilitate communication, even if the learner is not aware of the specific meaning and grammatical characteristics of each word that makes up the sequence. In addition to such readily identifiable sequences, **corpus analysis** has been useful in identifying formulaic sequences that are used by native speakers that may not be initially recognized as occurring frequently.

Conklin, K. and Schmitt, N. (2008) 'Formulaic sequences: are they processed more quickly than nonformulaic language by native and nonnative speakers?', *Applied Linguistics*, 29, 72–89.
Wray, A. (2008) *Formulaic Language: Pushing the Boundaries* (Oxford : Oxford University Press).

Fossilization

This term refers to the fact that most L2 learners do not reach the same level of **proficiency** as L1 speakers. When L2 learners' interlanguage permanently stops developing, it is said to fossilize, that is to say learners no longer improve in their use of the L2. The concept of fossilization is somewhat controversial. On the one hand, some researchers argue that humans' **innate** capacity for language learning ends after adolescence, and therefore individuals who start learning a language after this time will not be able to achieve native-like competence. In addition, numerous research studies have found that L2 learners often do not have the same grammatical, lexical, pragmatic and phonological abilities as L1 speakers. On the other hand, fossilization may be difficult to identify. If language learning is a complex, dynamic and evolving process, then there is the suggestion that even L1 speakers' language systems continue to develop into adulthood. Additionally, it is difficult to prove that someone's language system has permanently stopped developing. For this reason, some researchers prefer to use the term **stabilization**.

Han, Z. (2004) *Fossilization in Adult Second Language Acquisition* (Clevedon: Multilingual Matters).

Han, Z. and Odlin, T. (2006) *Studies of Fossilization in Second Language Acquisition* (Clevedon: Multilingual Matters).

Free variation

Although an L2 learner's **interlanguage** is assumed to be systematic, there may be occasions when learners use a specific linguistic form randomly rather than systematically. This free variation is especially likely to occur at the beginning stages of learners' use of the structure. For example, **form-function analysis** has shown that, in general, learners tend to use consistently the same form to express a given meaning, even though their systematic use may differ from the way in which L1 speakers use the form. Some researchers argue that free variation does not exist, and that all language use is systematic. Thus, if language use appears to be random, it is only because the variables that affect its use have not been clearly identified.

Towell, R., Hawkins, R. and Bazergui, N. (1993) 'Systematic and nonsystematic variability in advanced language learning', *Studies in Second Language Acquisition*, 15, 439–60.

Frequency

The number of times a linguistic item occurs. Frequency can be counted as the number of times a linguistic item occurs in the language **input** available to a specific learner, or it can be counted through the analysis of a **corpus** to determine the frequency of an item across a range of texts (e.g. newspaper articles published in the United Kingdom between 1999 and 2009) or speakers (e.g. speakers of Singapore English). Frequency is an important construct in **connectionist** approaches to SLA, as frequency is the driving force for learning because specific patterns that occur frequently in the input are reinforced in the learners' **interlanguage** systems.

See also **exposure**.

Anderson, B. (2007) 'Pedagogical rules and their relationship to frequency in the input: observational and empirical data from L2 French', *Applied Linguistics*, 28, 286–308.

Collins, L. and Ellis, N.C. (eds) (2009) 'Input and second language construction learning: frequency, form, and function', *The Modern Language Journal*, 93 (3)

Frequency analysis

A term used by Ellis and Barkhuizen (2005) to refer to a type of analysis used to investigate variability in the occurrence of different forms of a linguistic structure in a specific dataset. For example, a researcher may want to know what grammatical forms an L2 English learner uses to express past tense, as well as how frequently these forms are used. Consequently, the research would identify the ways in which the learner expressed past tense within a specific dataset. The researcher might identify forms such as the use of base form verbs, correct use of regular and irregular verbs, and over-generalization of *-ed*, before identifying how frequently each type of structure occurs in the learner's production. This type of analysis provides researchers with an idea of where learners might be in their interlanguage development, specifically as it relates to the **developmental sequences** of a specific grammatical feature.

Ellis, R. and Barkhuizen, G. (2005) *Analyzing Learner Language* (Oxford: Oxford University Press).

Frequency effects

This term addresses the role that the rate of exposure to specific linguistic features in the input plays in second language acquisition. Specifically, research into frequency effects proposes that the frequency of a linguistic item in the input is a major factor in its acquisition. Of course, frequency is not solely responsible for the acquisition of specific forms. Other factors, such as the **salience** and **difficulty** of linguistic forms, are also taken into consideration. Nevertheless, frequency is viewed as the driving force in acquisition. Frequency effects are supported by **connectionist** and **usage-based theories** of SLA.

See also **frequency hypothesis.**

Ellis, N.C. (2002) 'Frequency effects in language acquisition: a review with implications for theories of implicit and explicit language acquisition', *Studies in Second Language Acquisition*, 24, 143–88.

F

Frequency hypothesis

This hypothesis states that the frequency of linguistic forms in the **input** is a primary factor responsible for the order in which L2 structures are acquired. Research in the 1970s and 1980s investigated the relationship between input frequency and the accurate use of various morphological and syntactic structures. While there was some research support for the frequency hypothesis, it was also clear that other factors played a role in the order in which morphosyntactic features were acquired. In the last few decades, much research into frequency has been conducted within **connectionist** theoretical framework, which emphasizes the role of exposure, but does not specifically address the order in which linguistic features are acquired. The frequency hypothesis is a **usage-based approach** to SLA, and as such does not recognize an important role for **innate** linguistic knowledge. Instead, it is the frequency of items in the input that is important in accounting for success or failure in acquiring a second language.

See also **frequency effects, order of acquisition.**

Hatch, E. and Wagner-Gough, J. (1976) 'Explaining sequence and variation in second language acquisition', *Language Learning*, 4, 39–47.

Palmberg, R. (1987) 'Patterns of vocabulary development in foreign-language learners', *Studies in Second Language Acquisition*, 29, 201–20.

Functionalism/functionalist approaches to SLA

Based on work in linguistics, the functionalist theory of SLA examines how language functions, that is to say how it is used for communication. Thus, this approach considers which linguistic structures are used to communicate certain concepts in the language. The same function in language might be accomplished by more than one form, and conversely the same form might have two or more functions. For example, there are several ways (forms) of expressing plurality (function) in English, such as plural -*s*, numerals (e.g. *two, three*) and quantifiers (e.g. *many, some*). Additionally, the linguistic functions of tense and aspect have received considerable research in the functionalist framework. The role of the L2 learner is to match specific forms with specific functions.

Bardovi-Harlig, K. (2007) 'One functional approach to second language acquisition: the concept-oriented approach', in B. VanPatten and J. Williams (eds) *Theories in Second Language Acquisition: An Introduction* (Mahwah, NJ: Lawrence Erlbaum Associates), 57–75.

Becker, A. and Carroll, M. (1997) *The Acquisition of Spatial Relations in a Second Language* (Amsterdam: John Benjamins).

Fundamental difference hypothesis

Within a **universal grammar** framework, this hypothesis argues that the process of children learning their L1 is different from the process of adults learning their L2. The main difference, it is argued, is that L2 learners do not have access to universal grammar and therefore must learn the L2 in some other way. There are a series of differences that are used to support the hypothesis. One difference is that child L1 learners always master their L1, while L2 learners seldom achieve the same **proficiency** as L1 speakers of the target language. Another difference is that L2 learners already have a fully developed language system (their L1) while children learning their L1 have to learn the uses of language as well as its forms. Another difference is that while a child has the potential to learn any first language equally well, the same is not true for L2 learners. For example it is easier for adult English L1 speakers to learn Spanish or German than it is for them to learn Arabic or Chinese. However, children can learn any of those languages equally well, provided that they grow up in that specific language environment. Finally, motivation plays a role in L2 learning, but not in L1 learning.

The fundamental difference hypothesis suggest that L2 learners must rely on their L1 (and the information that their L1 supplies them about universal grammar) and their general learning skills, such as problem solving and hypothesis testing in order to learn the L2. As such, it differs from hypotheses that suggest that UG is available to help learners in the L2 learning process.

Montrul, S. (2009) 'Reexamining the Fundamental Difference Hypothesis. What Can Early Bilinguals Tell Us?', *Studies in Second Language Acquisition*, 31, 225–57.

Song, H. and Schwartz, B. (2009) 'Testing the fundamental difference hypothesis: L2 adult, L2 child, and L1 child comparisons in the acquisition of Korean wh-constructions with negative polarity items', *Studies in Second Language Acquisition*, 31, 323–61.

F

Generative grammar/generative theory

This theory assumes that language is an inborn human trait and that people possess abstract linguistic rules that they use for language learning, rather than relying on imitation and repetition. Language production proceeds from learners generating utterances based on their knowledge of these abstract rules. As a result, learners are able to produce an infinite number of sentences.

See also **universal grammar.**

Freidin, R. (2007) *Generative Grammar: Theory and its History* (New York: Routledge).

Genre

A genre is a style of language production that is used fairly consistently in a given context. Genres can be considered as patterns of language use that are specific to a certain area. For example, different types of writing, such as narrative, argumentative and expository texts, can be identified as different genres. Each of these genres will share general linguistic elements (e.g. they will all have basic grammatical structures), but they will also have components which are either unique to or more frequently found in their specific genre. For example, narrative writing is generally organized in a chronological order and uses linguistic elements, both lexical and grammatical, to indicate the passage of time. Researchers have identified specific language structures, patterns of expression, types of organization and cohesion that are often used in specific genres.

See also **academic language, English for academic purposes, English for specific purposes.**

Hyland, K. (2004) *Genre and Second Language Writing* (Ann Arbor, MI: University of Michigan Press).

GJT

See **grammaticality judgement test**

Global error

See **error.**

Grammar

(a) The explicit rules about language that are taught to learners. An example of such a grammar rule is the use of *-ed* to form the regular past tense in English.

In this sense of the term, grammar consists of explicit knowledge that learners can be taught, similar to other subjects such as maths and science. In this definition of grammar, one distinction that is made is whether a grammar is prescriptive or descriptive. A prescriptive grammar is based on external opinions of the way the language should be used. For example, learners of English may be taught that *whom* should be used to ask object pronoun questions such as *Whom did she ask?* However, a descriptive grammar would state that L1 users of English often use *who* in such instances: *Who did she ask?* Thus, a descriptive grammar is concerned with describing how L1 speakers actually use the language and not with how language experts think the language should be used. It is descriptive grammar, that is the way in which speakers actually use the language, that SLA research is interested in.

(b)   The set of systematic rules that learners possesses which constitutes their knowledge of the syntactic and morphological structures of a language. In this sense of the term, grammar refers to the abstract, often implicit, knowledge that individuals have about how to use the language. For L2 learners, this knowledge often differs from the target language norms; however, a learner's grammar is still considered to be a consistent system that the learner can draw upon. Additionally, there is some controversy about the effectiveness of teaching explicit rules for the development of this type of grammar, with some researchers arguing that learners cannot turn knowledge of rules into implicit grammar knowledge.

See also **interface hypothesis, interlanguage.**

Grammar-translation method

A method of L2 teaching that emphasizes the learning of explicit grammar rules and vocabulary. This linguistic knowledge is then applied as learners translate sentences from their L1 to their L2 and vice versa. The grammar-translation method has been seen as being ineffective in developing learners who are able to use the L2 for communicative purposes.

Grammaticality

Conforming to the systematic use of the target language. While grammaticality might seem like a straightforward concept, L1 speakers do not always agree in what they feel is grammatical. Such disagreement may be due to regional variation or feelings related to socially acceptable forms of the language.

See also **grammar.**

G

Grammaticality judgement test (GJT)

A test used for **assessment** or research purposes to measure participants' ability to recognize the grammaticality or ungrammaticality of linguistic items. Grammaticality judgement tests (GJT) are one of the most common tests of linguistic behaviour, and they may be used to assess both L1 and L2 speakers' knowledge of specific linguistic structures.

GJTs can differ in several ways. For instance, they can be either timed or untimed. In the timed variant, participants have to respond within a predetermined time-frame, which could be fixed across all items or variables, for example depending on sentence length. In untimed GJTs participants do not have to respond within a certain time. Performance on timed GJTs has been suggested to reflect **implicit knowledge**, and performance on untimed GJTs to reflect **explicit knowledge**. As an example, participants may be shown the following sentence and asked to respond within two seconds as to whether or not they think the sentence is grammatically correct:

John walked towards the girl who he had given the present to.

Another optional design feature is whether or not learners have to correct ungrammatical sentences. Asking learners to make corrections helps to ensure that they are indeed judging the sentence accurately and focusing on the actual ungrammatical part of the sentence.

There are several benefits of using GJTs for testing learners' grammatical knowledge. First, GJTs are relatively quick and easy to administer. Second, they allow researchers or teachers to test specific linguistic items that might otherwise be difficult to elicit from the students. There are also widely recognized potential drawbacks to GJTs. One of these is that it is unclear on what basis participants make a choice about the grammaticality of the items. If they do not have the necessary knowledge, they may simply guess – but the test results do not generally indicate whether guessing has occurred. It is also unclear whether participants judge sentences on the basis of the target structure or other linguistic features that they feel may be incorrect. Therefore, if a researcher is relying on a GJT to provide an indication of learners' knowledge regarding verb tense, and the learner is focusing on prepositional phrases, the researcher will not have an accurate measure of the linguistic structure that is being investigated. Another major issue is that it is not always clear how participants interpret grammaticality. They may judge an item as incorrect, for example when they feel it is not commonly used or if they would not use it themselves. This applies also to L1 speakers. In the example above some L1 speakers might judge the sentence as 'incorrect', preferring the use of *whom*. Other L1 speakers might decide that the sentence is grammatical because it is a commonly used form in everyday speech. In this way, it may difficult to determine a stable benchmark to judge participants' responses against. To some extent these issues can be mitigated through careful test preparation and participant training. GJTs should be accompanied by internal reliability measures to show response consistency across items.

See also **acceptability judgment.**

Han, Y. (2000) 'Grammaticality judgment tests: how reliable and valid are they?', *Applied Language Learning*, 11, 177–204.

Loewen, S. (2009) 'Grammaticality judgment tests and the measurement of implicit and explicit L2 knowledge', in R. Ellis, S. Loewen, R. Erlam, J. Philp, C. Elder and H. Reinders (eds) *Implicit and Explicit Knowledge in Second Language Learning and Teaching* (Clevedon: Multilingual Matters), 65–93.

Grammaticalization

This term describes the process involved when learners begin to use the L2. Initially learners may communicate by using vocabulary and communication strategies without the presence of grammatical markers, as in the phrase *No very good*. As learners' develop their interlanguage system, they are able to use grammatical structures to help express their intended meanings, rather than relying solely on lexical or communicative strategies. For example, as grammaticalization occurs, the previous phrase would become *It's not very good*.

See also **developmental sequences.**

G

Habit

In **behaviourist** views of learning, a habit was the pattern of behaviour that resulted from a stimulus and response. Therefore, behaviourist theories of language learning proposed that learners made connections between the sounds and meanings of a language by being repeatedly exposed to them. Language was viewed as a set of habits, and L2 learning was viewed as being the process of replacing the old habits of the L1 with the new habits of the L2. However, it is currently recognized that language learning goes far beyond the development of habits.

Head act

Within the study of **pragmatics** and **speech act** theory, a head act is the primary action that is being accomplished by an utterance. For example, language can be used to perform actions such as requesting, inviting, refusing, complimenting, complaining, etc. The head act is the main linguistic component that performs the action. As such, the head act is the main component of an entire **speech act**. Head acts can be accompanied by additional acts which modify the head act in some way. For example, a request is a type of head act which can be either upgraded or downgraded depending on the accompanying language, as seen in the examples below.

a. *Pass the salt.*
b. *Please pass the salt.*
c. *Pass the salt now!*

Heritage language

A second language that is being studied by someone who has some type of family relationship with the language. Heritage language contexts often occur in cases of immigration, with the language of the wider society being different from the heritage language. However, the languages of indigenous minorities can also be referred to as heritage languages. Often, the heritage language is spoken by older family members, such as grandparents or parents, but not by their grandchildren or children.

See also **heritage language learner.**

Heritage language learner

A person who is studying a language to which they have a family or cultural connection. In most instances, the target language is the language spoken by their parents, grandparents or other ancestors. Often, heritage language learners have been exposed to the heritage language in the family environment; however, that exposure may vary from minimal to substantial. An example of heritage language learners would be the third generation Italian immigrant children living in the United States. The children will have learned English, the dominant language of the country in which they are living. Nevertheless, they may also have heard Italian, the heritage language, being spoken by their parents and grandparents. As a result, they may have varying degrees of proficiency in Italian. Research suggests that the L2 learning needs and abilities of heritage language learners may differ from their non-heritage language learning peers. Consequently, some institutions offer L2 classes specifically for heritage learners.

Montrul, S. (2010) 'Current issues in heritage language acquisition', *Annual Review of Applied Linguistics*, 30, 3–23.
Potowski, K., Jegerski, J. and Morgan-Short, K. (2009) 'The effects of instruction on linguistic development in Spanish heritage language speakers', *Language Learning*, 59, 537–79.

Hybrid research
Research that combines various methods, such as **qualitative** and **quantitative**, descriptive and experimental. The use of multiple methods of investigation can help to provide different perspectives on the issue being researched.

Hypercorrection
A phenomenon in which language speakers overuse language rules in contexts where they do not apply. Often, the linguistic form being overused is seen as being socially more prestigious.

See also **over-generalization**.

Hypothesis
A hypothesis is an idea or assumption that a researcher holds about a specific aspect of L2 learning. As such, a hypothesis is something that can be investigated through research. In quantitative research, a null hypothesis is often used, stating that there is expected to be no significant difference between the options under investigation. For example, an investigation of corrective feedback might state a null hypothesis like 'There is no significant difference in the effects of recasts and metalinguistic feedback on L2 learners' subsequent accurate use of the targeted structure.' Researchers can then use statistical methods to reject or fail to reject the null hypothesis. However, researchers do not always use a null hypothesis, and it is perhaps more common for SLA researchers to state directional hypotheses in which they express their ideas about the expected results of the study. If the above null hypothesis were to be stated as a directional hypothesis, it might be 'Learners who receive metalinguistic feedback will be able to use the targeted linguistic structure more accurately than learners who receive recasts.'

H

Hypothesis testing

(a)   In SLA research, hypothesis testing refers to generating assumptions about L2 learning and then conducting empirical investigations to evaluate these assumptions. Usually, hypotheses come from theoretical claims made about L2 learning, as well as from previous research; however, hypotheses may also arise out of classroom experiences. Sometimes in quantitative research, a null hypothesis is used, stating that there are no differences among the groups that are being investigated. If researchers find differences among the groups, then they reject the null hypothesis, but if they do not find differences, then it is said that they fail to reject the null hypothesis.

(b)   In L2 learning, learners can form hypotheses about the rules and structures of the target language and then try out these ideas when they produce either oral or written language. Indeed, the **output hypothesis** proposes that one benefit of learners producing output is that they can test their ideas about how the target language works. After learners have produced language to test a specific hypothesis, they receive feedback on their output. If a specific hypothesis is correct, the communication should continue unhindered. However, if a hypothesis is not correct and the use of the L2 is ungrammatical, learners may receive negative feedback, indicating that they have made an error. In such cases, the information can help learners to reformulate their hypotheses about the rules of the L2.

H

i + 1

A metaphor proposed by Stephen Krashen to describe the type of input that is necessary for language acquisition. He argued that learners need input that is one step beyond their current level of L2 ability. In this way, learners can still understand most of the input, and this understanding helps them to comprehend the parts that are one step beyond their current state. The idea of *i* + 1 was initially appealing; however, it has come under criticism, in part because it is not clear how to determine, in practical terms, what constitutes the + 1 part of the equation.

See also **comprehensible input, monitor model.**

Identity

Identity is one type of social factor that influences language learning. Identity refers to how learners view themselves in relation to the world around them. Aspects of identity may include gender, culture, ethnicity, religion, vocation, among others. Although traditionally a learner's identity has been viewed as relatively fixed and stable, more recent conceptualizations of identity, such as **social identity theory**, view it as dynamic and fluid, changing both over time and in different contexts. Identity can impact L2 learning in several ways. A learner's identity can affect the opportunities that he or she has to interact in the target language. Identity may also affect a learner's motivation to acquire the target language.

Block, D. (2007) *Second Language Identities* (London: Continuum).
Norton, B. (2000) *Identity and Language Learning: Gender, Ethnicity and Educational Change* (Harlow: Longman).

Illocutionary act

In **speech act theory**, utterances are said to have various components. The illocutionary act is the intended effect that an utterance has on the hearer. For example, the illocutionary force of a request is for the hearer to provide the requested thing. Sometimes the illocutionary force of an utterance also matches the surface meaning of the utterance, such as when someone says *Please pass the salt*. Both the surface meaning and the illocutionary force of the utterance are a request for the salt. However, there are also times when the surface meaning of an utterance does not match the intended effect of the utterance. Thus, *Can you pass the salt?* is semantically a question about the hearer's physical ability to carry out a specific action. However, the question is generally understood as a request. Similarly, a person may make an utterance such as *Is it hot in here?* with the intended effect of having someone open a window for cooler air.

Croddy, W. (2002) 'Performing illocutionary speech acts: an analysis', *Journal of Pragmatics*, 34, 1113–18.

Sbisa, M. (2001) 'Illocutionary force and degrees of strength in language use', *Journal of Pragmatics*, 33, 1791–814.

Immediate recall

This is a type of research method in which L2 learners are asked to say what they were just thinking. Such a research method has been used in communicative activities in which a researcher and a learner are interacting. At a specific point in the interaction, the researcher will give a signal, such as a knock on the desk or a ring of a buzzer, which indicates that the learner should say what he or she was just thinking. The intention of this procedure is that the learner's immediate recall will provide the researcher with an indication of his or her cognitive processes, particularly in relation to what the learner was paying attention to in the immediately previous dialogue. Immediate recall is sometimes used in corrective feedback studies with the researcher providing the cue immediately after a **recast** or some other type of corrective response has been provided. If learners respond by saying that they were thinking about their own error or the teacher's correction, this is taken as evidence that the learners noticed the correction.

Egi, T. (2004) 'Verbal reports, noticing, and SLA research', *Language Awareness*, 13, 243–64.

Immediate report

A research method in which learners are involved in a communicative activity and are asked to repeat what has just been said in the interaction. At a specific point in the interaction, the researcher gives a signal, such as a knock on the desk, which indicates that the learner should repeat the last few words that were heard. This method is similar to **immediate recall**; however, instead of learners reporting what they were thinking, they are asked to repeat the last few words they have just heard. This research method is used to attempt to measure learners' noticing of linguistic items, particularly corrective feedback. If learners' repeat the teacher's correction rather than their previously incorrect utterance, then it is assumed that they noticed the correction.

Philp, J. (2003) 'Constraints on "noticing the gap": nonnative speakers' noticing of recasts in NS–NNS interaction', *Studies in Second Language Acquisition*, 25, 99–126.

Immersion education

A type of education that involves placing L2 learners in an environment primarily comprised of the target language. Learners study academic content, such as mathematics, science and history, in the target language. One well known example of immersion programmes is the French one in Canada where English L1 speaking children attended school classes conducted in French.

See also **content and language integrated learning, content-based instruction.**

De Courcy, M. (2001) *Learners' Experiences of Immersion Education* (Clevedon: Multilingual Matters)

Swain, M. and Lapkin, S. (2005) 'The evolving sociopolitical context of immersion education in Canada: some implications for program development', *International Journal of Applied Linguistics*, 15, 169–86.

Implicational scaling

A means of showing learners' progress on developmental structures, particular in the areas of grammar or phonology. Samples of learner language are analysed for a variety of specific linguistic structures, some that are acquired early and others that are acquired late. A **target-like use analysis**, measuring the percentage of accurate use of the various structures, is conducted, and the percentage accuracy scores are entered into a scale moving from early to late acquired structures. Learners with higher percentages extending further to the right-hand side of the scale (late structures) are considered to be at a higher developmental level. In Table 5, learner 1 is considered to be the most advanced because of the high accuracy scores with both early acquired (plural -*s*) and late acquired (third person -*s*) features. In contrast, learner 4 is the least advanced, as shown by the low scores on all features. Implicational scaling has been used in cross-sectional research to investigate multiple learners at different stages of development; however, there is some disagreement as to whether the accuracy orders seen in this type of research reflect those found in longitudinal studies of learner development.

See also **order of acquisition.**

Trofimovich, P., Gatbonton, E. and Segalowitz, N. (2007) 'A dynamic look at L2 phonological learning: seeking processing explanations for implicational phenomena', *Studies in Second Language Acquisition*, 29, 407–48.

Table 5   Implicational scaling, accuracy scores (%)

Learner	Plural -*s*	Irregular past tense	Regular past tense	Third person -*s*
1	100	100	98	95
2	99	95	80	75
3	75	60	50	20
4	30	10	0	0

Implicit corrective feedback

A response to learners' errors that does not draw overt attention to the error. Recasts (i.e. correct reformulations of learners' errors) are often considered to be relatively implicit types of feedback, particularly if the error is not isolated from the surrounding interaction or emphasized in any other way, as in the recast in the example below. Some researchers suggest that implicit feedback is better for L2 learners because it does not detract from the overall interaction; however, other researchers argue that it is often not noticed and is therefore not useful for L2 acquisition.

Example:
S: somebody steal my paper (·) stolen
T: someone stole your paper?
(Loewen and Philp, 2006: 550)

See also **explicit corrective feedback.**

Loewen, S. and Philp, J. (2006) 'Recasts in the adult English L2 classroom: characteristics, explicitness, and effectiveness', *The Modern Language Journal*, 90, 536–56.

Implicit instruction

Language teaching in which learners are not overtly taught linguistic items. Instead learners are left to deduce rules regarding the target language system from the input that they receive. Learners' attention is not actively directed to specific language forms. Implicit instruction can be considered to be a type of **focus on form** because it often occurs within the context of meaning-focused instruction. Examples of implicit instruction include **input flood** and **consciousness-raising tasks**. While implicit instruction can be beneficial for learning, **explicit instruction** is often considered to be more effective.

Norris, J. and Ortega, L. (2000) 'Effectiveness of L2 instruction: a research synthesis and quantitative meta-analysis', *Language Learning*, 50, 417–528.
Robinson, P. (1996) 'Learning simple and complex second language rules under implicit, incidental, rule-search, and instructed conditions', *Studies in Second Language Acquisition*, 18, 27–67.

Implicit knowledge

Implicit knowledge is knowledge of language that learners are not consciously aware of. Learners can draw on implicit knowledge to produce the language and to make grammaticality judgements, but they may not be able to explain on what basis they make these decisions. It is the type of knowledge that all L1 speakers have of their first language before they are explicitly taught the rules of their L1. Implicit knowledge is the primary type of linguistic knowledge used for spontaneous oral production, and it is sometimes known as **proceduralized knowledge**. It contrasts with **explicit knowledge**.

Ellis, R. (2002) 'Does form-focused instruction affect the acquisition of implicit knowledge?', *Studies in Second Language Acquisition*, 24, 223–36.
Ellis, R., Loewen, S., Erlam, R., Philp, J., Elder, C. and Reinders, H. (2009) *Implicit and Explicit Knowledge in Second Language Learning and Teaching* (Clevedon: Multilingual Matters).

Implicit learning

Learning without awareness of what is being learned. Implicit learning occurs, for example, when a learner sets out to do one thing (e.g. practise communicating in the second language) but learns something else about the language at the same time (e.g. a grammatical aspect). Implicit learning is sometimes confused with **incidental learning** as the learner does not deliberately set out to learn the (in this example) grammatical aspect of the language. However, with incidental learning, learners may be aware that they are learning something even if it was not their original intention; therefore the term 'incidental' learning should not be equated with implicit learning. Implicit learning also needs to be distinguished from **inductive** learning, which could be either implicit (such as when children acquire their L1) or explicit (when a learner is instructed to 'find the rule' that is present in a set of L2 input). Similarly, **deductive** learning can be explicit (traditional rule teaching) or implicit (**parameter setting**). Several researchers have argued that implicit and explicit learning operate on a continuum and that most learning situations involve a combination of both.

Many experiments have attempted to show the existence of implicit learning. In a typical experiment participants are exposed to sentences in an **artificial language.** When learners are subsequently asked to classify new sentences as grammatical or ungrammatical, participants usually perform above chance; however, they often cannot verbalize the rules of the underlying grammar. Researchers have taken this as evidence that implicit learning has taken place. Other researchers, however, have pointed out that in many cases it is difficult to be certain that participants did not develop any explicit knowledge in the course of the experiment. Not being able to verbalize knowledge may not be the same as not having any discrete knowledge of grammar. It has been argued that most experiments do not meet the following two criteria:

1. the information criterion (i.e. the information participants are asked to pro-vide on an awareness test must be the information that has caused improved performance);
2. the sensitivity criterion (i.e. the measure of awareness needs to be sensitive to all possible types of awareness of information).

Instead, it has been argued that most learning in such experiments involves the explicit learning of simple relationships between two or three items of information, rather than the abstraction of rules. Consequently, learners' decisions were not made on the basis of grammaticality but on the basis of similarity between items and the strength (e.g. reliability) of certain chunks. It is also not clear that gained knowledge transfers to new exemplars. Nonetheless, more recent experiments do seem to show evidence of implicit learning. A perhaps more relevant question is what contribution implicit learning makes to second language acquisition. Some have argued that it plays a very small role, but more research is needed to answer this question with certainty.

Hulstijn, J. (2005) 'Theoretical and empirical issues in the study of implicit and explicit second language learning', *Studies in Second Language Acquisition*, 27, 129–40.

Implicit memory

The storage area for implicit L2 knowledge that is not consciously available to the learner, or recollections that cannot be consciously retrieved. The activation of implicit memory is revealed when previous experiences facilitate task performance that does not require conscious or intentional recollection of those experiences. It has been argued that the existence of implicit memory is difficult to prove because it is often impossible to show that learners are indeed completely unaware of the previous experience, and, as a result, the term 'incidental memory' is more suitable for implicit memory, and 'intentional memory' for **explicit memory**.

Incidental L2 learning

Learning that happens without the learner intending for it to occur. For example, learners may be involved in a communicative activity in which they are discussing a specific topic. Thus, the primary intention is for them to practise speaking the L2. However, during that activity, a learner may notice and learn a specific lexical item or grammatical structure. Incidental learning can also occur when learners are focused on learning targeted grammatical structures (**intentional learning**), but become aware of other linguistic items that are not specifically the target of instruction at the moment. One area in which incidental learning has been a focus of investigation is vocabulary. In particular, research has investigated the role of extensive reading on learners' incidental learning of vocabulary.

Barcroft, J. (2009) 'Effects of synonym generation on incidental and intentional L2 vocabulary learning during reading', *TESOL Quarterly*, 43, 79–103.

Laufer, B. and Hulstijn, J. (2001) 'Incidental vocabulary acquisition in a second language: the construct of task-induced involvement', *Applied Linguistics*, 22, 1–26.

Indeterminacy

This refers to the fact that learners' L2 knowledge is often variable and incomplete. Thus, unlike L1 learners who have consistent knowledge of the rules of their L1 grammar, L2 learners' knowledge may be inconsistent and change from context to context. This characteristic can make it difficult to assess objectively an L2 learner's proficiency level.

Individual learner differences

This refers to a broad area of SLA research that investigates characteristics that L2 learners bring to the task of L2 learning and how those characteristics may differ from learner to learner. Some of the early research on individual differences began because researchers wanted to investigate why some language learners were better and more successful than others. In other words, they wanted to know what were the qualities of a good language learner. In subsequent decades, many individual difference topics have received considerable attention in their own right. Individual differences may directly influence L2 learning, as in the case of age or L1 transfer, or they may be moderating variables that have only indirect influence on L2 learning, as in the case of learning strategies and motivation.

See also **anxiety, aptitude, extroversion, intelligence, learning strategy, learning style, motivation, transfer.**

Dörnyei, Z. (2005) *The Psychology of the Language Learner: Individual Differences in Second Language Acquisition* (Mahwah, NJ: Lawrence Erlbaum).

Robinson, P. (2002) *Individual Differences and Instructed Language Learning* (Amsterdam: John Benjamins).

Induced error

An error that is purposefully prompted by the teacher or researcher in order to illustrate a point about the target language. When learners are made aware of the error, they are then more likely to be able to restructure their L2 knowledge of that grammatical structure. Induced errors are also used in studies of L2 processing to examine if learners are sensitive to grammatical violations. This is sometimes called the garden-path technique.

Inductive instruction

Teaching which does not directly tell learners what the targeted structure is nor gives them explicit information about that structure. Rather learners are provided with input and are then guided to work out the rules for themselves. Inductive instruction is considered to better reflect naturalistic language learning because learners extract rules and patterns from the input; however, studies of inductive instruction have not always found it to be more effective than **deductive instruction**.

See also **consciousness-raising task.**

Information-gap tasks

Pedagogical **tasks** in which different learners each have part of the information required to complete the task, usually to solve a problem or make a decision. For example, learners may be asked to find a lost friend and each be given different information about him, such as the country where he is or the type of work he does. To find the person, the learners have to exchange the information that they have. Information-gap tasks have been shown to increase student engagement in the task as each learner has an active role to play. Information gap tasks also increase the amount of student output as learners are required to exchange information in order to successfully complete the task. Because learners are working towards a common goal, they have to find ways to express themselves clearly (in other words, they have to produce **comprehensible output**) and they have to ensure they understand each other. As a result, **negotiation of meaning** is likely to occur. Information-gap tasks are common in L2 classrooms and have also been used extensively in SLA research as they provide L2 production data.

Jenks, C. (2009) 'Exchanging missing information in tasks: old and new interpretations', *The Modern Language Journal*, 93, 185–94.
Pica, T., Kang, H. and Sauro, S. (2006) 'Information gap tasks: their multiple roles and contributions to interaction research methodology', *Studies in Second Language Acquisition*, 28, 301–38.

Information processing

A **cognitive theory** that considers how human beings communicate and create meaning. Information processing theories have six general characteristics:

1. humans are viewed as autonomous and active;
2. the mind is a general purpose, symbol processing system;
3. complex behaviour is composed of simpler processes that can be divided into individual components;

4. these individual component processes can be isolated and studied independently of other processes;
5. processes take time, therefore predictions about reaction time can be made;
6. the mind is a limited-capacity processor.

In L2 learning, information processing is conceptualized as a process of information entering the learner's brain as detected input which is then analysed and assimilated into the learner's interlanguage system (which may be restructured to accommodate the new information). Then the new interlanguage system can be drawn upon in order to produce output. This approach is a cognitive approach to SLA that emphasizes mental processes and focuses less on the social aspects of L2 learning.

Initiate, respond, follow-up (IRF) sequence

A common classroom interaction pattern, originally identified by Sinclair and Coulthard (1975), whereby the teacher initiates an exchange, learners respond and the teacher provides feedback. For example, the teacher may ask *What is the past tense of go*? A student responds, for example with the answer *went*, and the teacher provides feedback, such as *that's correct*. IRF patterns have been shown to take up as much as 30 per cent of classroom interaction. IRF has the disadvantage that it involves the teacher doing most of the talking. It inhibits students from taking the initiative in classroom interaction and from benefitting from alternative interaction such as peer-feedback. Furthermore, the unequal relationship between students and teachers blocks more authentic communication in which negotiation of meaning can occur. In the IRF sequence teachers generally know the answers to the questions that they ask, and no negotiation is necessary. Most of the talking is done by the teacher, and it is the teacher who selects the topics for discussion and validates the responses. In this way the use of IRF diminishes student output and student responsibility for classroom interaction. In spite of these criticisms, the use of IRF sequences is not completely without benefit, as some studies have found that beginning learners can be helped by the predictable structure of the sequence.

Sinclair, J. and Coulthard, M. (1975) *Towards an Analysis of Discourse* (Oxford: Oxford University Press).

Waring, H. (2008) 'Using explicit positive assessment in the language classroom: IRF, feedback, and learning opportunities', *The Modern Language Journal*, 92, 577–94.

Innate(ness)

The idea that the capacity for language is preprogrammed in the human mind. Innateness is a central component of **universal grammar** and **generative approaches** to SLA. While the idea of innateness is somewhat controversial for L1 acquisition, there is even less agreement about its status in L2 learning. One of the questions being investigated by UG researchers is whether or not such innate knowledge of language, if it exists for L1 learning, is also available for L2 learning.

Pinker, S. (1994) *The Language Instinct: How the Mind Creates Language* (New York: HarperCollins).

Input

A term used to describe the language data that are potentially available to the learner. This includes all the visual and auditory language stimuli that surround the learner. These data could be in the form of authentically occurring language, such as an overheard conversation or written advertisement, or it could be in the form of intentionally provided examples of the language in the classroom. In other words, any example of the language that the learner can potentially perceive is considered input.

Input is different from **intake** or **acquisition** in that the term does not describe language data that have been processed by the learner. Input is a neutral term in the sense that it only describes the language information that is available to the learner, not a mental representation of that language. For the latter concept, other terms such as intake are used. Some researchers make a distinction between input as available language data, and perceived input, which are language data that have entered the brain.

The availability of input is widely agreed to be a prerequisite for learning a second language. In other words, without input the language cannot be learned. However, different theories of language acquisition give different weight to the importance of input. In nativist approaches to language acquisition, input is the information that potentially feeds into the **language acquisition device** and activates the setting of language-specific **parameters**. The input therefore serves primarily as a trigger of an innately endowed language system. In constructivist approaches, input is seen as data that have the potential to provide the building blocks for the language. Any encounter with the language adds to its development, and therefore the more input learners encounter, the more, on balance, they will potentially learn.

In the literature on second language acquisition, sometimes the term 'input' is used in a less neutral way, depending on the theoretical perspective of the authors. For example Krashen frequently talks about input with the meaning of comprehensible input, or input roughly attuned to the learner's level (or $i + 1$). When Krashen writes that learners only need sufficient input, he is referring to input of a certain type; that is, language data that match the developmental stage of the learner. This usage of the term differs from more common definitions of input, as it takes into account the learner's pre-existing mental representations of the language. It is more common, however, to reserve the term 'input' for all the language data potentially available, regardless of its characteristics, either in relation to the learner or its role in the surrounding context.

See also **input hypothesis, modified input.**

Input enhancement

Attempts to direct the learner's attention to a specific linguistic form, usually in written text, by emphasizing the forms in some way. Common types of enhancement include the use of underlining, bolding and using different colours. There is limited agreement as to the effectiveness of input enhancement for L2 learning. Some studies have found that learners can improve their ability to use the enhanced target structures, while other studies have found no difference between learners who read enhanced input and those who did not. Additionally, some studies have found that input enhancement can interfere with L2 learners' reading comprehension. Below is an example of an enhanced text used in an experiment investigating English L2 learners' use of the passive voice. Input enhancement is used as a type of **form-focused instruction**.

Birthday Celebration in Korea:
On the 100th day after a child's birth, there is a small feast, or 'baek-il feast.' It is to celebrate the child having survived this difficult period. At this time the Samshin Halmoni **is honored** with offerings of rice and soup. Also, to prevent disaster and to bring the child luck and happiness, red bean cakes **are** usually **placed** at every corner within the house.
(Lee, 2007)

Han, Z., Park, E. and Combs, C. (2008) 'Textual enhancement of input: issues and possibilities', *Applied Linguistics*, 29, 597–618.

Lee, S. (2007) 'Effects of textual enhancement and topic familiarity on Korean EFL students' reading comprehension and learning of passive form', *TESOL Quarterly*, 57, 341–73.

Input flood

The manipulation of a text to increase artificially the number of exemplars of a particular language structure in order to draw learners' attention to that structure. Input flooding is mostly done in writing but can also be done in listening texts. A text containing an input flood can also be said to have been *seeded* with the target structure. Input flood is considered to be an implicit type of **form-focused instruction**.

Loewen, S., Erlam, R. and Ellis, R. (2009) 'The incidental acquisition of third person -s as implicit and explicit knowledge', in R. Ellis, S. Loewen, R. Erlam, J. Philp, C. Elder and H. Reinders (eds) *Implicit and Explicit Knowledge in Second Language Learning and Teaching* (Clevedon: Multilingual Matters), 262–81.

Trahey, M. and White, L. (1993) 'Positive evidence and preemption in the second language classroom', *Studies in Second Language Acquisition*, 15, 181–204.

Input hypothesis

A central component of Krashen's **monitor model**, the input hypothesis argues that comprehensible input is necessary and sufficient for L2 acquisition. Input is made comprehensible by its linguistic and social context. For example, if learners were to encounter an unknown word, the best way for them to learn it is to rely on the context of the sentence/utterance that the word appears in or to be able to identify it from the context of the physical environment. As such, **interaction** or **negotiation of meaning** does not play an important role in the input hypothesis. Another component of the hypothesis is that output (i.e. speaking and writing) occurs as a result of input and acquisition, but it does not play a role in the learning process. The input hypothesis does not see an important role for explicit L2 instruction. Instead the role of a classroom teacher is to provide an acquisition rich environment for the learners. 'Acquisition rich' means that there is plenty of comprehensible input for the learners. When plentiful amounts of input are provided, learners will be able to progress along the **natural order** of acquisition.

See also **monitor model.**

Input processing

This is a model of L2 learning, proposed by Bill VanPatten, that addresses how learners comprehend utterances and how they make **form-meaning connections**. Input processing argues that learners rely on several principles when processing L2 input. First, they rely on the primacy of meaning principle, which argues that learners pay attention to meaning first and only secondarily to form. Another principle is the first noun principle, which states that learners tend to assign subject status to the first noun or pronoun in a sentence/utterance. Input processing suggests that these processing strategies may not help learners in acquiring specific features of the target language; therefore, **processing instruction** has been proposed as a teaching method to help learners overcome these processing strategies.

VanPatten, B. (2007) 'Input processing in adult second language acquisition', in B. VanPatten and J. Williams (eds) *Theories in Second Language Acquisition: An Introduction* (Mahwah, NJ: Lawrence Erlbaum), 115–35.

Instructed second language acquisition (ISLA)

Any type of L2 learning that occurs as a result of the teaching of the L2. It is an attempt by teachers, or instructional materials, to guide and facilitate the process of L2 acquisition. Instructed SLA contrasts with naturalistic language acquisition, which occurs outside the classroom as people use the target language in their everyday lives. The effectiveness of language teaching is somewhat controversial, with some researchers arguing that instruction does not help learners to acquire the ability to use the L2 for communicative purposes. Of course, L2 instruction can help learners gain metalinguistic knowledge about the language, but not everyone agrees that such explicit knowledge contributes to L2 acquisition. In spite of these arguments, there is some agreement that instruction can help to speed up the rate of acquisition as well as help learners to reach advanced levels of proficiency.

The methods of ISLA have changed over time. One early type was the **grammar translation** method which emphasized the explicit teaching of vocabulary and grammar rules to enable learners to translate texts both from and into the target language. A common type of instruction in the 1950s and 1960s was the **audio-lingual** method, which encouraged the use of repetitive drills and pattern practice to reinforce good language **habits**. In the 1980s, **communicative language teaching**, with its emphasis on using language as a means of communication in the classroom, became popular. However, researchers found that exclusive use of communicative activities in the classroom did not always result in learners who could use the L2 accurately. As a result, **focus on form** was suggested as method of integrating attention to form and meaning that could produce both accurate and fluent L2 learners. In addition to focus on form, several current methods for combining attention to L2 accuracy and fluency include **task-based language teaching**, **content-based instruction** and **processing instruction**. These numerous options for teaching language continue to receive attention as research-ers investigate the most effective means of language instruction.

Ellis, R. (2005) 'Principles of instructed language learning', *System*, 33, 209–24.
Housen, A. and Pierrard, M. (2005) *Investigations into Instructed Second Language Acquisition* (Berlin: Mouton de Gruyter).

Instrumental motivation

A type of motivation that is characterized by the learner's desire for some type of gain or advantage from L2 learning. For example, learners may wish to study the L2 because they believe that knowing the L2 will allow them to get a better job. Another example of instrumental motivation is when learners study a language in order to meet an institutional requirement. Instrumental motivation contrasts with **integrative motivation**, which involves a desire by learners to be associ-ated with the culture and speakers of the L2. In general, instrumental motivation is considered to be somewhat less effective than integrative motivation for L2 learning; however, it can be difficult to distinguish the two types of motivation. Additionally, in some research studies, instrumental learners have been found to be more successful than integrative learners. Instrumental motivation is similar to **extrinsic** motivation because often the goals that the learner is aiming for are imposed by external forces.

Gardner, R. and MacIntyre, P. (1991) 'An instrumental motivation in language study: who says it isn't effective?', *Studies in Second Language Acquisition*, 13, 57–72.
Masgoret, A. and Gardner, R. (2003) 'Attitudes, motivation, and second language learn-ing: a meta-analysis of studies conducted by Gardner and associates', *Language Learning*, 53, 123–63.

Intake

Intake refers to the intermediary stage between input and acquisition; however, the term has been used in slightly different ways by different researchers. For some researchers, intake refers to the mental representation of perceived input; for others, it is the process of assimilating this information into the learner's interlanguage. For both definitions, intake is clearly distinct from input, which consists of all the lan-guage data that are potentially available to, but not yet processed by, the learner.

Some researchers see intake not just as a mental representation but as a proc-ess of assimilating linguistic material into the interlanguage, which relies on the availability of apperceived and comprehended input. In this view, intake refers to language that has already been processed in some way, and may be processed fur-ther. Some researchers include the initial process of perceiving the input and/or the process of comprehending it; however, others include only the subsequent assimila-tion of intake. Other researchers take an even broader view of intake and include the entire process from initial perception to final assimilation. These researchers propose *intake factors* (e.g. age and affective factors), that determine which parts of the input may be engaged, and *intake processes* (e.g. inferencing, restructuring, transfer), that involve the processing of those parts of the input. It is difficult to see how such a conceptualization of intake differs from one of learning in general.

Further confusion occurs as a result of the sometimes divergent use of the term 'intake' to refer to a type of input. Krashen, for example, talks about certain types of input that contain a high proportion of intake. Generally speaking, however, a clear distinction is made between input, which is information that has not yet been processed in any way by the learner, but is simply available language data, and intake, which is linguistic input that has begun to enter the cognitive system.

Chaudron, C. (1985) 'Intake: on models and methods for discovering learners' processing of input', *Studies in Second Language Acquisition*, 7, 1–14.

Rosa, E. and O'Neill, M. (1999) 'Explicitness, intake, and the issue of awareness', *Studies in Second Language Acquisition*, 21, 511–56.

Integrative motivation

A type of motivation characterized by a desire on the part of the learner to associate with the target language and culture in some way. It is characterized by positive feelings towards the language and/or its speakers. An example of integrative motivation would be when a person studies the target language because he or she has a close relationship with a speaker of that language. Integrative motivation is considered to be an effective type of motivation for L2 learning.

See also **instrumental motivation.**

Gardner, R. (2001) 'Integrative motivation and second language acquisition', in Z. Dörnyei and R. Schmidt (eds) *Motivation and Second Language Acquisition* (Honolulu: University of Hawaii Press), 1–19.

Gardner, R., Masgoret, A., Tennant, J. and Mihic, L. (2004) 'Integrative motivation: changes during a year-long intermediate-level course', *Language Learning*, 54, 1–34.

Intelligence

This is an individual difference that has been investigated to see its effects on L2 learning, with the question being whether or not it is easier for smarter people to learn a second language. Although folk wisdom in some societies says that L2 learning is a sign of higher intelligence, there is little empirical evidence to suggest that this is a strong factor. However, **language aptitude**, which is separate from general intelligence, may play a more significant role in L2 learning.

Intentional L2 learning

This is the type of learning that learners consciously plan to do. It often involves the learning of specific grammar rules or vocabulary that are focused on in class. Intentional learning contrasts with **incidental learning**. Intentional learning is generally considered to be faster and more efficient than incidental learning, particularly when the topic to be learned is explicit information about the L2. However, there is less consensus about the benefits of intentional learning for the development of **implicit L2 knowledge**.

Barcroft, J. (2009) 'Strategies and performance in intentional L2 vocabulary learning', *Language Awareness*, 18, 74–89.

Interaction analysis

A type of research method that examines the language that occurs when people communicate with each other. It can be concerned with the type of input that is provided for learners during interaction, as well as how language is negotiated and modified during interaction. Another issue of interest in interaction analysis is turn-taking and topic control.

See also **interaction hypothesis.**

Interaction hypothesis

An approach to L2 learning that argues that conversational interaction in the L2 is crucial for learning. The interaction hypothesis proposes that learners receive **comprehensible input** as they interact with speakers of the L2. One of the ways that input can become comprehensible is through interactional modification. For instance, if learners do not understand what their interlocutors have said, they may make a clarification request to help them try to understand. This type of **negotiation of meaning** can help draw learners' attention to forms that might be unknown to them in the interaction. In addition to input, the interaction hypothesis also proposes a role for **output**. As learners produce output, they are able to test their knowledge of the L2 and to receive feedback on their language use. If they produce an incorrect form, learners may receive **corrective feedback** from their interlocutors on their production, particularly if the error leads to communication breakdown. The interaction hypothesis argues that this type of feedback can help learners to notice the gap between their own production and the norms of the target language.

See also **interactionist approaches, output hypothesis.**

Gass, S. (1997) *Input, Interaction and the Second Language Learner* (Mahwah, NJ: Lawrence Erlbaum).

Gass, S. and Mackey, A. (2007) 'Input, interaction, and output in second language acquisition', in B. VanPatten and J. Williams (eds) *Theories in Second Language Acquisition: An Introduction* (Mahwah, NJ: Lawrence Erlbaum), 175–200.

Interactionally modified input

Learners are not always able to understand the input that is provided for them in conversations. One way in which conversational utterances can be made more comprehensible is when interlocutors negotiate the meanings that they are trying to express. Negotiation might begin when learners signal that they do not understand something that has been said. This signalling may be done through a clarification request or some other indication of non-understanding. Interlocutors may then change their utterances in order to help learners understand the intended meaning. Such interactionally modified input can make the original input comprehensible to learners. It may also help learners to notice the gaps in their interlanguage system, which may help them to learn new linguistic information.

Interactionist approaches to SLA

This approach to SLA views conversational interaction as a crucial component for L2 learning. In interaction, learners receive input which can be modified in ways to make it more comprehensible to them. Such modifications may facilitate noticing and help the learners restructure their interlanguage knowledge. In addition learners can produce output which can provide opportunities for them to test their hypotheses about the L2. The **interaction hypothesis** forms the foundation of interactionist approaches to SLA.

> Gass, S. and Mackey, A. (2006) 'Input, interaction and output: an overview', *AILA Review*, 19, 3–17.

Interface hypothesis

The issue of whether or not explicit L2 knowledge can become implicit L2 knowledge. The implication of this hypothesis, put rather simplistically, is whether or not teaching learners grammatical rules helps them to use the L2 in spontaneous production. There are several views about this issue. The non-interface position argues that explicit knowledge and implicit knowledge are distinct and that the former has no influence on the latter. Thus, teaching learners grammar rules will not enable them to use those rules when communicating in the L2. The strong interface hypothesis argues that explicit knowledge becomes implicit knowledge through practice, and, therefore, teaching explicit grammar rules can benefit learners' L2 production. Finally, the weak interface position argues that it is possible for explicit knowledge to be converted into implicit knowledge and that explicit knowledge can facilitate implicit knowledge by helping learners to notice specific linguistic structures in the input and in their own production. The weak interface position is illustrated in Figure 4.

> Ellis, N. (2005) 'At the interface: dynamic interactions of explicit and implicit knowledge', *Studies in Second Language Acquisition*, 27, 305–52.
> Ellis, R. (2008) *The Study of Second Language Acquisition* (Oxford: Oxford University Press)

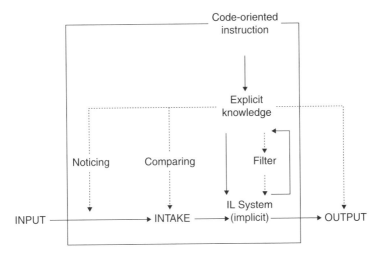

Source: Ellis (2008: 423).

Figure 4   Weak interface hypothesis

Interference

This term refers to the negative effects that a learners' L1 can have on learning the L2. Learners may have difficulty learning aspects of the L2 system because their knowledge of their L1 interferes with that process. For example, the strict word order rules of English in which the subject almost always occurs at the beginning of the sentence makes it difficult for English L1 learners to learn that other languages, such as Spanish, do not always require an overt subject nor must it always come at the beginning of the sentence. Interference can be considered to be a type of negative **transfer**.

Tagashira, K., Kida, S. and Hoshino, Y. (2010) 'Hot or gelid? The influence of L1 translation familiarity on the interference effects in foreign language vocabulary learning', *System*, 38, 412–21.

Interlanguage

The language system that is created by L2 learners as they develop their L2 knowledge towards the target language norms. The concept of interlanguage was first proposed by Larry Selinker (1972) to account for the status of learners' developing L2 knowledge. The concept was a reaction to the deficit description of L2 knowledge which viewed learners' non-target-like utterances as non-systematic errors that needed to be corrected. This deficit approach was a major component of early **behaviourist** theories of SLA. However, the concept of interlanguage proposes that learners progress towards target language competence in a systematic manner. Thus, at any one time, a learner's interlanguage is systematic and rule-governed, even though the system may differ from the target language grammar. Interlanguage systems do not remain static; they are dynamic and develop as learners continue to receive input and to restructure their L2 knowledge. The influences on an interlanguage system may include elements of the first language as well as general L2 stages of development. Instead of viewing errors as something to avoid, interlanguage theory recognizes that the 'mistakes' that learners make are to be expected as part of the learning process. Indeed current approaches would argue that learners must pass through non-target-like stages of production of certain structures as they progress towards more target-like production.

Selinker, L. (1972) 'Interlanguage', *International Review of Applied Linguistics*, 10, 209–31.
Selinker, L. (1992) *Rediscovering Interlanguage* (London: Longman).

Interlocutor

This term refers to a person who converses with another person. In interactionist approaches to SLA, an interlocutor is an important entity because he or she provides input and feedback for the learner. An interlocutor may be a native speaker of the target language or another learner.

Kim, Y. and McDonough, K. (2008) 'The effect of interlocutor proficiency on the collaborative dialogue between Korean as a second language learners', *Language Teaching Research*, 12, 211–34.

Internalization

A term from **sociocultural theory** that refers to the process of learners gaining greater control over the use of the L2. Sociocultural theory argues that learning consists of a progression from object-regulation to other-regulation to self-regulation, in which learners go from relying on external assistance in the performance of activities to being able to perform the activities on their own. For example, in L2 learning, learners may initially only be able to perform activities with the assistance of the teacher or a more advanced learner. However, as learners progress in their development, they are subsequently able to perform these activities on their own. This process constitutes internalization.

Lantolf, J. (2005) 'Sociocultural theory and L2', *Studies in Second Language Acquisition*, 28, 67–109.

Intrinsic motivation

This type of motivation is internal to the learner. It is characterized by positive feelings towards the language, its speakers and their culture. Examples of intrinsic motivation include: studying Japanese because a person likes anime and manga; learning a language because a person enjoys the challenge of analysing a language. For a time it was thought intrinsic motivation was superior to **extrinsic motivation**; however, there is no conclusive evidence that this is always the case. Also, the distinction between the two types of motivation is not always clear. Someone may choose to study a language to get a better job, but at the same time enjoy communicating with people from the target community. Intrinsic motivation is similar to **integrative motivation**, a term introduced by Gardner and Lambert (1972).

Gardner, R. and Lambert, W. (1972) *Attitudes and Motivation in Second Language Learning* (Rowley, MA: Newbury House).

Noels, K., Pelletier, L., Clement, R. and Vallerand, R. (2000) 'Why are you learning a second language? Motivational orientations and self-determination theory', *Language Learning*, 50, 57–85.

Introspective research methods

These are data collection methods that ask learners to reflect on their beliefs, feelings or cognitive processes. Because researchers cannot gain direct access to the learners' cognitive processes, they must rely on indirect methods for information about learners' thoughts. Areas of SLA research that use introspective methods include noticing and learner beliefs. Several methods have been used, including **stimulated recall**, retrospective reports, learner journals and **immediate recall**. There are several issues when considering the information that is provided by introspective methods. One is that learners must be able to verbalize their cognitive processes. While this may not be an issue for some things, like attitudes, it may be more difficult for constructs like **noticing** in which several levels of noticing have been proposed, some with and some without **awareness**. Furthermore, the choice of language in which learners are asked to verbalize can have an impact for low proficiency L2 learners who may have difficulty fully expressing themselves in the L2. Additionally, by definition some cognitive processes and representations of knowledge – such as implicit knowledge – are assumed to be largely non-verbalizable. Another issue to consider is the **veridicality** of introspective reports, meaning how closely do the verbalized reports correspond to the actual cognitive processes. For example, if learners are engaged in a stimulated recall in which they are watching a video of themselves and commenting on their thoughts at the time, how accurately does what they report thinking actually match their thoughts at the time? One factor that may help in obtaining more accurate reports is the immediacy with which learners are asked to engage in introspection. The sooner after the event learners respond, the less likely the reports will be subject to memory decay.

Introversion

See **extroversion.**

IRF sequence

See **initiate, respond, follow-up sequence.**

Item-based learning

Researchers such as Peter Skehan propose that there are two types of learning. Item-based learning involves the learning of linguistic features that are unique in their characteristics. Vocabulary learning is generally item-based because each lexical item must be learned on its own. Item-based learning can also occur with grammatical structures. For example, learning the irregular past tense in English requires learning the unique forms of irregular verbs. There is very little in the way of patterns to help learners; instead, they must simply commit the items to memory. This type of learning contrasts with **rule-based learning**.

Skehan, P. (1998) *A Cognitive Approach to Language Learning* (Oxford: Oxford University Press).

Jigsaw task

A communicative activity in which two or more interlocutors have differing pieces of information that must be combined in order to complete successfully the activity. For example, learners may be given different components of a character's daily activities, with the goal of the task being for the learners to recreate the character's routine. Learners must share their information in order to complete the entire routine.

See also **information-gap task.**

Swain, M . and Lapkin, S . (2000) 'Task-based second language learning: the uses of the first language', *Language Teaching Research*, 4, 251–74.

Keyword technique

A strategy for learning L2 vocabulary that involves making associations between the target language word and an L1 word. For example, if an English L1 speaker is trying to learn the Spanish word for 'woman' (*mujer*) he or she may come up with the keyword 'hair' which sounds very similar to the last syllable of the target word. Then the speaker may picture a woman with long, flowing hair to remind him or herself of the meaning of the Spanish word. Several studies have shown that the keyword technique is more effective for vocabulary learning than is rote memorization.

Sagarra, N. and Alba, M. (2006) 'The key is in the keyword: L2 vocabulary learning methods with beginning learners of Spanish', *The Modern Language Journal*, 90, 228–43.

Shapiro, A. and Waters, D. (2005) 'An investigation of the cognitive processes underlying the keyword method of foreign vocabulary learning', *Language Teaching Research*, 9 (2), 129–46.

L1

See **first language.**

L2

See **second language.**

Language Acquisition Device (LAD)

A metaphorical construct that refers to the part of the brain that is programmed for language learning. This concept was introduced by Chomsky in response to behaviourist theories that viewed language learning as consisting of repetition of input. However, Chomsky argued that children do not receive enough input to construct all of the sentences that they are able to generate. To account for this poverty of the stimulus, Chomsky proposed that the brain was pre-programmed for language learning, and his early term for this concept was the language acquisition device. Although less commonly used nowadays, this term belongs to **generativist** and **nativist** theories, such as **universal grammar**, that view humans as having an **innate** capacity for language.

> Hulstijn, J. (2002) 'What does the impact of frequency tell us about the language acquisition device?', *Studies in Second Language Acquisition*, 24, 269–73.

Language aptitude

See **aptitude.**

Language distance

In an attempt to consider cross-linguistic influences without accepting the **contrastive analysis hypothesis** idea that differences between the L1 and L2 necessarily result in learning difficulties, Kellerman (1979) proposed the idea that the perceived distance between an L1 structure and a target language structure might influence whether or not a learner would transfer that structure. The concept of language distance proposes that learners have ideas about what are common language structures in all languages, perhaps things such as nouns and verbs, or ways of marking plurality. Additionally, learners also have ideas about which structures are unique to their own L1. Structures that learners feel are unique to their own language will not influence their L2 learning, while those structures that are felt to be common to many languages will be transferred. In an investigation of language distance, Kellerman tested how L1 Dutch learners of English would translate the word *break* in different contexts. He found that those meanings of *break* which could be considered as core meanings were translated as equivalent to the Dutch word. (Examples of core meanings include, *I broke my leg. The cup broke.*) However, uses of English *break* that might be considered non-core or idiomatic were translated differently (for example, *His voice broke. The news broke*).

In addition to referring to the relationship between specific linguistic structures, language distance can also refer to the overall relationships of languages to each other. Consequently, English and German would be considered closer languages than English and Chinese.

Corder, P. (1979) 'Language distance and the magnitude of the language learning task', *Studies in Second Language Acquisition*, 2, 27–36.

Kellerman, E. (1979) 'Transfer and non-transfer: where we are now', *Studies in Second Language Acquisition*, 2, 37–57.

Language exchange

See **tandem learning.**

Language laboratory

A practical manifestation of the **audiolingual** method was the creation of language laboratories where learners could individually complete mechanical drills on the computer or on audiorecorders and receive immediate feedback (usually in the form of correct/incorrect statements). There was a strong belief at that time that the computer might one day replace the teacher. In reality the repetitive drills were often boring to all but the most motivated students and could only offer practice in decontextualized aspects of the language. Activities performed in language laboratories were found to help learners acquire certain types of explicit knowledge (for example verb conjugations) but this knowledge often did not translate to increased fluency and improved communicative skills outside the lab. Language laboratories were gradually replaced from the late 1970s by self-access centres, which focused more on the learner and the learning process. Alternatively, labs were modified to be used with a wider range of more communicative **computer-assisted language learning** materials. In many cases language labs or computer labs are now used by whole classes with the teacher directing group activities on the computers or supporting students in their (remedial) self-study.

Vanderplank, R. (2010) 'Deja vu? A decade of research on language laboratories, television and video in language learning', *Language Teaching*, 43, 1–37.

Language processing

This refers to the cognitive activities that are necessary for learners to comprehend, store and produce language. For comprehending oral input, learners must take the auditory stream and decode the sounds. Once the sounds are decoded, the cognitive system must parse the sounds, meaning that the incoming sounds need to be divided into syntactic segments, which are then processed for meaning. For example, if a learner of English hears the question *Howareyoutoday?*, he or she must be able to divide the speech into meaningful units (*how*, *are*, *you*, *today*) in order to understand the question.

For storage and production of language, theories of processing are concerned with issues such as **automaticity** and **restructuring**. Automaticity refers to the spccd with which languagc units can be processed, while restructuring concerns the ability to change the mental representations of the linguistic system and to integrate new linguistic information into the linguistic system. As for language production, language processing is concerned with how ideas are conceptualized and formulated into speech or writing. In other words, what mental processes are involved in encoding specific ideas into units of language that can be understood by other individuals? Specific theories which address language processing include **processability theory**, **input processing**, **information processing** and **Levelt's model of speech production**.

Clahsen, H., Felser, C., Neubauer, K., Sato, M. and Silva, R. (2010) 'Morphological structure in native and nonnative language processing', *Language Learning*, 60, 21–43.

Sabourin, L. and Stowe, L. (2008) 'Second language processing: when are first and second languages processed similarly?', *Second Language Research*, 24, 397–430.

Language related episode (LRE)

A term that is used to refer to segments of discourse in which learners pay attention to language in some way. LREs may occur in communicative activities when learners switch from using language as a tool to communicate, and instead focus on language as an object to be learned. LREs may occur when learners ask questions about, reflect on or correct the language they are producing. In the example below, the learners are narrating a story. As they convey their meaning, they also focus on which verb to use (*va*, *part* or *marche*) as well as whether or not to use the pronominal form *se*. After they have decided which forms to use, they continue telling the story. It is suggested that focusing attention on language during communication can be beneficial for learners because they may notice the target language forms at the moment that they need them for communication. **Focus on form episodes** and **corrective feedback** are terms that are similar in meaning to LREs.

Example of an LRE:
B: Yvonne va à l'école.
    (Yvonne goes to school.)
A: Se part à l'école.
    (Yvonne leaves [uses non-existent pronominal form] for school.)
B: Oui. Elle … se marche
    (She walks [uses non-existent pronominal form])
A: Se part, parce que …
    (Leaves [uses non-existent pronominal form], because)
A: Est-ce que c'est part ou se part?
    (Is it leaves or leaves? [in the non-existent pronominal form])
B: Part.
    (Leaves.)

L

A: Part? Just part?
     (Leaves, Just leaves?)
B: Ya.
A: Ok. Yvonne part à l'école, um ...
(Swain and Lapkin, 2001: 108–9)

Jackson, D. (2001) 'Language-Related Episodes', *ELT Journal*, 55, 298–9.
Swain, M. and Lapkin, S. (2001) 'Focus on form through collaborative dialogue: Exploring task effects', in M. Bygate, P. Skehan and M. Swain (eds) *Researching Pedagogic Tasks, Second Language Learning, Teaching and Testing* (Harlow: Longman).

Language socialization

An approach to language learning that examines how novices are socialized into participation in the target community. Coming from linguistic anthropology, language socialization has looked at first language acquisition and how children are socialized into their own language. Some research has suggested that simplified language is used when adults speak to children to help them learn the language; however, a seminal study of carer/child interaction in New Guinea and Samoa (Ochs and Schieffelin, 1984) revealed that not all cultures use modified carer talk to achieve this socialization. In the second language context, language socialization studies focus primarily on classroom interaction and examine how participants in the classroom become proficient members of that speech community. The view of L2 learning is primarily one of participation in which L2 learners move from the periphery to a more central and legitimized participatory status.

Friedman, D. (2010) 'Speaking correctly: error correction as a language socialization practice in a Ukrainian classroom', *Applied Linguistics*, 31, 346–67.
Ochs, E. and Schieffelin, B. (1984) 'Language acquisition and socialization: three developmental stories and their implications', in R. Schweder and R. LeVine (eds) *Culture and its Acquisition* (New York: Cambridge University Press).

Language transfer

See **transfer.**

Languaging

A term coined by Merrill Swain to refer to the use of language to make meaning. As learners are involved in this meaning-making process, they are also involved in learning. That is to say, their own language production helps to mediate their learning process. As learners produce language, they are able to reflect on their own language output in an iterative process of production and learning. Their language production may be directed towards other individuals or it may be self-directed, as in the case of **private speech**.

Swain, M. (2006) 'Languaging, agency and collaboration in advanced language proficiency', in H. Byrnes (ed.) *Advanced Language Learning: The Contribution of Halliday and Vygotsky* (London: Continuum), 95–108.

Swain, M., Lapkin, S., Knouzi, I., Suzuki, W. and Brooks, L. (2009) 'Languaging: university students learn the grammatical concept of voice in French', *The Modern Language Journal*, 93, 5–29.

Learnability

The relative difficulty of acquiring a linguistic item, depending on the learner's developmental readiness or developmental stage. The concept of learnability is based on studies which have found that the acquisition of syntactic structures and morphemes often occurs in a fixed order. Linguistic items that are several stages beyond the learner's current level have low learnability. Thus, learnability is not an inherent quality of a specific structure, since the learnability of an item cannot be measured independently from the learner's level. Therefore, a structure that would not be learnable for one learner might be learnable for a learner at a higher level.

> *See also* **developmental sequence, developmental readiness, order of acquisition.**

Learner autonomy

A set of learner characteristics related to the ability and willingness to engage critically with the learning process. The concept of autonomy in language learning developed in the 1980s and builds on a general shift of attention to the language and an increased recognition of the role of learners as active participants in the language learning process. It is influenced by humanism and constructivism in general education. In recent years it has itself influenced language teaching practice through greater attention to learners' ability manage their own learning, both inside and outside the classroom. In addition, it has influenced the development of specific approaches to learning and teaching designed to give learners more responsibility for their learning and to teach the necessary skills for independent learning, such as the provision of self-access facilities, language advising or language counselling and learner training.

The relationship between learner autonomy and second language acquisition is unclear. Learner autonomy is a multidimensional and interdisciplinary concept that relates to, builds on, and in some cases overlaps with, other educational concepts, such as motivation, interaction and awareness. For this reason it has proven difficult to isolate and investigate the development of learner autonomy and to control for confounding variables. It is also not clear whether being an autonomous learner causes success in acquiring a second language or whether it simply correlates with it.

Some have argued that learner autonomy should not be measured through formalized tests, but rather that it needs to be regarded as a fundamental educational aim that underlies human development and determines the value of education to the individual. Others have argued that it may be possible to identify and measure specific *aspects* of learner autonomy or the skills that underlie it.

The related term 'teacher autonomy' is used to refer to the teacher's ability and willingness to engage critically with the teaching and his or her own learning process. It is considered interrelated with learner autonomy in that both are interdependent of each other.

Benson, P. (2000) *Teaching and Researching Learner Autonomy* (Harlow: Longman).
Lamb, T. and Reinders, H. (eds) *Learner and Teacher Autonomy: Concepts, Realities, and Responses* (Amsterdam: John Benjamins).

Learning

(a)   The process of becoming a more able user of the target language.

See also **acquisition.**

(b)   Stephen Krashen used this term to refer specifically to the memorization of explicit rules about the L2. He argued that such explicit L2 knowledge is of limited use in helping learners to produce language in spontaneous communication. The only role for learned knowledge is to help learners monitor their production, but given the limitations of attentional resources, such monitoring can only help with relatively easy rules, such as English regular past tense rather than hypothetical conditionals. Krashen contrasted 'learning' with 'acquisition', with the latter referring to the process of gaining knowledge that allowed learners to use the language in spontaneous communication. This distinction between learning and acquisition is still relevant in SLA; however, recently different terms have been used to refer to the two types of L2 development and knowledge. One example is the distinction between **implicit** and **explicit L2 knowledge**. Another is the contrast between **procedural** and **declarative knowledge**. As a result of the challenges to Krashen's theories, the terms 'learning' and 'acquisition' are often now used interchangeably rather than in the strict sense that Krashen proposed.

Learning strategy

The different ways in which learners go about learning and/or studying the L2. Learning strategies involve conscious decisions that learners make about how to reach their language learning goals. Strategy research has identified a number of different types of strategies. Metacognitive strategies involve thinking about the learning process and may involve activities such as planning one's studying. Cognitive strategies are the mental processes that learners employ such as memorization or the keyword strategy for vocabulary learning. Social strategies involve activities with other people such as speaking with a language partner or an L1 speaker. Affective strategies involve managing one's emotional state, for example by providing positive rewards for achieving L2 goals. An instrument commonly used to measure strategy use is the **strategy inventory for language learning (SILL)**, which contains a series of statements regarding specific learning activities. Learners are asked to indicate how frequently they engage in the different types of activities. Once all of the questions have been answered, learners are instructed to group the strategies according to the previously mentioned categories in order to identify their learning strategy profile.

Strategy research has been concerned with identifying the types and the number of strategies that successful language learners use. In addition, there has been research to investigate the effectiveness of teaching language learning strategies in the classroom. One of the criticisms of strategy research is that the assigning of various activities to specific categories of strategies is often imprecise. For example, planning to study with a language partner could be an example of a metacognitive strategy, as well a social strategy. Learning strategies are seen as being different from **communication strategies**.

Cohen, A. and Macaro, E. (2007) *Language Learner Strategies: 30 Years of Research and Practice.* (Oxford: Oxford University Press)

Plonsky, L. (2011) 'The effectiveness of second language strategy instruction: a meta-analysis', *Language Learning*, 61.

Learning style

An individual difference in how learners approach the learning process. Some learners are more analytic and like to know the rules and components of the language. Other learners are more holistic and prefer to be provided with language input without being told about all the individual components of the input. It was originally thought that certain learning styles might be more facilitative for language acquisition, and that certain styles of learning might be better suited to specific types of instruction. For example, analytic learners might learn better with explicit teaching methods. Recently, it has been argued that learning styles may not be static traits, but rather that individuals' learning styles might vary depending on the learning situation they find themselves in.

Bailey, P., Onwuegbuzie, A. and Daley, C. (2000) 'Using learning style to predict foreign language achievement at the college level', *System*, 28, 115–33.

Ehrman, M. and Leaver, B. (2003) 'Cognitive styles in the service of language learning', *System*, 31, 393–415.

Levelt's model of speech production

This is an explanatory model of how language is produced. Levelt, in his model (see Figure 5), proposed five components in speech production. The first component is conceptualization, and it involves the individual in formulating an idea. The next component, formulation, is where the preverbal idea is expressed in language. The formulation process involves selecting the appropriate lexical items and grammatical forms to convey the intended meaning. The third component is articulation, which occurs when the vocal system produces the language that was formulated in the previous step. In the fourth component, audition, the overt speech is guided into the speech comprehension system (the fifth component) where it is checked for any errors in production. While each of these components can be described as discrete stages, it is argued that in fact it is necessary for considerable overlap in the component processes to occur in order to produce uninterrupted speech. Thus, as some thoughts are being articulated and monitored, others are already in the process of being conceptualized and formulated.

Izumi, S. (2003) 'Comprehension and production processes in second language learning: in search of the psycholinguistic rationale of the output hypothesis', *Applied Linguistics*, 24, 168–96.

Levelt, W. (1989) *Speaking: From Intention to Articulation* (Cambridge, MA: Massachusetts Institute of Technology Press).

L

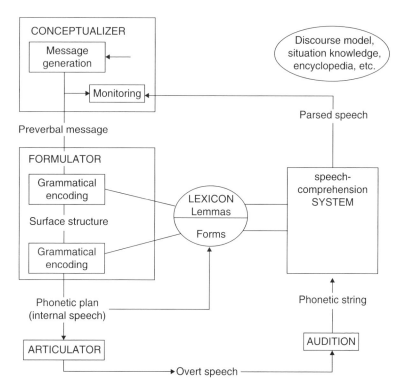

Source: Levelt (1989).

Figure 5 Levelt's speech production model

Lexical item

See **Lexicon.**

Lexicon

(a) The lexical items (i.e. vocabulary) that belong to a specific language. Thus, one can refer to the vocabulary words that comprise English as the English lexicon.

(b) The set of lexical items that are a part of an L2 learner's **interlanguage** system. Thus, learners may have different lexicons based on the range of words that they know. Learners' knowledge of the lexicon can be characterized both by how many words they know (**breadth of knowledge**) and how well they know those words (**depth of knowledge**).

Wolter, B. (2001) 'Comparing the L1 and L2 mental lexicon: a depth of individual word knowledge model', *Studies in Second Language Acquisition*, 23, 41–69.

Zareva, A. (2007) 'Structure of the second language mental lexicon: how does it compare to native speakers' lexical organization?', *Second Language Research*, 23, 123–53.

Local error

Errors that are specific to one or two components of an utterance or sentence and that do not interfere with the overall meaning of the sentence. For example, the sentence below contains a local error in the use of past tense. Despite the error in the verb tense, it is clear that the sentence refers to the past tense, because of the use of the adverb 'yesterday'.

Yesterday, I eated pizza for dinner.

See also **error.**

Long-term memory

The place in which mental representations of language are permanently stored. In one sense, it can be argued that the process of language learning involves getting the language from the input into long-term memory. Long-term memory contrasts with **working memory** which is a limited capacity storage system. Language that enters working memory can enter into long-term memory if that language is attended to in sufficient detail; however, language may also exit the working memory without being committed to long-term memory.

Longitudinal research

A research study in which data are collected over a period of time, usually for at least a month, although longer studies of six months or more are also possible. Longitudinal research often consists of case studies involving only a few participants; however, a large amount of detail about those participants is provided. An advantage of longitudinal research is that it can track the development of a learner's interlanguage system, a process that takes time. However, longitudinal studies are often difficult to conduct because participants may not be available for such long periods of time. In addition, the data collected from only a few participants may not be generalizable to other learners in other contexts. Nevertheless, these studies provide rich insight into specific instances of L2 learning, and they are valued in SLA research.

See also **cross-sectional research.**

Huebner, T. (1983) *A Longitudinal Analysis of the Acquisition of English* (Ann Arbor, MI: Karoma).
Munro, M. and Derwing, T. (2008) 'Segmental acquisition in adult ESL learners: a longitudinal study of vowel production', *Language Learning*, 58, 479–502.

L

LRE

See **language related episode.**

Markedness

In languages there are some linguistic forms that are common, systematic and prototypical, while there are other forms that are uncommon, irregular and atypical. Unmarked features refer to those that are more common in the world's languages and marked features refer to the more uncommon ones. An example of a marked feature in phonology is the sound [ð], which is the initial sound in *the*. It is not found in many languages and is therefore relatively marked. On the other hand, the sound [m] is found in many languages, and is thus unmarked. Markedness also occurs at a conceptual level. For example, when providing an example of *bird*, a person would be more likely to mention *robin* or *chicken* as prototypical birds, rather than *kiwi* or *ostrich*. The first two are the unmarked examples of the category, while the latter two are marked. In SLA, it is argued that learners have more difficulty learning marked meanings and forms than they do unmarked ones.

Eckman, F. (2008) 'Typological markedness and second language phonology', in J. Hansen Edwards and M. Zampini (eds) *Phonology and Second Language Acquisition* (Amsterdam: John Benjamins), 95–115.

Meaning-focused instruction

Meaning-focused instruction is based on the idea that in the classroom the L2 should be treated as a tool for communication and not as an object of study in itself. As a result, the overall emphasis of L2 instruction should be on the communication of meaning. Proponents of meaning-focused instruction argue that learning discrete linguistic items and grammar rules does not help learners to develop their interlanguage systems. Examples of meaning-focused instruction include **communicative language teaching**, **content-based instruction** and **task-based language teaching**. Meaning-focused instruction contrasts with **form-focused instruction** which contains varying degrees of attention to linguistic items and rules.

Mediation

A **sociocultural theory** concept that expresses the idea that human cognition does not engage directly with the world, but that it is affected indirectly through symbolic artefacts such as language, society and culture. Thus, for example, language mediates the relationships between humans and the social and physical world. That is to say, language allows humans to control their own psychological processes and to connect with their environment. An important component of mediation is **regulation**, which occurs as individuals come to rely less on physical objects and other individuals as they perform activities, and are consequently more able to self-regulate.

Memory learning strategies

A type of learning strategy that is concerned with memorization. Examples include: using flashcards to remember new L2 words, using new L2 words in a sentence in order to remember them, and making mental pictures of a situation in which the word might be used. Memory strategies are one type of **cognitive learning strategy**, all of which involve identifying, remembering, storing or retrieving words, sounds or other aspects of the target language.

Mentalist theories of language learning

Theories of L2 learning that are concerned with the **innate** structure of the brain that is held to be primarily responsible for language learning. These theories are less concerned with external and environmental aspects of L2 learning. **Universal grammar** is an example of a mentalist SLA theory.

Metacognition

Metacognition refers to knowledge of cognitive processes, or 'knowing about knowing'. A distinction is made between (1) metacognitive knowledge, which is defined as thinking of what one knows; (2) metacognitive skill/regulation, which is knowledge of what one is doing and the ability to regulate how one does it; and (3) metacognitive experience, which is described as knowledge of one's current cognitive or affective state. The development of metacognition is an important goal of **learning strategy** instruction and particularly relates to learners' ability to identify learning needs, select learning resources, plan their learning and self-assess. Although there is ample evidence to show that successful learners are more metacognitively aware than less successful learners, it is not clear if attempting to develop metacognitive awareness leads to learning gains, although there is some evidence that it may do so. Metacognitive awareness is a key component of **learner autonomy**. Metacognition in language learning is usually measured through **introspection**, but there is no general consensus on which instruments to use.

Flavell, J. (1970) 'Developmental studies of mediated memory', in J. Flavell, W. Reese and L. Lipsitt (eds) *Advances in Child Development and Behavior* (New York: Academic Press).

Vandergrift, L., Goh, C., Mareschal, C. and Tafaghodtari, M. (2006) 'The metacognitive awareness listening questionnaire: development and validation', *Language Learning*, 56, 431–62.

M

Metacognitive learning strategy

A type of L2 learning strategy that involves learners thinking about the learning process. Examples include setting goals, monitoring performance or deciding on the best way to approach a learning task.

See also **metacognition.**

Metalanguage

The language that is used to talk about language. Metalanguage may consist of both technical or non-technical terms. Examples of technical metalinguistic terms in SLA would be *present perfect tense* and *subject verb agreement*. Examples of non-technical metalinguistic terms would include *word* and *sentence*. There is some debate about the usefulness of technical metalanguage in L2 learning and teaching. Some researchers argue that metalanguage is not helpful for developing learners' ability to produce the language and that it does not have a place in the classroom. Additionally, critics argue that it is just one more set of terminology that learners have to learn. In contrast, other researchers claim that technical metalanguage can be an efficient means of communicating information about the L2, especially when it would be difficult to describe specific rules or features of the L2 in non-technical terms.

Berry, R. (2005) 'Making the most of metalanguage', *Language Awareness*, 14, 3–20.
Fortune, A. (2005) 'Learners' use of metalanguage in collaborative form-focused L2 output tasks', *Language Awareness*, 14, 21–38.

Metalinguistic awareness

Learners' understanding of how the various components of language work. This awareness may involve the use of technical terminology that is used to describe language, although metalinguistic terms are not necessary for awareness. Often, L1 speakers have very limited metalinguistic awareness regarding their own L1; however, when learners study an L2, particularly if it involves focusing on grammar rules, they may gain explicit awareness of the structure of language and the terms that are used to describe it.

Golonka, E. (2006) 'Predictors revised: linguistic knowledge and metalinguistic awareness in second language gain in Russian', *The Modern Language Journal*, 90, 496–505.
Renou, J. (2001) 'An examination of the relationship between metalinguistic awareness and second-language proficiency of adult learners of French', *Language Awareness*, 10, 248–67.

Metalinguistic feedback

When teachers correct learners' errors, they can include specific, explicit information about the nature of the error. For example, if a student says *yesterday I eated pizza,* the teacher could respond by saying that *eat* is an irregular past tense verb. Some researchers argue that such an explicit type of feedback disrupts the communicative process and should not be used in classroom interaction. However, others claim that metalinguistic feedback can be beneficial because it makes the error more salient by providing precise information about the nature of the error.

See also **explicit correction.**

Metalinguistic knowledge

Knowledge about language that is verbalizable and explicit. Generally, this knowledge can be expressed in the technical terminology that is often taught and used in the classroom. Learners are aware of the metalinguistic knowledge that they possess, and often they have learned such knowledge explicitly and intentionally. Metalinguistic knowledge can take the form of rules, such as 'to form regular past tense in English, add -ed to the simple verb form', or other types of knowledge about language, such as the fact that Chinese is a tonal language. Metalinguistic knowledge is sometimes equated with **explicit knowledge**. Metalinguistic knowledge contrasts with **implicit knowledge**, which refers to knowledge of how to use the language.

Berry, R. (2009) 'EFL majors' knowledge of metalinguistic terminology: a comparative study', *Language Awareness*, 18, 113–28.

Roehr, K. (2008) 'Metalinguistic knowledge and language ability in university-level L2 learners', *Applied Linguistics*, 29, 173–99.

Mistake

An L2 learner's inaccurate production of the target language. However, in contrast to an **error**, a mistake is a one-off occurrence, rather than a systematic deviation from the target language. As such, mistakes can be considered slips of the tongue or **performance** errors, similar to those made by L1 speakers. Mistakes are not considered to represent deficiencies in the learners' **competence**.

Modern language aptitude test (MLAT)

A collection of tests that measure individuals' ability to learn languages. The tests cover a number of different aspects of aptitude such as phonemic coding ability (the ability to distinguish the difference between sounds), analytic ability (the ability to find patterns in language) and inductive language learning (the ability to deduce rules from samples of language). The MLAT is used both as a selection tool (for example to select those students showing the greatest promise) and as a placement tool to help determine what level of instruction is most suitable for learners. The MLAT is also sometimes used, in conjunction with other tools, to identify language disabilities.

Carroll, J. and Sapon, S. (1959) *Modern Language Aptitude Test-form* (New York: The Psychological Corporation).

Modified input

Input that has been changed in some way from its original, authentic form. One type of modification is simplification, in which the language is made less complex by using shorter sentences, simpler grammatical forms or more commonly occurring vocabulary. Another type of modification is elaboration which includes restating ideas in different ways or repeating segments of the input. There has been some suggestion that simplified talk may help with learner comprehension but that it is not helpful for longer-term development. Elaborated talk, on the other hand, has been shown to have a positive effect on acquisition. Examples of simplified and elaborated texts from Oh (2001: 75–6) are:

Baseline text:
We are less credulous than we used to be. In the nineteenth century, a novelist would bring his story to a conclusion by presenting his readers with a series of coincidences – most of them wildly improbable ...

M

Simplified text:
We are less believing than we were. In the nineteenth century, a novelist would end his story by many accidental events. Most of the events were not likely to happen in reality ...

Elaborated text:
We are less credulous than we used to be in the past. We don't easily believe coincidences, or accidental happenings. In the nineteenth century, a novelist would bring his story to a conclusion by presenting his readers with a series of such coincidences, though most of them were wildly improbable. That's why so many nineteenth century novels end by some accidental events which are never likely to happen in real life ...

See also **caretaker talk, foreigner talk, structured input.**

Ellis, R. and He, X. (1999) 'The roles of modified input and output in the incidental acquisition of word meanings', *Studies in Second Language Acquisition*, 21, 285–301.
Oh, S. (2001) 'Two types of input modification and EFL reading comprehension: simplification versus elaboration', *TESOL Quarterly*, 35, 69–96.

Modified output

Learner production that has been altered in some way, usually in response to a **noticing-of-the-gap**, the realization on the part of the speaker that his or her original utterance was ill-formed in some way or that it was not understood by the recipient. For example, when two speakers exchange information and there is a communication breakdown, the conversation can be abandoned, but more commonly the speakers will make attempts to continue the conversation by finding a different way to convey the message. This **negotiation of meaning** can be done in several ways, for example by using simpler language or by rephrasing the information. In SLA, modified output has been said to be beneficial because it enables the communication to continue and thus increases the amount of exposure to the target language. Producing modified output also helps learners to develop their communicative abilities and stretches them to produce language that is grammatically more complex and accurate than their original utterance.

See also **comprehensible output hypothesis, pushed output.**

Egi, T. (2010) 'Uptake, modified output, and learner perceptions of recasts: learner responses as language awareness', *The Modern Language Journal*, 94, 1–21.
Sheen, Y. (2008) 'Recasts, language anxiety, modified output, and L2 learning', *Language Learning*, 58, 835–74.

Monitor model

Stephen Krashen's theory of language acquisition, in which he proposed five main hypotheses:

1. The acquisition–learning hypothesis states that there are two types of L2 development. Acquisition is the development of implicit L2 knowledge that

can be used to produce language in real time. Learning is the development of the knowledge about L2 rules, which can only be of limited use in helping learners to monitor their language production, but does not help in general with L2 production.

2. The natural order hypothesis states that the L2 develops in a specific order, similar to the development of L1 speakers of the language.
3. The monitor hypothesis states that learners use their learned knowledge (see hypothesis 1) to monitor and, where necessary, self-correct their language production.
4. The input hypothesis states that input that is slightly above a learner's current interlanguage level is necessary for L2 development ($i + 1$). Such input can be made comprehensible by the linguistic and social context. Output, in this view, does not contribute to acquisition.
5. The affective filter hypothesis states that input can only become **intake** if learners have a low **affective filter**, that is to say if they view the target language and the learning context favourably. If they have a high affective filter, then their resistance towards the language will interfere with their learning.

Krashen's monitor model has been very influential in the field of SLA; however, the model itself has been largely superseded.

Krashen, S. (1982) *Principles and Practice in Second Language Acquisition* (Oxford: Pergamon).

Monitoring

Paying attention to one's language output. In doing so, learners may realize that they have made a mistake in their production, and this realization may lead them to self-correct. However, there are certain conditions that must be met for monitoring to occur. First, learners need to have explicit knowledge of the L2 grammar rules that are being used in production. Second, these rules need to be simple enough to be accessed during online speech production because, in order for monitoring to occur, learners need time to think about L2 rules and how they could apply them to their output. Learners also needed to be paying attention to language forms because, even if they had time, they might only be focused on their intended meaning rather than the forms used to express those meanings. Thus, monitoring might be more likely to occur in L2 writing because learners have time to reflect on their language production. In contrast, in oral interaction learners have much less time to monitor because of the ongoing, real-time nature of speech production. Finally, it should be noted that monitoring was a component of Krashen's **monitor model**.

M

Kormos, J. (1999) 'Monitoring and self-repair in L2', *Language Learning*, 49, 303–42.
Kormos, J. (2000) 'The role of attention in monitoring second language speech production', *Language Learning*, 50, 343–84.

Monolingualism

The ability to speak only one language.

See also **bilingualism.**

Morpheme

The smallest unit of meaning in a language. For example, *word* has a meaning in English, and therefore it is a morpheme. However, *word* cannot be broken down into smaller meaningful units. *Wo, wor, ord* and *rd* do not have any meaning in English. Morphemes can be free, meaning that they can stand alone or be bound, meaning that they must be attached to another morpheme. Thus, *word* is a free morpheme, but plural *-s* is a bound morpheme. It expresses the meaning of plurality but it must be attached to another morpheme. Thus, *words* contains two morphemes.

Morpheme (order) studies

A series of influential studies in the 1970s and 1980s that were initiated by Brown's (1973) investigation into L1 child acquisition. He found that L1 children followed similar developmental patterns when learning English. Early learned features included plural *-s* and verb + ing, while late acquired features included regular past tense *-ed* and third person *-s*. Several studies then replicated this research in the L2 context, particularly with child L2 learners. Dulay and Burt (1974) investigated the English language systems of Spanish and Chinese speaking children. They found similar patterns of development between the two groups, suggesting that L1 influences on L2 learning were minimal. Bailey et al. (1974) conducted a similar study with adults and found a comparable developmental order, and no differences between an L1 Spanish speaking group and a mixed L1 group. The results of the morpheme studies have been somewhat disputed for methodological reasons. In addition, the assumption that accuracy order is equal to acquisition order has been questioned, particularly since most of the morpheme studies were **cross-sectional** and they did not account for individual variability because most relied on group averages. Nevertheless, the studies largely showed that L2 learners followed similar developmental patterns to L1 children. The L1 of the learners did not alter the order of acquisition. Furthermore, instruction seemed to have little effect on altering the path of acquisition. One of the criticisms of morpheme studies is that they only investigated a few of the morphemes in English. Such studies have largely gone out of fashion, but they have had a strong influence on the field.

See also **order of acquisition.**

Bailey, N., Madden, C. and Krashen, S. (1974) 'Is there a "natural sequence" in adult second language learning?', *Language Learning*, 24, 235–43.

Brown, R. (1973) *A First Language: The Early Stages* (Cambridge, MA: Harvard University Press).

Dulay, H. and Burt, M. (1974) 'Natural sequences in child second language acquisition', *Language Learning*, 24, 37–53.

Krashen, S., Houck, N., Biunchi, P., Bode, S. Birnbaum, R. and Strei, G. (1977) 'Difficulty order for grammatical morphemes for adult second language performers using free speech', *TESOL Quarterly*, 11, 338–41.

Larsen-Freeman, D. (1975) 'The acquisition of grammatical morphemes by adult ESL students', *TESOL Quarterly*, 9, 409–30.

Larsen-Freeman, D. (1976) 'An explanation for the morpheme acquisition order of second language learners', *Language Learning*, 26, 125–34.

Porter, J. (1977) 'A cross-sectional study of morpheme acquisition in first language learners', *Language Learning*, 27, 47–62.

Rosansky, E. (1976) 'Method and morphemes in second language acquisition research', *Language Learning*, 26, 405–25.

Villiers, J. de and Villiers, P. de (1973) 'A cross-sectional study of the acquisition of grammatical morphemes in child speech', *Journal of Psycholinguistic Research*, 2, 267–78.

Morphology

The study of the elements of language that make up words. These elements are called **morphemes**. In some cases, words cannot be divided into smaller units of meaning. For example, *play* cannot be broken down into smaller words. However, other elements of language can be added to it to come up with words such as *replay*, *player*, *played*. In each of these cases, the elements that were added contain meaning in themselves and slightly change the meaning of *play*.

Mother tongue

The language that a child first learns.

See also **first language, native language.**

Motivation

Motivation is a psychological construct that refers to the desire and incentive that an individual has to engage in a specific activity. In the study of SLA, motivation has been considered an important area of investigation because it has been assumed that increased motivation will result in increased learning. However, the research into motivation has not been so straightforward. First there are different types of motivation that have been proposed and investigated in SLA. One of the earliest distinctions was between **integrative** and **instrumental motivation**. Integrative motivation refers to an individual's desire to identify with speakers of the target language. Thus, learners might like the target language culture. In contrast, instrumental motivation refers to a need to fulfil some objective. For example, learners may be studying a language because they feel that it will help them get a better job, or because it is a school requirement. It has been argued that integrative motivation generally results in better language learning.

Another, slightly different, way in which motivation has been characterized is **intrinsic** and **extrinsic**. Intrinsic motivation comes from within an individual. Similar to integrative motivation, it may be the case that the learner likes certain aspects of the target language, its speakers and their culture. Extrinsic motivation is imposed on the learner by external forces. For example, a student's parents may require him or her to study a language. Again, intrinsic motivation is seen as being superior to extrinsic motivation for L2 learning.

Although motivation is often thought to be a causative factor in L2 learning, it is also possible that L2 learning causes motivation. Resultative motivation occurs when learners experience success in L2 learning and this success then brings about increased levels of motivation.

The previous conceptualizations of motivation tend to view it as a static trait that does not change; however, recent conceptualizations of motivation propose that it is much more fluid, dynamic and changing than is reflected in the above descriptions. Recent studies have looked at motivation during tasks and have found that it may be high at the beginning, but that it may drop off as the activity continues. Dörnyei has conceptualized the dynamic nature of motivation as occurring in three stages: pre-actional, actional and post-actional. The pre-actional stage is the one in which learners' motivation gets generated and they decide which goals they would like to attain. The actional stage refers to the carrying out of the intended activity and sustaining it over a period of time. The post-actional stage refers to the completion of the activity, the learner's reflection upon the process and the possibility that such reflection brings about for further activity.

Dörnyei, Z. (2001) *Teaching and Researching Motivation* (Harlow: Pearson).
Dörnyei, Z. (2005) *The Psychology of the Language Learner: Individual Differences in Second Language Acquisition* (Mahwah, NJ: Lawrence Erlbaum).

Multicompetence

A term used by Vivian Cook to refer to the knowledge of two or more languages in the same mind. Multicompetence suggests that a learner's L2 influences the L1, and therefore a bilingual speaker's knowledge of his or her first language differs from the knowledge that a monolingual speaker has of that language. Additionally, speakers of more than one language are argued to have greater cognitive flexibility.

See also **bilingualism**.

Cook, V. (2003) *Effects of the Second Language on the First* (Clevedon: Multilingual Matters).
Hall, J., An, C. and Carlson, M. (2006) 'Reconceptualizing multicompetence as a theory of language knowledge', *Applied Linguistics*, 27, 220–40.

Multidimensional model

A model of L2 learning that argues that different features of language develop differently. Some language features, such as word order and grammatical morphemes, are developmental and follow a prescribed order based on **processing** constraints. Other features are variational, meaning that they can be acquired at any time and in any order depending on a variety of factors, including **motivation**, social context and **input frequency**. The multidimensional model was a precursor to **processability theory**.

Meisel, J., Clahsen, H. and Pienemann, M. (1981) 'On determining developmental stages in natural second language acquisition', *Studies in Second Language Acquisition*, 3, 109–35.

Multilingual acquisition

The process of learning more than one **additional language**, either simultaneously or sequentially. While many of the aspects of multilingual acquisition are the same as for second language acquisition, the fact that two or more languages other than the learner's first language are involved changes some aspects of the learning process. For example, learners may combine syntactic or lexical elements of the L2 and L3. In addition, they may use knowledge of the L2 to help them learn the L3.

Multilingualism

The ability to use three or more languages.

Todeva, E. and Cenoz, J. (2009) *The Multiple Realities of Multilingualism* (Berlin: Mouton de Gruyter).

Multimethod research

Research that incorporates both **qualitative** and **quantitative** research methods. The use of multiple methods of investigation can provide additional information into the topic under investigation.

Lam, W. (2009) 'Examining the effects of metacognitive strategy instruction on ESL group discussions: a synthesis of approaches', *Language Teaching Research*, 13, 129–50.

M

Native language

The language that is first learned by an individual. This language is also referred to as a **first language** or **mother tongue**. In many instances, it is easy to identify people's native language because they have only learned one language or because they did not start learning a second language until after their native language was developed (for example by the age of five or six). However, in bilingual contexts it is sometimes more difficult because they have been exposed to, and have learned, two languages simultaneously.

Native speaker

A person who has been exposed to and has spoken the **target language** since birth. As such, native speakers have implicit knowledge of their native language and are able to speak it accurately and fluently, assuming that they possess normal mental capacity. Native speakers are often considered to be the baseline by which to compare L2 learners, and quasi-experimental studies often include a group of native speakers who undergo the same procedures as L2 learners in order to compare the performance of the two groups. However, there has been some debate over the status of the native speaker in SLA research. It is unclear for example whether or not L2 learners can achieve native-like proficiency in the target language. Furthermore, there is debate about whether or not L2 learners should aspire to native speaker proficiency. Some researchers argue that intelligible communication, rather than native speaker proficiency, should be the goal for L2 learners.

Davies, A. (2003) *The Native Speaker* (Clevedon: Multilingual Matters).
Foster, P. and Tavakoli, P. (2009) 'Native speakers and task performance: comparing effects on complexity, fluency, and lexical diversity', *Language Learning*, 59, 866–96.

Nativist approaches to SLA

This approach argues that at least some aspects of L2 learning are **innate**. That is to say, the human brain contains prewired components that assist in language learning. Consequently, nativist approaches differ from usage-based approaches to language learning, which do not claim that humans possess a special language acquisition device, but instead see language learning as resulting from the frequency of input exposure. While nativist approaches are very much associated with theories of L1 learning, they can also be applied to L2 learning.

See also **universal grammar**.

Naturalistic language acquisition

The type of L2 learning that occurs outside of a classroom or formal learning environment. Learners are simply exposed to the target language in their everyday activities. As a result, learners may not be aware of L2 rules or have **metalinguistic knowledge** about the target language. However, the cognitive processes that are involved in naturalistic language acquisition are argued to be the same as for **instructed language learning**. In addition, at least one study has found that the order in which naturalistic learners of English acquired certain morphemes did not differ substantially from the order learned by instructed learners, with both types of learners conforming to the natural order of acquisition. Because the term 'naturalistic' implies that classroom learning is unnatural, sometimes the term 'non-classroom learning' or 'uninstructed learning' is used.

Muñoz, C. (2008) 'Symmetries and asymmetries of age effects in naturalistic and instructed L2 learning', *Applied Linguistics*, 29, 578–96.

Pica, T. (1983) 'Adult acquisition of English as a second language under different conditions of exposure', *Language Learning*, 33, 465–97.

Natural order hypothesis

A hypothesis from Krashen's **monitor model** which claims that specific morphemes in a language are acquired in a predictable order. This sequence is referred to as natural because it largely follows the order that L1 children follow in language development. Research has shown that L2 learners do not necessarily learn structures in the order that they are taught. For example, although English regular past tense is often taught relatively early in L2 classes, it is not a structure that is acquired early by learners. In addition, learners do not necessarily learn the structures that are most frequent in the input. Instead they acquire structures in a similar order to L1 children. Krashen (1982) proposed the order shown in Figure 6.

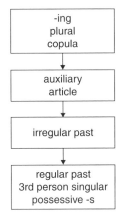

Source: Krashen (1982: 13).

Figure 6   Order of acquisition

See also **order of acquisition.**

Krashen, S. (1982) *Principles and Practice in Second Language Acquisition* (Oxford: Pergamon).

Negative evidence

Information about what it is not possible to do linguistically in the target language. The role of negative evidence in SLA is controversial. Some argue that children do not receive negative evidence when they are learning their L1, and therefore negative evidence is not necessary for L2 learning. Others argue that in fact L1 learners do receive negative evidence and that it is useful for L2 learning. Additionally, at least one study (White, 1991) has found that negative evidence was necessary for French L2 learners of English to learn correct English adverb placement. In English, there are certain places in the sentence where the adverb can be placed (sentence initial, between the subject and verb, and at the end of the sentence; see examples below) and learners would presumably receive many examples of **positive evidence** in the input, indicating these possibilities. However, in English it is not possible for the adverb to go between the verb and the direct object, but in French and Spanish such placement is allowed. In authentic input, learners would not be exposed to incorrect sentences such as example 4 below. In addition, if they produced such a sentence, it is probable that it would be understood by the hearer since adverb placement does not generally affect the meaning of the sentence. Therefore, L1 speakers of French and Spanish may continue to produce sentences with incorrect adverb placement unless they receive negative information indicating that such utterances are not correct. Such negative evidence could come in the form of **corrective feedback** or **explicit instruction** in the target structure.

Examples:
1. I usually drink coffee in the morning.
2. Usually, I drink coffee in the morning.
3. ?I drink coffee in the morning usually.
4. *I drink usually coffee in the morning.

Kang, H. (2010) 'Negative evidence and its explicitness and positioning in the learning of Korean as a heritage language', *The Modern Language Journal*, 94, 582–99.
White, L. (1991) 'Adverb placement in second language acquisition: some effects of positive and negative evidence in the classroom', *Second Language Research*, 7, 133–61.

Negative transfer

This occurs when the learner's L1 knowledge interferes with learning the target language. For example, there may be L1 grammatical rules that the learner tries to apply to the L2, or there may be interference from the L1 lexicon. For example, L1 French learners of English may incorrectly assume that the English word *demand* is equivalent to the word *ask*, since the French word *demander* is translated as *ask* in English. Negative transfer may also occur when learners use their L1 phonology when speaking the L2.

See also **contrastive analysis hypothesis, cross-linguistic influences, interference.**

Negotiation of form

A term coined by Lyster (1998) to contrast with **negotiation of meaning**. It involves interlocutors paying attention to the incorrect usage of linguistic items during communication, even when no breakdown in communication has occurred. In particular, it refers to the use of prompts to elicit a correction from the learner, rather than providing the correction for the learner in the form of a recast. It is argued that a considerable amount of **focus on form** constitutes negotiation of form, rather than **negotiation of meaning**. Nevertheless, this term has not become common in the research on focus on form.

Lyster, R. (1998) 'Negotiation of form, recasts, and explicit correction in relation to error types and learner repair in immersion classrooms', *Language Learning*, 48, 183–218.

Negotiation of meaning

A term coined by Michael Long to describe the process that can occur when there is a breakdown in communication between two or more interlocutors. If one of the speakers says something that the other person does not understand, the latter can indicate his or her lack of comprehension and then try to figure out the intended meaning. Meaning may be negotiated through discourse moves such as **clarification requests** and **confirmation checks**. Long claims that this type of interaction can be beneficial for L2 learning because learners are able to focus on specific linguistic forms while the general meaning of the utterance is clear to them. Negotiation of meaning is an important component of the **Interaction Hypothesis**.

See also **focus on form.**

Bitchener, J. (2004) 'The relationship between the negotiation of meaning and language learning: a longitudinal study', *Language Awareness*, 13, 81–95.

Long, M. (1996) 'The role of the linguistic environment in second language acquisition', in W. Ritchie and T. Bhatia (eds) *Handbook of Second Language Acquisition* (San Diego, CA: Academic Press), 413–68.

Neurolinguistics

The study of the neural mechanisms involved in processing language. Neurolinguistic studies have contributed primarily to our understanding of L1 acquisition, but in recent years L2 research has also been influenced by neurolinguistics. Neurological changes that occur over time, such as the degree of brain plasticity (the ability of the brain to change at the neuronal level), are said to affect whether a learner can achieve native-speaker proficiency in a second language. Such changes are related to the **critical period hypothesis**, or **sensitive period**, which suggests that complete acquisition of an L2 is only possible, or at least easier to achieve, when the brain is more plastic. Other areas in which neurolinguistic research has informed SLA include studies of **bilingualism** and, to a lesser extent, language impairments.

N

Arabski, J. and Wojtaszek, A. (2009) *Neurolinguistic and Psycholinguistic Perspectives on SLA* (Clevedon: Multilingual Matters).

Paradis, M. (2004) *A Neurolinguistic Theory of Bilingualism* (Amsterdam: John Benjamins).

Non-interface position

See interface hypothesis.

Non-native speaker

A person who learns or speaks an additional language other than their first language. The term implies that the knowledge or proficiency level of the speaker differs from that of a **native speaker**. As a result of this negative connotation, some researchers prefer to use terms such as 'L2 speaker' or 'L2 user'.

Noticing hypothesis

The noticing hypothesis was proposed by Richard Schmidt to account for the role of attention in L2 learning. Schmidt proposed that learners must attend to linguistic items in the input in order for those forms to have the potential to become **intake** and eventually a part of the learner's interlanguage system. Thus, noticing requires paying attention with some level of **awareness**. Schmidt argues that subconscious or implicit learning has a very limited role in L2 acquisition. Rather, learners must first consciously notice a form before it can be learned.

Schmidt, R. (1995) *Attention and Awareness in Foreign Language Learning* (Honolulu, HI: University of Hawaii).

Schmidt, R. (2001) 'Attention', in P. Robinson (ed.) *Cognition and Second Language Instruction* (Cambridge: Cambridge University Press).

Noticing the gap

This concept, related to the **noticing hypothesis**, suggests that learners need to discover the difference between their own interlanguage forms and the target language forms. One way to help learners do this is by providing them with corrective feedback when they make L2 production errors. For example, if a learner's incorrect utterance is **recast** by the teacher, it is hoped that the learner will notice that the reformulated correction is different from his or her own, original utterance. By noticing this gap, learners can intake the input for learning purposes. Another way in which learners may notice the gap in their L2 ability is in tasks such as **dictogloss**, in which learners are asked to reconstruct texts which they have previously heard. As learners work to recreate the text, they may realize that they do not always possess the linguistic ability that they need in order to reconstruct the text accurately. Again, this awareness of the incompleteness of their interlangauge ability can create the conditions for learning.

Swain, M. (1995) 'Three functions of output in second language learning', in G. Cook and B. Seidlhofer (eds) *Principles and Practice in Applied Linguistics* (Oxford: Oxford University Press), 125–44.

Noun phrase accessibility hierarchy

See **accessibility hierarchy.**

Novelty effect

The idea that an L2 structure that is very different from structures in the L1 will be easier to learn because it is more salient and 'novel' to the learners. In addition, the use of new materials or methods in the classroom might also have a positive effect that might disappear over time, as the novelty wears off.

N

Obligatory occasion analysis

A type of analysis used to determine if a learner, or a group of learners, has acquired a particular morpheme. The basic procedure is to identify all the occasions in a text where a particular morpheme has to be used (hence 'obligatory') and then to calculate the number of times the learner supplies this item correctly. The resulting percentage is an indication of a learner's mastery of the morpheme in question. Obligatory occasion analysis has been criticized because it does not take into account learners' overuse of morphemes; therefore, **target-like use analysis** has been proposed to rectify this oversight. The following formula is used to calculate obligatory occasion usage:

$$\frac{Number\ of\ correct\ suppliances}{Number\ of\ obligatory\ occasions} = Obligatory\ use$$

Observer's paradox

A term coined by William Labov to refer to the fact that by simply observing something, that thing becomes changed. For example, if researchers go into an L2 classroom, even if they do not participate in the classroom activities, their presence changes the dynamics of the classroom. The goal of researchers is to minimize as much as possible the effects of their observations.

One-to-one principle

This principle states that learners, especially in the beginning stages of learning, tend to associate one linguistic form with only one meaning. For example, L2 learners of English might learn that *will* is used to express future events, and they may therefore think that *will* is only used in regard to the future, and that the only way to express future events is by using *will*. In order for interlanguage development to occur, learners need to break the one-to-one principle and learn that forms can have multiple meanings and that the same meaning can be expressed in different ways.

Andersen, R. (1984) 'The one-to-one principle of interlanguage construction', *Language Learning*, 34, 77–95.

Bardovi-Harlig, K. (2004) 'The emergence of grammaticalized future expression in longitudinal production data', in B. VanPatten, J. Williams, S. Rott and M. Overstreet (eds) *Form-meaning Connections in Second Language Acquisition* (Mahwah, NJ: Lawrence Erlbaum), 115–37.

Online planning

The type of planning that learners engage in while they are conducting a task. As such there is only limited time for them to plan their language production.

Consequently, learners have to rely primarily on their **proceduralized** or **implicit L2 knowledge**, and they are able to access only the most basic grammatical rules to help them with language production. Online planning contrasts with **pre-task planning**, and is a variable that is investigated in **task-based language teaching**.

OPI

See **oral proficiency interview.**

Opinion-gap task

A communicative activity in which learners must present and discuss their thoughts and ideas about a specific topic. The purpose of the task is for learners to use the target language to communicate with other learners. Opinion-gap tasks may be open, allowing learners to express their own opinions. An example of an open task would be for learners to answer a question such as *How do you feel about banning smoking in public places?* In contrast, a closed task requires learners to come to a consensus regarding their opinions. An example of a closed task would be for learners to be presented with a list of candidates for a job and then to discuss and agree upon which one they feel is most qualified for the job.

See also **task-based language teaching.**

Oral proficiency interview (OPI)

A test that is used to assess a learner's speaking ability. The OPI consists of authentic communicative tasks in which the learner interacts with the test administrator. The interaction is recorded and then rated according to a predetermined scale of proficiency levels. The **American Council on the Teaching of Foreign Languages (ACTFL)** OPI is an example of one of the more commonly used speaking assessment instruments.

Segalowitz, N. and Freed, B. (2004) 'Context, contact, and cognition in oral fluency acquisition: learning Spanish in at home and study abroad contexts', *Studies in Second Language Acquisition*, 26, 173–99.

O

Order of acquisition

The finding that language acquisition occurs in a systematic manner, with certain linguistic structures being acquired before others, regardless of such characteristics as type of instruction, frequency of the structure in the input, learner L1 and age. The **morpheme order studies**, which were based on child L1 acquisition, found that, in general, L2 learners followed a similar pattern of development to that of L1 children. Thus, morphemes which were acquired early in the learning process included plural *-s* and verb + *ing* (e.g. going, talking). Morphemes that were acquired later in the learning process included regular past tense *-ed* and third person singular *-s*. The order of acquisition represents a developmental approach to L2 learning similar to that which is found in **developmental sequences**. However, the order of acquisition refers to the learning of different syntactic and morphological structures. In contrast, developmental sequences are the stages that learners go through in acquiring one specific morphosyntactic feature, such as English negation or question formation.

See also **natural order hypothesis.**

Luk, Z. and Shirai, Y. (2009) 'Is the acquisition order of grammatical morphemes impervious to L1 knowledge? Evidence from the acquisition of plural -s, articles, and possessive 's', *Language Learning*, 59, 721–54.

Output

The language, either written or oral, that is produced by learners. Some theories of SLA, such as **universal grammar** and Krashen's **monitor model** view output as merely a result of learning; however, **interactionist approaches** and **sociocultural theory** view output as part of the learning process. In fact, Swain proposed the **comprehensible output hypothesis** to account for the role of output in interactionist approaches to SLA. Regardless of the theoretical approach, one of the functions of output is that it helps learners to practise the L2, thereby developing **fluency** and **automaticity** in the target language.

Mennim, P. (2007) 'Long-term effects of noticing on oral output', *Language Teaching Research*, 11, 265–80.
Shehadeh, A. (2003) 'Learner output, hypothesis testing, and internalizing linguistic knowledge', *System*, 31, 155–71.

Output hypothesis

See **comprehensible output hypothesis.**

Over-generalization

The phenomenon in which learners apply a rule in contexts in which it should not be used. For example, learners may have just learned the present progressive, so they use it frequently, even when it is not appropriate. Another example is when learners apply the English regular past tense rule to irregular verbs to produce forms such as *eated/ated* or *goed.*

See also **U-shaped development.**

Overproduction

See **over-generalization.**

Parallel distributed processing (PDP)

Parallel distributed processing (PDP) is a **connectionist** model in which information is considered to be stored in the form of a neural network that consists of nodes and pathways. In this view, words are not stored as discrete separate items; for example, the words 'is' and 'was' do not exist as separate items, but instead are distributed across the network. As learners are exposed to input containing these words, their pathways in the network are strengthened. Learners also make new associations between nodes as they encounter new forms in the input.

See also **connectionism.**

Parameter

A concept in **universal grammar** that refers to the ways in which the underlying rules or **principles** that apply to all languages are realized in language. There are a limited number of parameter options that are available for the way in which specific principles can be realized in individual languages. Chomsky likens parameters to a switch which has several settings, and learners of a specific language must determine which position the switch should be in.

One of the issues for L2 learning concerns the resetting of parameters, when the L1 has one setting and the L2 has a different setting. If UG is accessible to L2 learners, then parameter resetting should be possible. However, if UG is only available through the L1, then the learner would not be able to reset the parameter, if the parameter differed in the L2. Nor would learners be able to reset the parameter if UG is entirely unavailable to them. It should also be noted that parameter resetting, and indeed all UG activities, are performed unconsciously by the brain. Learners cannot consciously access UG and decide, for example, that they would like to reset a parameter.

An example of a parameter is the pro-drop or null subject parameter. It states that some languages require the presence of a subject pronoun while others do not. English is a [–pro-drop] language, and therefore requires the presence of a subject pronoun. Thus, sentence 1 is grammatical, but sentence 2 is not.

1.   He sings.
2.   *Sings.

However, Spanish is a [+pro-drop] language, and therefore does not require a subject pronoun. Therefore, both sentences 3 and 4 are grammatical.

3.   El canta.
He sings.
4.   Canta.
He/she sings.

In addition, there are other aspects of grammar that are associated with the pro-drop parameter settings. For example, a language such as Spanish is [+pro-drop], allowing pronouns to be omitted. It also allows subject-verb inversion. However, English is [–pro-drop], and also does not allow subject-verb inversion, as seen in the examples below.

La mujer canta.
The woman sings.

Canta la mujer.
*Sings the woman.

> Flynn, S. (1987) *A Parameter-setting Model of L2 Acquisition* (Dordrecht: Reidel).

Parsing

(a) The psycholinguistic process that learners engage in when they are confronted with oral or written input. Learners must make sense of the incoming language data in real time, and they do so by analysing and categorizing the incoming input into meaningful units. Parsing is generally viewed as a syntactic process in which learners identify different sentence parts. For example, in order for learners to understand fully a written or spoken sentence such as, *The boys walked to the house*, they need to identify the subject of the sentence, as well as the plural -s marker that it contains. Furthermore, learners need to identify and process the past tense -ed marker on the verb. Finally, they need to identify the prepositional phrase and its various components. Sometimes parsing is also said to involve semantic and phonological processing.

> Dussias, P. (2004) 'Parsing a first language like a second: the erosion of L1 parsing strategies in Spanish–English bilinguals', *International Journal of Bilingualism*, 8, 355–71.
> Papadopoulou, D. and Clahsen, H. (2003) 'Parsing strategies in L1 and L2 sentence processing: a study of relative clause attachment in Greek', *Studies in Second Language Acquisition*, 25, 501–28.

(b) A type of data analysis carried out by applied linguists or by computer programs to determine the syntactic structure of sentences and larger texts. This definition of parsing contrasts from the previous one in that it is done consciously and the primary goal is to produce linguistic descriptions of the sentences being analysed rather than to comprehend the meaning of the sentences. This type of parsing is associated with traditional grammar instruction in which, for example, learners might have to identify the following syntactic categories in a sentence: subject, verb, indirect object, direct object.

Participation metaphor

Some theories of language do not view acquisition as the goal of L2 learning. Rather they view participation as the goal. That is to say, L2 learning is seen to occur as learners are able to participate in more activities in the target language and to participate in more appropriate ways. This view of SLA focuses more on the social than the cognitive aspects of L2 learning.

> *See also* **language socialization, sociocultural theory.**

Pavlenko, A. and Lantolf, J. (2000) 'Second language learning as participation and the (re)construction of selves', in J. Lantolf (ed.) *Sociocultural Theory and Second Language Learning* (Oxford: Oxford University Press), 155–77.

Young, R. and Miller, E. (2004) 'Learning as changing participation: discourse roles in ESL writing conferences', *The Modern Language Journal*, 88, 519–35.

Pattern

Patterns, also called **formulaic sequences** or **chunks**, are combinations of words that act as a unit and that have at least one open class item. For example, *no me gusta X* would be a pattern that beginning learners of Spanish learn to express *I don't like X*. Although it is made up of three words and an unspecified object (the open class item), together the words act as a unit with one meaning. In many cases, the meanings of the individual components of such patterns are not recognized by learners; instead, learners simply know the overall meaning of the pattern.

PDP

See **parallel distributed processing.**

Perception

(a) The ability to recognize the auditory and visual components of language. Perception may be used in several different ways. In the first, more general meaning, perception refers to the detection and recognition of linguistic items, often with an accompanying awareness of those items. For instance, studies of L2 phonology have investigated learners' ability to perceive the difference between different sounds in the target language that may be difficult for learners to distinguish. Examples include the English [r/l] distinction for L1 Japanese and Korean speakers, and the Japanese single versus double vowel [o/oo] or consonant [p/pp] distinction for L1 English speakers. Another, more technical use of the term perception occurs in discussions of the **noticing hypothesis**. In this case, perception is defined as the unconscious registration of the existence of linguistic items, which is the first step in the process of awareness.

Altenberg, E. (2005) 'The perception of word boundaries in a second language', *Second Language Research*, 21, 325–58.

Hardison, D. and Saigo, M. (2010) 'Development of perception of second language Japanese geminates: role of duration, sonority, and segmentation strategy', *Applied Psycholinguistics*, 31, 81–99.

(b) Perception can also be used to refer to learners' beliefs and **attitudes** towards the target language or the learning environment. For example, researchers may investigate topics such as learners' perceptions of their own proficiency, or L1 and L2 speakers' perceptions of various accents.

Polio, C., Gass, S. and Chapin, L. (2006) 'Using stimulated recall to investigate native speaker perceptions in native–nonnative speaker interaction', *Studies in Second Language Acquisition*, 28, 237–67.

Watanabe, Y. and Swain, M. (2008) 'Perception of learner proficiency: its impact on the interaction between an ESL learner and her higher and lower proficiency partners', *Language Awareness*, 17, 115–30.

P

Performance

The actual production of language by a speaker. Performance is sometimes distinguished from **competence**. The latter is used to describe the learners' idealized, abstract knowledge of the language. In reality, however, a person's linguistic performance may be less than ideal and may not represent the full extent of the speaker's knowledge. For example language production may contain mistakes due to situational factors such as distraction or anxiety. L1 speakers of a language, by definition, have competence in their L1, that is to say, they know (even though they may not be able to verbalize) the systematic rules of their L1. However, when L1 speakers actually produce the language, they may make **mistakes** or slips-of-the-tongue which do not reflect their competence. L2 speakers' performance may also contain mistakes; however, the status of L2 speakers' underlying competence is less clear, and thus it is harder to determine if a learner's use of a non-target-like language form represents a performance error or gap in the learner's competence. Traditionally, studies of L1 linguistics, particularly from a **generativist position**, have been interested in competence. In contrast, L2 studies have been much more focused on learners' performance.

> Eckman, F. (1994) 'The competence-performance issue in second language acquisition theory: a debate', in E. Tarone, S. Gass and A. Cohen (eds) *Research Methodology in Second-language Acquisition* (Hillsdale, NJ: Lawrence Erlbaum), 3–15.

Phonological loop

See **working memory.**

Phonological working memory

See **working memory.**

Phonology

The study of the sound systems of languages. Phonology is concerned with both segmental and suprasegmental features. Segmental features are often what people think of when they consider pronunciation. They are the individual units of sounds, often called vowels and consonants. So, for example, *cat* is made up of three segmental features [k], [æ] and [t]. Suprasegmental features include pitch, emphasis and stress patterns. L1 speakers know which sounds or combinations of sounds are possible in their language and which ones are not. L2 learners must learn the sound system of the target language. Sometimes the sounds are the same between the L1 and L2; however, sometimes there are sounds in the L2 that do not exist in the L1. In the latter case, learners must either master the novel sounds, approximate them as best they can or substitute an L1 sound for the L2 sound. Differences in L2 speakers' pronunciation of target language phonology accounts for their accent in the L2. Phonology is considered to be one of the hardest components of language for L2 learners to achieve native-like proficiency in, especially if they begin studying the language after puberty.

Eckman, F. (2004) 'From phonemic differences to constraint rankings: research on second language phonology', *Studies in Second Language Acquisition*, 26, 513–49.
Hansen Edwards, J. and Zampini, M. (2008) *Phonology and Second Language Acquisition* (Amsterdam: John Benjamins).

Picture description task

A communicative activity that can be used to elicit L2 production. Learners are given a series of pictures that they must describe. Sometimes the pictures are unrelated to each other and are to be described individually. Other times, learners must use the pictures to create a narrative, based either on the order of pictures provided for them or by putting the pictures into a logical order themselves. Learners can perform these tasks either by themselves or with other learners in an **information gap task**. The oral or written language that is produced in these tasks can then be analysed for a variety of linguistic features.

Planning

The opportunity for learners to think about the language that they are going to produce. Planning may occur either before a task (**pre-task planning**) or during it (within-task or **online planning**). Research into planning has been concerned with how various aspects of planning might affect language production, with an underlying assumption being that learners have a limited amount of attention that they can devote to online, spontaneous language production. Consequently, there may be trade-offs among **accuracy**, **fluency** and **complexity** in production, depending on the distribution of attentional resources. For example, some research has found that pre-task planning may increase learners' accuracy during the task, but it may hinder their fluency.

Ellis, R. (2005) *Planning and Task Performance in Second Language Learning* (Amsterdam: John Benjamins).
Ellis, R. (2009) 'The differential effects of three types of task planning on the fluency, complexity, and accuracy in L2 oral production', *Applied Linguistics*, 30, 474–509.

Portfolio

The term 'portfolio' is used to describe an instrument for recording progress (process) and ability (product) in the target language. This could be as simple as a pen and paper notebook, or as extensive as a computer-based record-keeping tool. Portfolios can be used to support learning, for example by encouraging learners to reflect on the language learning process, to record experiences in using the language, and to motivate learners by recording their achievements. Teachers can use portfolios to gain insight into the types of practice learners engage in, the difficulties that they face, and the ways in which their language improves. Portfolios are often used in learner-centred approaches to encourage critical reflection and to give some degree of control over the learning process to the language learner. In these cases, portfolios are used as learning or teaching aids. However, they can also be used simply as a record of achievement, for example listing all vocabulary acquired, courses completed or certifications obtained by a learner.

P

A major portfolio project is the European Language Portfolio, developed by the Council of Europe. This project aims to support the learning process, but it also includes a Language Passport, which learners can use to demonstrate their language proficiency, for example to future employers or to educational institutions. The European Language Portfolio makes use of the **Common European Framework** for comparability between countries.

Cummins, P. and Davesne, C. (2009) 'Using electronic portfolios for second language assessment', *The Modern Language Journal*, 93, 848–67.

Little, D. (2005) 'The Common European Framework and the European Language Portfolio: involving learners and their judgements in the assessment process', *Language Testing*, 22, 321–36.

Positive evidence

Positive evidence consists of examples of what is possible in a language. Thus, all **input** is potentially evidence to a learner of which linguistic structures and items can occur in the target language. There is agreement amongst all theories of SLA that positive evidence is *necessary* for L2 learning; however, there is controversy as to whether it is *sufficient* for L2 learning, with some researchers arguing that **negative evidence** is also necessary.

Leeman, J. (2003) 'Recasts and second language development: beyond negative evidence', *Studies in Second Language Acquisition*, 25, 37–63.

Sanz, C. and Morgan-Short, K. (2004) 'Positive evidence versus explicit rule presentation and explicit negative feedback: a computer-assisted study', *Language Learning*, 54, 35–78.

Positive transfer

This occurs when the learner's L1 knowledge facilitates learning the target language. For example there may be L1 grammatical rules that are similar in the L2, or there may be lexical cognates in the two languages.

See also **contrastive analysis hypothesis, cross-linguistic influences, transfer.**

Poverty of the stimulus

This is one of the puzzles of language acquisition. How can learners acquire the underlying rules of a language and be able to generate an infinite number of grammatical sentences when learners are only exposed to a finite amount of input? Furthermore, the input that children receive is sometimes simplified and not always entirely grammatical; nevertheless, children develop full **competence** in their first language. This poverty of the stimulus is one of the phenomena that led Noam Chomsky to formulate his theory of **universal grammar**, arguing that language learning is not based on input alone, but that humans also have an innate capability for language learning which is activated by language input. However, not all theories of language acquisition accept that the poverty of the stimulus argument necessarily supports the existence of an innate language capacity. Such usage-based theories appeal to **frequency effects**, and general learning strategies are able to overcome the poverty of the stimulus.

Hara, M. (2007) 'Input, triggering and poverty of the stimulus in the second language acquisition of Japanese passives', *Second Language Research*, 23, 419–58.

PPP (presentation, production, practice)

A method of language instruction that involves the explicit presentation of specific linguistic forms, such as vocabulary items or grammar rules. This presentation is followed by controlled learner production of the target forms. Finally, freer practice in using the forms is allowed. PPP is often associated with more traditional types of L2 instruction, in which the target language is presented in a largely decontextualized, non-communicative context. PPP has been criticized because it does not take into account learners' **order of development**, nor does it allow learners to use the language items for primarily communicative purposes. Finally, PPP is based on the idea that teaching explicit L2 knowledge can result in learners developing their implicit L2 knowledge; however, this assumption is controversial.

See also **interface hypothesis.**

Fuente, M. de la (2006) 'Classroom L2 vocabulary acquisition: investigating the role of pedagogical tasks and form-focused instruction', *Language Teaching Research*, 10, 263–95.

Pragmatics

The study of the way that language is used for communication. Pragmatics is concerned with how speakers express their intended meanings and how those meanings are interpreted in specific contexts. In some cases, speakers' utterances are relatively easy to interpret based on their literal meanings of the words used. However, in other cases, a speaker's intended meaning may be less clear from the surface meaning of the words. For example, *Pass the milk* is an obvious request for milk. In contrast, *Can you pass the milk?* appears on the surface to be a question about the hearer's ability; nevertheless, such a question is also often interpreted as a request for milk. These types of **speech acts** in which language is used to accomplish social action are an important aspect of pragmatics research. In addition to requests, other common speech acts include inviting, refusing, complaining and complimenting. Another area of pragmatics research investigates how social context and interlocutor status affect speech. For example, requests or complaints are expressed differently in a language depending on the context and the level of politeness required. A request from a student to a professor for an extension on his or her essay deadline may require a higher level of politeness than a request from a student to a classmate to borrow a sheet of paper. In addition to different rules within the culture of one language, different languages and cultures have different rules about the way language should be used to achieve things. Some languages consider it important to be direct when making a request, while others prefer indirectness. Part of the L2 learning process is learning the pragmatics of the target language; however, pragmatic ability is often one of the last components of language that an L2 speaker learns.

Alcón Soler, E. and Martínez-Flor, A. (2008) *Investigating Pragmatics in Foreign Language Learning, Teaching and Testing* (Clevedon: Multilingual Matters).

Kasper, G. and Rose, K. (2003) *Pragmatic Development in a Second Language* (Malden, MA: Blackwell).

Pre-modified input

Language that is changed in some way before it is presented to the learner. Changes may include using more common vocabulary items, using simpler grammatical structures, and including more redundancy. Pre-modified input contrasts with **interactionally modified** input and **authentic** input. While pre-modified input may assist learners with comprehension, it is argued to be less effective for L2 learning because it does not always contain language that is new to the learner.

See also **modified input.**

Pre-task planning

See **planning.**

Pretest–post-test design

A common research method in quantitative studies involving the assessment of learners before and after they have been exposed to a specific teaching technique or other type of language input. Generally, the content of the pretest and post-test are the same so that the researcher can see if there are any gains in learners' scores. For example, learners may be pretested on their knowledge of English past tense. Then the learners may engage in a communicative activity in which their incorrect use of past tense is corrected. After that activity, the learners take the post-test. If their test scores improve, the researcher can claim that the treatment (in this case the corrective feedback) has been beneficial for L2 learning.

Several issues are important in this type of research design. First, it is important to consider the construct **validity** of the tests. Do the tests measure the same thing that is being targeted in the treatment stage? Often researchers may give learners several different types of tests to assess different components of the language, such as implicit and explicit knowledge. Another factor to consider is the timing of the tests. If the pretest is given immediately before the treatment, there is the possibility that the learners will become aware of the target structure. In general, such awareness is not desired by the researcher because then any improvement in test scores may not be due solely to the treatment. One way to solve this problem is to include distractor items in the pretest, so that learners will not figure out the targeted linguistic structure. Another option is to administer the pretest several days before the treatment. Timing is also an issue for the post-test. Often researchers try to administer both an immediate post-test and a delayed post-test. An immediate post-test may be given right after the test or perhaps one or two days later. Such a test can obviously measure if the treatment had an immediate effect on the learners. However, L2 development is not always an immediate process. Furthermore, the effects of a treatment may not always be long-lasting. Therefore, delayed post-tests which occur anywhere from a week to a month after the treatment are also considered important. Two considerations concern delayed post-testing. The first is that it can be difficult for learners to come back after such a length of time, with the result that important data can be lost for individual research participants. Second, it is also possible that learners may come into contact with the target language structure during the intervening time. As a result, any gains in test scores might not be due to the treatment alone.

Priming

A form of conditioning in which previous exposure to language affects future linguistic production. For example, studies have found that individuals are more likely to use a word after they have heard it in prior language input. In addition, a specific word may activate related words in the individual's cognitive system. Thus, a learner who is exposed to the word *teacher* will be able to retrieve related words, such as *classroom* and *test* more quickly. Priming studies have been used to demonstrate the existence of implicit memory and learning without conscious recollection of exposure to the language. In second language acquisition research, priming studies have been used in the discussion about the importance of **noticing** and **consciousness** in acquiring new language.

McDonough, K. and Kim, Y. (2009) 'Syntactic priming, type frequency, and EFL learners' production of wh-questions', *The Modern Language Journal*, 93, 386–98.

McDonough, K. and Trofimovich, P. (2008) *Using Priming Methods in Second Language Research* (New York: Routledge).

Principles

A term from **universal grammar** that refers to the underlying structural properties of language contained in the human mind. These principles are abstract rules that apply to all languages. Principles are not learned by individuals; rather they are part of the hardware package of the human brain. An example of a UG principle is the structure dependency principle which states that sentences in all languages consist of structured elements, rather than just assorted words that can be put together in any way. One type of structured element is a noun phrase, another type is a verb phrase. These phrases have distinct boundaries and properties which are structured as well. As an example, each sentence below answers the question *who ate the cake?*, and in each case it is the noun phrase that answers this question, even though the noun phrases have different surface features.

Patrick ate the cake.
Alice and John ate the cake.
The dog ate the cake.

P

These examples are greatly simplified, and in reality the principles expressed in UG are much more abstract and complex. However, the important idea is that these principles are common to all languages. Additionally, language is comprised of parameters, which account for the different ways in which the abstract principles are manifested in specific languages.

Freidin, R. (1992) *Principles and Parameters in Comparative Grammar* (Cambridge, MA: Massachusetts Institute of Technology Press).

Private speech

A concept from **sociocultural theory** that argues that individuals can use speech that is directed to themselves to help regulate the activities in which they are involved. As a result, private speech is argued to allow individuals to gain control over the activities that they are engaged in. Thus, while performing a challenging writing task, learners may produce language subvocally in order to help them complete the task. One study of private speech in the L2 classroom found that learners who observed their classmates receiving oral correction often repeated that correction softly to themselves.

Lee, J. (2008) 'Gesture and private speech in second language acquisition', *Studies in Second Language Acquisition*, 30, 169–90.

Ohta, A. (2001) *Second Language Acquisition Processes in the Classroom: Learning Japanese* (Mahwah, NJ: Lawrence Erlbaum).

Procedural knowledge

Knowledge of how to do something without having to think explicitly about it. This is the type of knowledge that L1 speakers have of their first language. It is also the type of knowledge that develops when repeatedly doing certain activities, such as driving a car or playing a sport. Sometimes procedural knowledge is referred to as 'knowledge to' do something, and it contrasts with **declarative** 'knowledge of' something. The fact that L2 learners can develop proceduralized knowledge is not controversial, and this procedural knowledge may be developed by repeated use, just as with other activities. However, there is some controversy as to whether or not **declarative** or **explicit knowledge** of something can become proceduralized. In addition, there is some suggestion that the ability to develop procedural knowledge in an L2 may diminish with age.

See also **skill acquisition theory.**

Processability theory

Manfred Pienamann's theory stating that language production and language learning are constrained by the way in which the human brain processes language. One of the main components in processability theory is that language is processed in constituent forms. Initial processing operations are fairly simple, occurring with single lexical items or chunks. As learners progress, they are able to process forms that are close together in the sentence, such as in a noun phrase. This processing ability would be demonstrated, for example, by being able to mark plurality and gender in a phrase such as *los dos gatos* (*the two cats*). Further development occurs when learners are able to process forms that cross constituent boundaries, as in subject-verb agreement when the noun phrase and the verb phrase are involved. Processability theory states that learners must go through these acquisitional stages and that L2 instruction is not able to alter these stages. Table 6 illustrate the stages of processability theory.

Dyson, B. (2009) 'Processability theory and the role of morphology in English as a second language development: a longitudinal study', *Second Language Research*, 25, 355–76.

Pienemann, M. (1998) *Language Processing and Second Language Development: Processability Theory* (Amsterdam: John Benjamins).

Table 6 A hierarchy of acquisition in L2 English

Stage	L2 process	Morphology/syntax
6	Main and subordinate clauses	Embedded questions: 'I wonder why she sold the car.'
5	Subject-verb agreement involving non-salient morphology	3rd person -s: 'This man owns a dog.'
4	Inversion	Yes/no inversion: 'He has seen you?'
3	Noun phrase agreement	Plural: 'He own many dogs.' Adverb: 'He sleep always.' Do fronting: 'Do he like you?'
2	Plural/possessive pronoun	Canonical order (subject-verb-object: 'He buy car.')
1	Invariant forms	Single constituent (including formulaic chunks: 'eating'/'I don't know.')

Source: Ellis (2008: 98; based on Pienemann, 1998: 171).

Processing

See **language processing**.

Processing instruction

A type of language teaching based on Bill VanPatten's **input processing** theory, which argues that learners use certain processing strategies to understand the L2. Sometimes these strategies are based on the L1 and do not work in the L2. Processing instruction explicitly identifies the incorrect processing strategy and teaches learners the correct L2 processing strategy. An example of an incorrect processing strategy occurs for English learners of Spanish. English uses word order (subject–verb–object) to identify the subjects and objects in sentences. However, in Spanish, direct object pronouns come before the verb, and subjects can come after the verb. Therefore, the learners' English processing strategies can lead them to misinterpret such utterances in Spanish. Processing instruction explains the incorrect strategy to learners, teaches them the new strategy, and then gives them the opportunity to use the new processing strategy.

Processing instruction is entirely comprehension-based. Learners are given target language input but are not required to produce it. Although research has shown that processing instruction can be beneficial for learners, it does not necessarily work better than output-based instruction. Furthermore, the types of linguistic structures that can be taught using processing instruction is limited to those where there is a mismatch between L1 and L2 processing strategies.

Figure 7 illustrates the pedagogical intervention of processing instruction.

VanPatten, B. (2004) *Processing Instruction: Theory, Research, and Commentary* (Mahwah, NJ: Lawrence Erlbaum).
VanPatten, B. and Cadierno, T. (1993) 'SLA as input processing: a role for instruction', *Studies in Second Language Acquisition*, 15, 225–43.

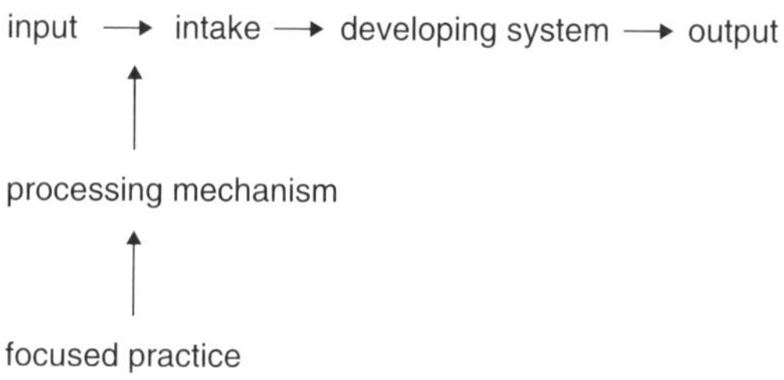

input ⟶ intake ⟶ developing system ⟶ output

↑

processing mechanism

↑

focused practice

Source: VanPatten and Cadierno (1993: 46).

Figure 7   Processing instruction in foreign language teaching

Productive knowledge

The type of knowledge that learners can use to produce language. It is typically used to refer to vocabulary knowledge and contrasts with **receptive knowledge**. Learners' productive vocabulary knowledge is generally smaller than their receptive knowledge.

Proficiency

A term used to refer to learners' knowledge of and ability to use the target language. Proficiency is often viewed in global terms, that is to say, a learner's overall ability in the L2; however, it may also refer to specific aspects of the language, such as grammar proficiency or pragmatic proficiency. Additionally, it can be used to refer to the ability to use a specific linguistic feature, such as past tense. The measurement of proficiency in SLA is not without difficulties. Often global proficiency is measured with standardized tests such as the Test of English as a Foreign Language (TOEFL) or the International English Language Testing System (IELTS); however, these tests have been criticized for focusing only on specific aspects of language knowledge. Another way of referring to proficiency that is often used in SLA research is assignment to class level, such as beginner, intermediate and advanced. While there is some merit in such measurements, these are fairly blunt indicators and it is possible for learners of differing L2 ability to be placed in the same level classroom.

Thomas, M. (2006) 'Research synthesis and historiography: the case of assessment of second language proficiency', in J. Norris and L. Ortega (eds) *Synthesizing Research on Language Learning and Teaching* (Amsterdam: John Benjamins), 279–98.

Prompts

A type of **corrective feedback** that elicits the correct form from the learner rather than providing the correction. Often the elicitation occurs in the form of a **clarification request**, as seen in the example below; however, prompts may also involve repetition of the incorrect form with interrogative intonation or clues provided by the teacher as to the correct form that should be used. Since prompts do not provide the correct form for learners, they have to draw on their own cognitive resources in order to supply it. It is argued that this deeper type of cognitive processing is more beneficial for L2 learning, particularly in comparison to **recasts** which provide the correct form. Although research studies have shown that prompts can result in learner improvement, the effects of prompting have not always been found to be superior to the effects of recasts.

Example:
Researcher: Je suis comme une ville mais plus petite et `a la campagne. [*I am like a city but smaller and in the country.*]
Participant: Une village. [*A village-F.*]
Researcher: Pardon? [*Pardon me?*]
Participant: Un village. [*A village-M.*]
Researcher: Oui, on continue. [*Yes, let's continue.*]
(Lyster and Izquierdo, 2009: 472)

Ammar, A. (2008) 'Prompts and recasts: differential effects on second language morpho-syntax', *Language Teaching Research*, 12, 183–210.
Lyster, R. and Izquierdo, J. (2009) 'Prompts versus recasts in dyadic interaction', *Language Learning*, 59, 453–98.

Psycholinguistics

The interdisciplinary study of the cognitive, or mental, processes involved in the use or acquisition of a language. Mental processes include the ways in which learners notice, memorize, practise and recall different aspects of the language. Psycholinguistics is important in the study of second language acquisition, as understanding how learners acquire a language can help us to understand not only what happens, but also why it happens. For example, we can observe that producing the target language develops fluency. Psycholinguistic research has shown that fluency is as a result of the shortening of the 'retrieval route', or the speed with which a learner is able to locate the required linguistic information in the brain. Such findings can help to lead to the identification of factors that influence the development of fluency, thereby influencing L2 teaching and learning. For example, we could hypothesize that learners need to be given ample opportunity to produce the target language, and we could empirically determine if increased production has an effect; furthermore, we could explore how much and what type of language production is needed. In other words, the study of psycholinguistics helps to make some of the claims and hypotheses in second language acquisition testable.

One of the areas where psycholinguistics has made important contributions to the study of second language acquisition is the area of vocabulary acquisition. This is probably because the study of vocabulary acquisition is closely linked with the study of memory and this, in turn, has been an important area of study of psycholinguistics. Questions that have been investigated include, for example: how often does a new word need to be encountered before it is stored in long-term memory? Does giving word glosses (additional information about a word, for example by providing definitions or translations in the margins of a text) help with vocabulary acquisition?

Bilingualism is another area where psycholinguistics has made important contributions by investigating how different languages are stored (e.g. separately or together), activated (e.g. how people recognize a word) and used (e.g. the factors that influence interference from one language onto the other).

Psycholinguistics is also related to **neurolinguistics**, or the study of neural processes in the brain. By locating and measuring the intensity of brain activity during the execution of a language learning task it may be possible to understand, for example, how difficult the task is for the learner, and how the level of difficulty relates to acquisition. Related to this is the study of language disorders such as dyslexia or aphasia. These areas of research can help us to understand which parts of the brain contribute to, for example, speech production or comprehension.

TESOL Quarterly (2008) 'Special issue: psycholinguistics for TESOL', 42 (3).

Pushed output

Merrill Swain's **output hypothesis** argues that encouraging learners to produce language that is syntactically slightly more advanced than their actual ability can be beneficial for learning. The utterances that learners produce in such a context is called pushed output. In the example below, the learner is encouraged to use the correct verb tense by the teacher's provision of a recast. The learner's response to the correction can be considered pushed output.

L: so he is in prison for six years
T: he has=
L: =has been in prison for six years
T: yes
L: I don't know how long he should be
(Loewen, 2005: 369)

Loewen, S. (2005) 'Incidental focus on form and second language learning', *Studies in Second Language Acquisition*, 27, 361–86.

P

Qualitative research

A type of research that aims to provide a rich and detailed account of complex phenomena or contexts in order to understand them better. For that reason, qualitative researchers usually avoid quantifying variables, manipulating aspects of the research context or intervening in other ways. Often in this type of research, the number of participants is relatively small and the context is very specific. Furthermore, the purpose is not to be able to generalize the results but rather to provide insight into the specific context. Traditionally in SLA, qualitative research has not been the predominant approach; nevertheless it has been accepted as a useful means by which to gain insight into the L2 learning process. A variety of research techniques are used in qualitative research, including **ethnography**, **case study**, interview, observation, **conversation analysis** and **discourse analysis**.

Benson, P., Chik, A., Gao, X., Huang, J. and Wang, W. (2009) 'Qualitative Research in Language Teaching and Learning Journals, 1997–2006', *The Modern Language Journal*, 93, 79–90.

Dörnyei, Z. (2007) *Research Methods in Applied Linguistics: Quantitative, Qualitative, and Mixed Methodologies* (Oxford: Oxford University Press).

Quantitative research

At its most basic, quantitative research involves using numeric values to describe and/or summarize data. To do this, researchers use descriptive statistics such as frequencies and averages. A further goal of much quantitative research is to be able to generalize from a specific sample to a larger population. To achieve this, researchers attempt to take a large enough sample from a population so that the individual variation in the group is averaged out. Ideally, a **random sample** should be selected; however, many times a convenience sample, comprised of easily available participants such as learners in an intact class, is selected. Often, quantitative research involves controlling and manipulating variables so that researchers can investigate the effects of a specific variable on several different groups. The groups are then compared using inferential statistical methods, such as analysis of variance (anova), one of the most commonly used statistics in SLA research. A variety of research techniques are used, including **quasi-experimental** and **cross-sectional**. The data that are analysed in quantitative research often consist of learners' scores on L2 proficiency measures, such as grammaticality judgement tests, elicited imitation tests, metalinguistic knowledge tests and spontaneous production activities.

In SLA research, quantitative research has traditionally been the predominant type of research, although qualitative research is growing in popularity. Additionally, there has been a call for increased rigour in the conducting and reporting of quantitative research. For example, researchers have been urged to investigate the reliability of their testing instruments, to test the assumptions of the statistics that they use and to report more detailed information, such as effect sizes, regarding the statistical outcomes.

Larson-Hall, J. (2010) *A Guide to Doing Statistics in Second Language Research using SPSS* (New York: Routledge).

Loewen, S. and Gass, S. (2009) 'Research timeline: the use of statistics in L2 acquisition research', *Language Teaching*, 42, 181–96.

Quasi-experimental research

Research that aims to investigate the effects of some type of intervention on the abilities or performance of L2 learners, often by means of a **pretest–post-test design**, with the treatment between the two tests. Before the experiment, a target structure and type of treatment are identified. For example, a researcher might wish to investigate the effects of error correction (the treatment) during a communicative task on learners' ability to use the *passé composé* and *imparfait* in French (the target structure). Sometimes, the treatment consists of different options administered to two or more groups. For example, a study of error correction might wish to compare recasts and metalinguistic feedback. One group of learners would receive one type of treatment, while another group receives a different type of treatment. In addition to treatment groups, it is also possible to have a comparison group and/or control group. A comparison group completes the same activities as the treatment group (such as the communicative task from the above example), but does not receive the treatment (e.g. error correction). A control group, on the other hand, participates only in the pretest and post-test components of the research and not in the treatment activities. If group scores increase or decrease from the pretest to post-test at statistically different rates, then the researcher may have reason to believe that the treatment has affected the groups' performance. Quasi-experimental research differs from experimental research in that it does not include **random sampling**, thereby limiting somewhat the generalizability of the results.

Mackey, A. and Gass, S. (2005) *Second Language Research: Methodology and Design* (New York: Routledge).

Q

Random sample

In **quantitative research**, a random sample is obtained when each and every member of a population has an equal chance of being included in an experimental procedure. For example, if a research study wants to investigate the effects of different types of L2 instruction for intermediate learners at a specific language school, then each student should have an equal opportunity of being chosen to participate in the study. Such random sampling increases the generalizability of the results of the study because it lessens the biases that may occur in the data if only certain types of participants are chosen. Random sampling is often difficult in SLA research, particularly if it is conducted in a classroom setting. In many such cases, participants are assigned to the study based on the classes that they are enrolled in, not on random selection. Random sampling is a primary characteristic of experimental research studies, while quasi-experimental studies lack random sampling.

Rate of acquisition

The amount of time it takes to learn a language. There are numerous variables that may determine the speed with which a learner acquires the L2, including the amount and type of L2 exposure, and the **age** of the learner. One of the goals of L2 instruction is to speed up the L2 learning process. Indeed, there is evidence to suggest that instruction can increase the rate of L2 acquisition; nevertheless, learners must still progress through the natural **order of acquisition** and **developmental sequences**.

Reaction time

The amount of time it takes a learner to respond to a stimulus. Studies of reaction times occur in several different research areas of SLA. In studies of L2 **processing**, reaction times are used to investigate the mental processes that are involved in understanding and producing language. Differences in the amount of time it takes learners to respond to various input is taken as evidence for differences in the cognitive resources involved in processing the input. Another research area involves **priming** studies in which learners are exposed to specific linguistic input after which their reaction times on subsequent recognition or performance tasks involving the targeted language items are measured. A shortening of participants' reaction times is considered to be evidence of sensitivity to the targeted linguistic items. Reaction times can also be measured in studies using **grammaticality judgement tasks**. Since different types of L2 knowledge may be accessed more or less quickly, the amount of time learners take to make their judgements may reflect the type of knowledge they are using to make their judgements. Learners who make quick judgements may be accessing **proceduralized** or **implicit L2 knowledge**, while learners who take more time to make their judgements may be using **declarative** or **explicit L2 knowledge**.

Clahsen, H. and Hong, U. (1995) 'Agreement and null subjects in German L2 development: new evidence from reaction-time experiments', *Second Language Research*, 11, 57–87.

Reactivity

The extent to which performing a task for research purposes alters the nature of the task. One example of reactivity is the Hawthorn effect, whereby the introduction of a new method or material affects participants' performance because of its novelty, not because of its intrinsic qualities. Another example of reactivity is the observer's paradox, in which the mere presence of an observer affects the context that is being observed, and yet such observation is a necessary part of research. Consequently, researchers try to take measures to minimize these effects by, for instance, familiarizing the participants with the research methods being used in the study and limiting the intrusiveness of the research methods.

Reactivity may also be an issue in **introspective research methods** when the act of reflecting may increase learners' attention to specific linguistic items, thereby increasing the likelihood of those items being learned. Because researchers frequently rely on learner introspection data from **think-aloud** and **stimulated recall** tasks, there has been considerable effort given to investigating reactivity in this context.

Egi, T. (2008) 'Investigating stimulated recall as a cognitive measure: reactivity and verbal reports in SLA research methodology', *Language Awareness*, 17, 212–28.

Sanz, C., Lin, H., Lado, B., Bowden, H. and Stafford, C. (2009) 'Concurrent verbalizations, pedagogical conditions, and reactivity: two CALL studies', *Language Learning*, 59, 33–71.

Recast

A response to an error in learners' oral production that involves the reformulation of the incorrect linguistic element while maintaining the overall meaning of the utterance. Recasts are considered to be an important type of **corrective feedback** because they allow interlocutors quickly and briefly to address problematic language items while continuing with communication. Recasts are said to be implicit ways in which learners' attention can be drawn to the correct use of linguistic items. However, some researchers argue that recasts are not as effective as other types of corrective feedback, in part because they may be too implicit to be noticed during interaction. In addition, because learners are provided with the correct form, they may simply parrot the form back rather than comparing their own incorrect utterance to the correct form provided in the recast. Nevertheless, recasts are a common feature of classroom interaction and a frequent topic of SLA research. The examples below illustrate teachers' recasts of students' incorrect utterances.

S: *to her is good thing (·) to her is good thing*
T: *yeah for her it's a good thing*   recast

S: *because she got a lot of money there*
(Loewen and Philp, 2006: 538)

S: *I was in pub*
T: *in the pub?*   recast
S: *yeah and I was drinking beer with my friend*
T: *which pub did you go to?*
(Ellis et al., 2001: 299)

See also **negative evidence, prompt.**

Ellis, R., Basturkmen, H. and Loewen, S. (2001) 'Learner uptake in communicative ESL lessons', *Language Learning*, 51, 281–318.
Loewen, S. and Philp, J. (2006) 'Recasts in the adult English L2 classroom: characteristics, explicitness, and effectiveness', *The Modern Language Journal*, 90, 536–56.

Receptive knowledge

The ability of learners to understand what is said to them even if they are not able to produce a comparable utterance. This term is particularly used with vocabulary knowledge when learners know the meaning of a word they hear, but they would not be able to come up with the word on their own. It is generally accepted that learners' receptive knowledge of vocabulary is greater than their productive knowledge. Receptive knowledge is also sometimes referred to as passive knowledge.

Mochida, A. and Harrington, M. (2006) 'The yes/no test as a measure of receptive vocabulary knowledge', *Language Testing*, 23, 73–98.
Webb, S. (2008) 'Receptive and productive vocabulary sizes of L2 learners', *Studies in Second Language Acquisition*, 30, 79–95.

Register

The style of language that is appropriate in a given context. Thus, the different types of language that are used in more or less formal contexts are examples of different registers. For example, *Ain't got no lovin'* and *I don't have a significant other in my life* both express a similar meaning, but that meaning is expressed in different registers. In addition, register may refer to specialist language that is used in different professions or hobbies. For example, *ruck, maul* and *line-out* are part of the register that is used to talk about rugby. *Morpheme, interlanguage* and *focus on form* are part of the register of SLA. Sometimes L2 classes are offered to focus on a specific register, such as academic language, business language or language specific to professions such as nursing or engineering.

See also **English for specific purposes, English for academic purposes.**

Ruhlemann, C. (2008) 'Register approach to teaching conversation: farewell to standard English?', *Applied Linguistics*, 29, 672–93.

Regulation

A term from **sociocultural theory** that is used to refer to the learning process. Regulation is the ability that individuals have to perform certain tasks. Individuals start out being object-regulated, that is to say they use objects to help them perform activities. For example, children might use marbles or other objects to help them learn basic mathematics skills such as addition and subtraction. Learners progress from object-regulation to other-regulation. Other-regulation occurs when other individuals assist in performing a task. The goal of the learning process is to become self-regulated, whereby individuals have the ability to perform an action on their own. In terms of L2 learning, it is possible to see how learners go from being other-regulated in which they require considerable amounts of assistance to being self-regulated in the production of the L2.

Aljaafreh, A. and Lantolf, J. (1994) 'Negative feedback as regulation and second language learning in the zone of proximal development', *The Modern Language Journal*, 78, 465–83.

Rehearsal

(a)   An aspect of some definitions of **noticing** in which linguistic **input** is repeated in **short-term memory**. Such rehearsal is said to be an important component of turning **intake** into learned knowledge.

(b)   The act of practising or repeating an utterance or task before producing it. Rehearsal can take place internally in the learner's mind or it can be done verbally. Although learners may choose to rehearse language production on their own, rehearsal is also a component of studies into the effects of teacher-guided **pre-task planning**.

Repetition

(a)   The repeating of learning activities. Repetition can be one **learning strategy** that learners engage in. For example, when trying to learn vocabulary, learners may repeat the forms and meanings of words in order to try to remember those words. Repetition can also refer to classroom instruction when lessons or activities are repeated more than once. An underlying assumption of repetition in these contexts is that language learning is a type of **habit** formation; therefore, the more frequently learners repeat the word or grammatical structure, the more likely they are to learn the items. However, such a behaviourist approach to learning has been largely discredited, with the result that mere repetition apart from meaningful, communicative interaction is not viewed as being beneficial for L2 learning. It should be noted, however, that studies of **task-based learning** have found that repetition of communicative tasks can result in improved linguistic performance and possibly acquisition.

(b)   In studies of teacher–student interaction and **corrective feedback**, it has been found that not only do teachers **recast** learners' incorrect utterances but they also repeat their correct utterances. Therefore, it is argued that learners may have difficulty knowing whether they are receiving confirmation of a correct utterance or correction of an incorrect utterance. Such ambiguity is argued to diminish the effectiveness of recasts.

Lyster, R. (1998) 'Recasts, repetition, and ambiguity in L2 classroom discourse', *Studies in Second Language Acquisition*, 20, 51–81.

Replication

This term refers to conducting a research study that entirely or partially copies a previous research study, with the purpose of either confirming or disconfirming the results of the previous study. Because many SLA studies involve relatively few participants, it is important for additional studies to be conducted in order to assess the generalizability of previous studies. In addition, many research studies have been conducted on young adult L2 learners of English. Therefore, replicating these studies with other languages and other types of learners can increase understanding of the phenomena under investigation. Some replications may keep the design of the study the same, but use participants with different L1s or L2s in order to see if similar results are obtained. Other replications may slightly alter the design of the previous study.

Polio, C. and Gass, S. (1997) 'Replication and reporting: a commentary', *Studies in Second Language Acquisition*, 19, 499–508.

Restructuring

The process by which a learner's internal grammar changes and develops. Learning therefore involves bringing new information into the learner's interlanguage system and reordering that system. Restructuring does not merely consist of the addition of new information, but rather involves making changes to the pre-existing system.

Rule-based language learning

The learning of grammatical systems in a language. These systems apply generally to a large number of exemplars in the language. For example, when L2 learners of English learn the regular past tense they are learning a rule that applies to the majority of English verbs. Rule-based learning contrasts with **item-based learning**.

See also **dual-mode model.**

R

Salience

Salience refers to how noticeable or explicit a linguistic structure is in the **input**. Some researchers argue that learners must **notice** L2 structures before they can learn them; therefore, more salient structures may be more easily learned because they are more noticeable. There are several different ways in which salience increases. First, it is possible that **frequency** may affect saliency, with structures with either very high or very low frequency being more salient. Second, salience can increase through enhancing the form of the input either through the manipulation of written or spoken structures. This might take the shape of bolding, underlining words in a passage or giving extra stress or emphasis to a spoken form. The relative size of a structure and its meaning load may also be a factor. Lexical words, such as *dog* and *cat*, that carry essential meaning may be more salient than function words, such as *and* and *in*.

See also **input enhancement**.

Goldschneider, J.M., and DeKeyser, R.M. (2001) 'Explaining the "natural order of L2 morpheme acquisition" in English: a meta-analysis of multiple determinants', *Language Learning*, 51, 1–50.

Scaffolding

A concept in **sociocultural theory** that refers to the help that an expert language user provides to a novice. This scaffolding can help the L2 learner gain further control over the language. While often this concept is used to refer to the novice–expert context, novices can also help scaffold each other, so that, when working in pairs or in groups, the language production of the group is greater than that which any one of the students could have produced on his or her own.

See also **zone of proximal development**.

SCT

See **sociocultural theory**.

Second language (L2)

A language that is learned subsequent to the one that is first learned as a child. While a learner may learn a third or fourth language, often any additional language is referred to as a second language, even if the language is not chronologically second. The term 'additional language' is sometimes used as a more accurate alternative.

Second language acquisition (SLA)

(a)   The process of learning a language other than one's **first language**.

(b)   The academic field of investigating how languages other than one's **first language** are learned.

Second language learning

(a)   The process of learning a language other than one's **first language**.

(b)   The study of an additional language in a context where the target language is the dominant language of society. For example, if an L1 speaker of Korean is studying English in New Zealand, he or she is in a second language learning context. Conversely, if an L1 speaker of English is studying Korean in Korea, he or she is also engaged in second language learning. This term contrasts with **foreign language learning**.

(c)   Stephen Krashen used the term 'learning' to refer specifically to the memorization of explicit rules about the L2. He argued that such **explicit L2 knowledge** was of limited use in helping learners to produce language in spontaneous communication. The only role for learned knowledge was to help learners monitor their production, but given the limitations of attentional resources, such monitoring could only help with relatively easy rules. Krashen contrasted 'learning' with 'acquisition'. This distinction is still relevant in SLA; however, different terms have generally been used to refer to the two types of L2 development/knowledge. Thus, currently the terms 'learning' and 'acquisition' are often used interchangeably.

Self-correction

This occurs when learners repair their own incorrect language production. Self-correction can be the result of learners monitoring – that is paying attention to – their own **output**. Monitoring is argued to involve the use of learners' **explicit knowledge** about the language, rather than their implicit, proceduralized knowledge. Because of the limitations of **working memory**, it is difficult for speakers to remember explicit rules about language while they are speaking. There simply is not enough time to think about a rule and still keep speaking. However, self-correction can be seen as an indication that learners have noticed an error in their own production and are able to correct it. Therefore, self-correction may be one way in which explicit L2 knowledge can be used to help learners produce accurate language while they are speaking.

Another perspective on self-correction is that it reflects the difference between **performance** and **competence**. If learners are able to self-correct, then the error may be seen as more of a performance error than as a limitation in the learners' underlying competence. However, learners who are not able to self-correct an error may not have fully developed **interlanguage** proficiency in the target structure.

See also **monitor model**.

Self-regulation

A term from **sociocultural theory** that represents the goal of the learning process. Sociocultural theory argues that learners go from being other-regulated, meaning that they require assistance from other people or objects in order to complete a specific task, to self-regulated, where they no longer require additional assistance. For example, a novice L2 learner might need a teacher to provide vocabulary items or grammatical structures in order to perform a discussion activity. However, as learners becomes more skilful, they need less and less **scaffolding** and are able to perform the activity without external help.

See also **regulation.**

Self-report

A type of **introspective research method** in which learners describe their internal thought processes. Such reports may occur retrospectively, with learners reflecting on their previous experiences, or the reports may be given while learners are involved in a specific task. Self-reports may be in a written form, such as a journal that learners keep about their learning experiences. Self-reports may also be oral. For example, a **stimulated recall** is a type of self-report in which learners describe their thoughts after they have performed a task. It is also possible for learners to **think aloud** while they are performing reading or writing tasks.

Semantics

A branch of linguistics that studies the meanings that are expressed in language. Semantics is concerned with meaning both at the word and the sentence level. At the word level, it investigates the relationship between the word, often referred to as a sign, and its reference, that is the symbolic concept that the word represents. Often in semantic analysis, words are reduced into component elements of meaning. For example, the word *boy* might be analysed as including the following components [+animate, +human, +child, +male] while the word *dog* might be analysed as [+animate, –human, +canine]. At the sentence level, semantics examines how people make sense of larger segments of language. One approach, drawing on the field of logic, is to evaluate the truth value of sentences and the larger propositions that sentences represent. Such an approach can explain why a sentence such as *The sun shines during the day.* corresponds with our real-world knowledge and is therefore semantically interpretable, while the sentence *The sun shines at night.* does not match our real-world knowledge and therefore does not make sense. While the field of linguistics has paid considerable attention to semantics, the field of SLA has not done the same. There is some concern about the relationship between semantics and syntax in SLA; nevertheless, the amount of research in this area has not equalled the investigations into grammar, vocabulary, phonology and pragmatics.

Juffs, A. (1996) 'Semantics-syntax correspondences in second language acquisition', *Second Language Research*, 12, 177–221.
Slabakova, R. (2006) 'Is there a critical period for semantics?', *Second Language Research*, 22, 302–38.

Semantic memory

A memory store of general knowledge about the world. It is comprised of meanings or understandings of knowledge that are decontextualized and distinct from specific events. Thus, semantic memory differs from **episodic memory**. Psycholinguistic studies of SLA have examined how language is stored in memory.

Semi-lingualism

A condition in which people learn neither their first or second language to a native-speaker level of proficiency.

Sensitive period

A weaker version of the **critical period hypothesis**, the sensitive period hypothesis suggests that the age at which a person begins learning a second language is not as crucial for achieving native-like proficiency. In addition, the cut-off age of the sensitive period is less precise and more fluid, and the effects of reaching that period may be less drastic. Thus, learners may have a harder time achieving native-like proficiency after reaching adolescence; however, they still may be able to do so. In addition, the age at which this transition happens may be wider in range than that suggested by the critical period hypothesis.

> Uylings, H. (2006) 'Development of the human cortex and the concept of "critical" or "sensitive" periods', *Language Learning*, 56, 9–90.

Sequence of development

> *See* **developmental sequence.**

Short-term memory

A temporary memory store used to process language input in real time. In SLA research, this term has now been largely superseded by the term **working memory**.

Silent period

A period of time in which learners do not produce language. Some researchers argue that, similar to L1 acquisition when babies go through a period of time when they only receive language **input** and do not produce language, L2 learners can go through a stage when they do not, and should not be forced to, produce the L2. However, the fact that learners may not be producing language does not mean that they are not learning. The silent period is an optional stage in L2 learning, and not all learners go through it.

> Iddings, A. and Jang, E. (2008) 'The mediational role of classroom practices during the silent period: a new-immigrant student learning the English language in a mainstream classroom', *TESOL Quarterly*, 42, 567–90.

S

SILL

> *See* **strategy inventory for language learning.**

Simplification

> *See* **modified input.**

Skill acquisition theory

This **cognitive theory** addresses learning in a general sense, and therefore it is not focused only on SLA. Skill acquisition theory attempts to explain how learners proceed from basic to advanced proficiency in a given skill, in this case L2 ability. The theory proposes that learners go through a series of stages as they develop. In the case of L2 learning, learners begin with knowledge about the L2. Such knowledge is often in a **declarative** form, with learners being able to verbalize what they know. For example, a beginning learner of L2 Japanese might know that in Japanese the subject of a sentence is marked with the particle *ga*; however, they might not be able to apply that rule when they are producing language. As learners develop, they are involved in **proceduralizing** their knowledge, meaning that they are able to put their knowledge about the language into use in producing the language. Proceduralization occurs through practice. As learners practise using the language, their knowledge becomes more **automatic**. While at first learners may need considerable time and effort to draw on their declarative knowledge as they produce language, as they practise, they will become more and more proficient, until ideally they are able to produce language without needing to think explicitly about the language forms they are producing.

DeKeyser, R. (2007) 'Skill acquisition theory', in B. VanPatten and J. Williams (eds) *Theories in Second Language Acquisition: An Introduction* (Mahwah, NJ: Lawrence Erlbaum), 97–113.

SLA

See **second language acquisition.**

Social distance

The perception that learners have of themselves in relation to speakers of the target language. If learners feel an affinity for the target language speakers and culture, then the social distance is lessened. In contrast, if learners feel isolated from the target language culture or are antagonistic to it, the social distance is greater. It is argued that less social distance will help L2 learning because it can help bring learners into contact with L1 speakers of the target language. However, if there is a greater social distance, then learners will distance themselves from opportunities to engage with the target language. Social distance is not only a matter of the learner's perspective. Speakers of the target language may have negative views of the target language learners, resulting in increased social distance in spite of potential efforts by the learners.

See also **acculturation model.**

Schumann, J. (1976) 'Social distance as a factor in second language acquisition', *Language Learning*, 26, 135–43.

Social identity theory

An approach to L2 learning that argues that an important factor in L2 acquisition is how learners perceive themselves in relation to the target language community and, in return, how the target language community perceives the learners. In current views, social identity is a fluid and dynamic construct that can change depending on contexts in which learners find themselves. An important construct in social identity theory is that of investment, which refers to the motives and desires that learners have in learning the L2. Additionally, language learning can be seen as a process in which learners invest in their own identities.

See also **identity.**

Norton Peirce, B. (1995) 'Social identity, investment and language learning', *TESOL Quarterly*, 29, 9–31.

Social learning strategies

These are activities that learners engage in with other people in order to help them learn the target language. Examples of social strategies include asking to be corrected when speaking the L2, trying to learn about the culture of the L2 speakers, and practising the L2 with other students.

See also **learning strategy.**

Sociocultural theory (SCT)

A social theory of learning that was first developed by Lev Vygotsky, a Russian child psychologist in the 1920s. His works were translated into English in the 1960s and have become influential in the field of education. In the 1990s, SLA researchers began to draw on SCT as a theory for explaining L2 acquisition. SCT views learning as a **mediated** process in which the individuals develop as they interact with their environment. Such interaction is mediated by tools such as culture and language, which allow individuals to participate in social settings. An important SCT concept for SLA is the **zone of proximal development**, which is a metaphorical concept that refers to the distance between what novices or learners can do on their own and what they can do with the assistance of an expert. **Regulation** and **private speech** are also common constructs from SCT that are applied to the L2 learning context.

Lantolf, J. and Beckett, T. (2009) 'Sociocultural theory and second language acquisition', *Language Teaching*, 2009, 42, 459–75.
Lantolf, J. and Thorne, S. (2006) *Sociocultural Theory and the Genesis of Second Language Development* (Oxford: Oxford University Press).

S

Sociolinguistics

The study of how language is used in society and the social factors that influence language use and development. Sociolinguistics is not a field of study that is primarily or exclusively concerned with SLA; however, the field of SLA has been influenced by sociolinguistics, for example in terms of examining how context and **variation** play a role in L2 learning. The role of context in SLA has been investigated in several different ways. One concerns how different **registers** and types of language are used in different social contexts. Such contextual variation may influence the variety (whether **standard** or non-standard) of language that learners are exposed to and therefore consequently acquire. In addition, L2 learners need to learn that different types of language are used in different social contexts. **Pragmatics** research has investigated the role of social context and social factors in influencing the ways in which learners use language when, for example, making requests or accepting an invitation.

Another aspect of sociolinguistic research investigates what happens when languages, and the speakers of those languages, come into contact with each other. One issue concerns individuals' **social identities** and how learners' identities may influence their access to the target language. Another issue relates to the use of two or more languages in social settings. Often such research examines the role of **bilingualism** or **multilingualism** in various contexts. Another aspect of interest involves **code-switching**, which is the use of more than one language within a conversation or text. In particular, the advantages and disadvantages of using both the L1 and the target language in the L2 classroom has been an issue of considerable interest.

Gatbonton, E., Trofimovich, P. and Magid, M. (2005) 'Learners' ethnic group affiliation and L2 pronunciation accuracy: a sociolinguistic investigation', *TESOL Quarterly*, 39, 489–511.

Tarone, E. (2007) 'Sociolinguistic approaches to second language acquisition research: 1997–2007', *The Modern Language Journal*, 91, 837–48.

Speech accommodation theory

A theory proposed by Howard Giles stating that the interlocutor with whom one is speaking can affect one's own language production. Giles proposed that speakers may converge by making their language more similar to each other's as a way of identifying with their interlocutor. However, speakers may also diverge in their language, thereby accentuating the differences between them. For example, L1 speakers may modify their language when speaking with an L2 speaker in order to express solidarity with the L2 speaker. One positive aspect of accommodation theory is that it acknowledges the effects of interlocutors on speech production; however, it does not account for all types of variability in language production.

Giles, H. and Smith, P. (1979) 'Accommodation theory: optional levels of convergence', in H. Giles and R. St Clair (eds) *Language and Social Psychology* (Oxford: Basil Blackwell), 45–65.

Speech act

A term used to describe the things that speakers can do with language. Thus a speech act is the use of language to achieve a specific end or to perform some social activity. For example, common types of speech acts that have been identified and investigated include requesting, refusing, inviting and complaining. Speech act theory is concerned with how these acts are accomplished through language. In doing so, the theory has proposed three types of speech acts: locutionary, illocutionary and perlocutionary. 'Locutionary act' is used to refer to the surface meaning of an utterance. '**Illocutionary act**' is used to refer to the intended meaning of the utterance. 'Perlocutionary act' refers to the effect that an utterance has on the hearer.

To illustrate these acts, we can imagine two people walking into a room and one of them saying *It's cold in here.* The locutionary act is one of commenting on the temperature in a room. The illocutionary act of the utterance may be to complain about the temperature or to request that something be done about the temperature. The perlocutionary act is what the hearer does in response to the utterance, in this case perhaps apologizing for the temperature or turning up the heat. For SLA, the primary consideration is how L2 learners learn these speech acts and how their linguistic and pragmatic resources enable them to perform these speech acts. Speech act theory is closely related to **pragmatics**.

See also **head act.**

Cohen, A. (2005) 'Strategies for learning and performing L2 speech acts', *Intercultural Pragmatics*, 2, 275–301.
Taguchi, N. (2006) 'Analysis of appropriateness in a speech act of request in L2 English', *Pragmatics*, 16, 513–33.

Stabilization

A concept that refers to the fact that a learner's **interlanguage** system may cease to develop before it achieves target-like accuracy. However, unlike **fossilization**, stabilization does not imply that a learner's knowledge of a specific structure cannot develop further, but rather it implies that there is no further learning at the moment. Stabilization is typically used to refer to specific linguistic structures rather than to the learner's interlanguage system as a whole. Stabilization acknowledges that as long as a learner is alive, there may be the possibility for further L2 development.

Stages of development

Another term for **developmental sequences**, which states that learners progress through clearly identifiable stages as they acquire specific grammatical structures. English question formation, negation and regular past tense are structures which have been identified as having specific stages of development.

Standard variety

A type of language that is given social privilege and prestige. Most linguists believe all languages and varieties of language are equally valid linguistic systems that express the meanings that are needed by the speakers. However, society often ranks some varieties of language as better than others. The standard language is usually one that is taught in school and spoken by the educated populace. For instance, sentence one below is an example from the standard variety of English. Sentence two is an equally valid expression of the same meaning; however, it represents a non-standard (and often stigmatized) variety of English.

1. *He doesn't have any money.*
2. *He ain't got no money.*

One of the questions for SLA is which variety of language a learner should learn. Generally it is the standard variety that is taught in L2 textbooks and in **foreign**

language learning contexts. However, the standard variety may or may not be the variety of language that learners are exposed to or are most likely to use, particularly if they are in a **second language** context where they are surrounded by speakers of the non-standard variety. As a result, some researchers argue that the standard variety should not be the default variety of the target language, but rather the local norms of the speech community should be considered.

Jenkins, J. (2009) *World Englishes. A Resource Book for Students*, 2nd edn (London: Routledge).

Stimulated recall

An **introspective research method** in which learners report their thoughts retrospectively. Learners are audio or video-recorded either during class or as they are engaged in a lab-based activity. Shortly after the activity, they are presented with segments of the activity and asked to say what they were thinking at the time. The purpose of stimulated recall is to try to gain insight into learners' cognitive processes. Thus, learners may be shown a section of video in which the teacher is correcting one of their grammatical errors. By presenting this stimulus to learners, it is hoped that they will be able to comment on whether or not they noticed their own error and the teacher's correction. Thus, the stimulated recall might provide some evidence of learner **noticing**. There are several issues to consider when doing stimulated recall. One is that the recall session should occur as soon as possible after the event in order to avoid memory decay. Another issue is the **verdicality** of learners' recall statements. That is to say, whether learners are accurately reporting what they were thinking at the time. One difficulty here is that learners may report what they are thinking at the time of the recall session rather than what they were thinking at the time of the recording. Similarly, learners might report what they think the researcher wants them to say rather than what they were actually thinking. To avoid this, researchers are advised not to have learners try to explain their thoughts, and to assure them that it is okay to say that they do not remember what they were thinking or that they were not thinking anything in particular. Another issue with stimulated recall is its **reactivity**, meaning that the act of doing a stimulated recall may influence subsequent task performance since the recall serves as another encounter with the stimulus. Reactivity is not generally an issue if a researcher is only interested in the learner's thoughts at the time; however, if a researcher is also interested in whether or not the learner learned from the stimulus, they might consider giving the learner a **post-test** on the item. However, the post-test must be performed before the stimulated recall because if it is conducted afterwards, it will be measuring not only the effects of the first exposure to the linguistic item, but also the effects of the secondary exposure during the stimulated recall. In spite of these limitations, stimulated recall is becoming a popular research tool in SLA.

Gass, S. and Mackey, A. (2000) *Stimulated Recall Methodology in Second Language Research* (Mahwah, NJ: Lawrence Erlbaum).

Stimulus-response

A **behaviourist** concept in which learning is viewed as resulting from the repeated exposure to a stimulus and the ensuing response. For example, if a young child sees a spherical object and hears the word *ball*, he or she will associate the object and the word. Then, if the child says *ball*, he or she might be given one. If the stimulus and response happen repeatedly, this will solidify the meaning of *ball* for the child, and thus the word-meaning association will become a **habit** for the child. This approach to language learning has been criticized as being unable to account for the complex nature of language acquisition.

Strategy

A type of activity that learners are involved in to help them in L2 learning, L2 production or L2 comprehension.

> *See also* **communication strategy, learning strategy.**

Strategy inventory for language learning (SILL)

A questionnaire designed to investigate L2 learners' use of language **learning strategies**. The SILL consists of numerous statements regarding different types of language learning strategies, and learners are asked to rate themselves according to how frequently they engage in each activity. Data obtained using the SILL have shown eight distinct types of strategies: general study habits (such as time management); functional practice (seeking opportunities for communication in the L2); seeking and communicating meaning; studying or practising independently; using mnemonic devices; reliance on L1 or another speaker (a negative factor); formal practice (e.g. practice of grammar rules); and use of metacognitive strategies.

> Oxford, R.L. (1990) *Language Learning Strategies: What Every Teacher Should Know* (Boston: Heinle & Heinle).

Structured input

A type of language that has been modified to draw learners' attention to specific linguistic forms. Structured input is most frequently associated with **processing instruction**, which is a method of language teaching that provides learners with language that has been manipulated to draw learners' **attention** to the fact that they may be relying on a **strategy** for processing language that does not work in the target language. Thus, structured input might contain language that cannot be understood correctly by using L1 strategies. For example, English speakers rely on word order to determine subjects and objects in a sentence. Generally, the noun before the main verb is the subject and the noun after the verb is the object. Thus, the two sentences below contain different subjects.

1. *Mary saw them.*
2. *They saw Mary.*

However, word order is not always a reliable processing strategy in other languages, such as Spanish. Therefore, structured input for English L2 learners of Spanish would include sentences that are not interpreted correctly if the first word in the sentence is the subject. For example, in both sentences below, Mary is doing the seeing, even though the word order is different. Learners must rely more on the conjugation of the verb, rather than the order of the nouns to determine their roles in the sentence.

Maria los vió.
Mary them saw [third person singular].
Mary saw them.

Los vió Maria.
them saw [third person singular] Mary.
Mary saw them.

The purpose of providing structured input is to help learners identify faulty processing strategies and to change them to more target-like ones.

See also **modified input.**

Erlam, R. (2003) 'Evaluating the relative effectiveness of structured-input and output-based instruction in foreign language learning: results from an experimental study', *Studies in Second Language Acquisition*, 25, 559–82.

Farley, A. (2005) *Structured Input: Grammar Instruction for the Acquisition-Oriented Classroom* (New York: McGraw-Hill).

Study abroad

A period of study in a country where the **target language** is spoken as the predominant language. The purported benefits of study abroad include ample opportunity for **interaction** with L2 speakers, extensive exposure to L2 **input**, increased opportunities for L2 **output**, the acquisition of cultural information about the target language community, and increased **motivation**. Research on the effects of study abroad on L2 acquisition has found mixed results, especially for shorter stays. Longer periods of study do appear to affect positively L2 acquisition and socio-affective aspects of learning the target language.

Kinginger, C. (2008) 'Language learning in study abroad: case studies of Americans in France', *The Modern Language Journal*, 92, supplement, iii–131.

Pellegrino Aveni, V.A. (2005) *Study Abroad and Second Language Use: Constructing the Self* (New York: Cambridge University Press).

Syntax

The aspect of language that concerns itself with how words can be combined to form sentences. As such, syntax investigates the rules that determine whether a sentence is acceptable or not in a given language. While first language learners develop complete knowledge of the syntax of their L1, second language learners often do not acquire similar knowledge of their L2. As a result, the acquisition of syntactic structures by L2 learners has been an important area of SLA research. Syntax, along with **morphology**, is a technical term for what people often refer to as **grammar**.

Tandem learning

A method of language learning involving pairs of students who want to learn each other's first language. Students may communicate face-to-face or online, and they generally spend equal amounts of time practising each of the target languages. Part of the rationale for tandem learning is that it provides learners with access to the target language, increases responsibility for their own learning and offers opportunities for the development of intercultural communicative competence. Tandem learning is also referred to as language exchange.

Chung, Y., Graves, B., Wesche, M. and Barfurth, M. (2005) 'Computer-mediated com-munication in Korean–English chat rooms: tandem learning in an international languages program', *The Canadian Modern Language Review/La Revue canadienne des langues vivantes*, 62, 49–86.

Schwienhorst, K. (2003) 'Learner autonomy and tandem learning: putting principles into practice in synchronous and asynchronous telecommunications environments', *Computer Assisted Language Learning*, 16, 427–43.

Target language

The language that is being studied by a learner. For instance, if university students in the United States or the United Kingdom are studying French, then French is the target language. Alternatively, high school students in China may be studying English as their target language. An issue in language teaching concerns how much of the instruction should be in the target language. Often in communicative language teaching or in multilingual classrooms, the target language is used exclusively. However, in monolingual contexts or during explicit grammar instruction, much of the instruction may occur in the learners' **first language** rather than the target language.

Humphreys, G. and Spratt, M. (2008) 'Many languages, many motivations: a study of Hong Kong students' motivation to learn different target languages', *System*, 36, 313–35.

Turnbull, M. and Arnett, K. (2002) 'Teachers' uses of the target and first languages in second and foreign language classrooms', *Annual Review of Applied Linguistics*, 22, 204–18.

Target-like use analysis

An analysis of learners' oral or written language production that is used to determine how accurately they use specific linguistic structures. To conduct a target-like use analysis, researchers identify and tally all the obligatory occasions in which a specific linguistic structure should have been used by the learner. For example, if learners talk or write about what they did last week, then they have created an obligatory context for the past tense. Consequently, all verbs they use in the narrative should be in the past tense. Researchers then count the number of times the target structure is supplied correctly in the obligatory contexts. Additionally, researchers tally the number of over-generalizations in which the target structure was used, but should not have been. Once these three frequencies have been identified, the following formula is used to calculate the percentage of target-like use, which in turn provides an indication of learners' proficiency in using the target structure.

$$\frac{Number\ of\ correct\ suppliances}{Number\ of\ obligatory\ occasions\ +\ Number\ of\ over\text{-}generalizations} = Target\text{-}like\ use$$

Target-like use analysis is similar to **obligatory-occasion analysis**; however, the former incorporates over-generalizations while the latter does not. As such, target-like use analysis is generally preferred to obligatory-occasion analysis as a means of investigating **accuracy** in language use.

Pica, T. (1983) 'Methods of morpheme quantification: their effect on the interpretation of second language data', *Studies in Second Language Acquisition*, 6, 69–78.

Task

In the broad sense of the word, a task is any language learning activity that learners engage in. However, the term has taken on a more technical meaning with the advent of **task-based language teaching (TBLT)**, which is one type of **communicative language teaching**. Although there are several different definitions of tasks in TBLT, there are several common characteristics. (1) Tasks should have a real-world connection; in other words, they should resemble something that learners do in real life. (2) Tasks have a primary focus on meaning. (3) Tasks allow learners to use their own linguistic resources. (4) Tasks can involve listening, speaking, reading and/or writing. (5) Tasks have a non-linguistic goal as their outcome. For example, learners might need to agree on something in an **opinion gap task**, or they may need to draw something in a picture description task.

Several characteristics of tasks have been identified. One such characteristic concerns the outcome of the task. Closed tasks have only one correct outcome. For example, in a map task, learners may have to identify the one correct route to reach a destination. Alternatively, in an opinion-gap task, learners may need to reach agreement regarding a specific topic. In contrast, open tasks allow learners to arrive at multiple outcomes. An example of an open task would be an opinion-gap task in which learners are required to express an opinion but do not have to come to an agreement.

Another distinction in the design of tasks relates to the flow of information. In a one-way task, one person has all of the information while the other person does not have any. An example of a one-way task would be a picture-drawing task in which one person has a picture that he or she has to describe, and the other person has to draw the picture. A two-way, or **jigsaw**, task involves both of the participants having some of the information, which they need to exchange with each other in order to complete the task. For example, in a map task, learners may each have differing maps which contain some, but not all, of the information that is needed to reach a specific destination. By sharing the information which each other, learners can successfully complete the task.

Finally, a distinction can be made between focused and unfocused tasks. Focused tasks have specific linguistic items that are targeted. In other words, the teacher/ researcher intends for the learners to use specific linguistic structures, with the hope that encountering specific forms will help with learning. For example, the input for a task might contain multiple exemplars of a specific feature. Such an **input flood** could help focus learners' attention on that feature. In contrast, unfocused tasks do not contain specific targeted linguistic items.

Garcia Mayo, M. (2006) *Investigating Tasks in Formal Language Learning* (Clevedon: Multilingual Matters).

Tavakoli, P. and Foster, P. (2008) 'Task design and second language performance: the effect of narrative type on learner output', *Language Learning*, 58, 439–73.

Task-based language teaching (TBLT)

Language instruction that uses **tasks** as a means to engage learners in **authentic** communicative activities as well as to draw attention to specific linguistic features. Proponents of TBLT argue that using a syllabus consisting of tasks rather than a series of isolated grammatical structures is a preferable type of language instruction because it allows learners to develop communicative ability. In addition, it allows learners to follow the natural **order of acquisition**, rather than attempting to teach structures that may be beyond their current **interlanguage** system.

Ellis, R. (2003) *Task-based Language Learning and Teaching* (Oxford: Oxford University Press).

Van den Branden, K. (2006) *Task-based Language Education: From Theory to Practice* (Cambridge: Cambridge University Press).

Teachability hypothesis

Manfred Pienemann proposed that in order for linguistic structures to be learned, they must be relatively close to a learner's current **interlanguage** status. Structures that are too far beyond the learner's interlanguage are not teachable. Pienemann therefore argued that the linguistic structures that are taught in the L2 classroom should follow the learner's **stages of acquisition**. Two difficulties with such a proposal are (1) the stages of acquisition are known for only a limited number of linguistic structures in only a few languages, and (2) learners within the same class may be at different stages of acquisition. The limitations of the teachability hypothesis have been addressed in Pienemann's subsequent **processability theory**.

Pienemann, M. (1984) 'Psychological constraints on the teachability of languages', *Studies in Second Language Acquisition*, 6, 186–214.

Pienemann, M. (1989) 'Is language teachable? Psycholinguistic experiments and hypotheses', *Applied Linguistics*, 10, 52–79.

Teacher talk

Teachers' production of language in the classroom. Teacher talk may differ from **authentic** language in that it may be modified for learners, either through

T

simplification or elaboration. Teacher talk is similar to **caretaker talk** and **foreigner talk**, and its role in promoting or hindering L2 learning has been an object of investigation in SLA.

See also **modified input.**

Kim, S. and Elder, C. (2005) 'Language choices and pedagogic functions in the foreign language classroom: a cross-linguistic functional analysis of teacher talk', *Language Teaching Research*, 9, 355–80.

Walsh, S. (2002) 'Construction or obstruction: teacher talk and learner involvement in the EFL classroom', *Language Teaching Research*, 6, 3–23.

Theory

A coherent set of reasoned arguments, supported by evidence, intended to explain aspects of second language acquisition. As such, a theory does not simply describe aspects of L2 learning; rather it provides an explanation of and makes predictions about how various aspects of the L2 learning process occur. Some theories used to explain SLA have come from other disciplines such as linguistics and psychology. Such theories include **behaviourism, connectionism, socio-cultural theory, skill acquisition theory** and **universal grammar**. Other theories are specific to SLA, for example the **monitor model, processability theory, input processing** and **autonomous induction theory**.

Mitchell, R. and Myles, R. (2004) *Second Language Learning Theories*, 2nd edn (London: Arnold).

VanPatten, B. and Williams, J. (2007) *Theories in Second Language Acquisition: An Introduction* (Mahwah, NJ: Lawrence Erlbaum).

Think-aloud task

A type of research method in which learners verbalize their thoughts as they perform an activity. For example, learners may be asked to do a writing task and concurrently say aloud the things they are thinking as they write. The purpose of think-alouds is to provide insight into the cognitive processes that learners use when performing the task in question. It is therefore important that the activity of thinking-aloud does not interfere with students' completion of the task at hand. Participants are usually instructed simply to say out loud what goes through their mind, rather than to speak to someone. A related research method is a **talk-aloud**, in which participants are asked simply to describe their actions, but not to attempt to explain them. Think-aloud and talk-aloud protocols have been used to investigate how learners solve problems, how they construct sentences in writing tasks, and what information in the input they pay attention to, amongst others. As such, think-alouds can provide insight into the process of second language learning.

See also **introspective research methods.**

Bowles, M. (2010) *The Think-aloud Controversy in Second Language Research* (New York: Routledge).

Leow, R.P. and Morgan-Short, K. (2004) 'To think aloud or not to think aloud: the issue of reactivity in SLA research methodology', *Studies in Second Language Acquisition*, 26, 35–57.

Tip-of-the-tongue

A phenomenon in which a person knows a specific grammatical or lexical item, but has difficulty in retrieving that item from memory. Tip-of-the-tongue experiences, which occur for both L1 and L2 speakers, have been investigated to explain **implicit memory** processes.

Ecke, P. (2008) 'Cross-linguistic influence on word search in tip-of-the-tongue states', *TESOL Quarterly*, 42, 515–27.

Top-down processing

This term refers to a type of cognitive process in which learners draw on their general knowledge and world experiences in order to help them understand the language they encounter. For example, before having learners read a specific text, the teacher may ask them what they know about the topic. Another example is when learners draw on their knowledge of how texts are organized to help them make sense of what they are reading. Thus, learners might use their knowledge that chronological narratives often start at the beginning of an event and continue until its completion to help them understand a story. Another way in which learners might use top-down processing is by recognizing whole words as they are reading, rather than by focusing on each individual letter in order to understand the word. Top-down processing contrasts with **bottom-up processing**.

Field, J. (1999) '"Bottom-up" and "top-down"', *ELT Journal*, 53, 338–9.
Field, J. (2004) 'An insight into listeners' problems: too much bottom-up or too much top-down?', *System*, 32, 363–77.

Total physical response (TPR)

A method of language instruction developed by James Asher in the 1970s that involves learners responding physically to instructions in the target language. Thus a teacher might have a lesson in which learners have to perform actions based on imperatives such as *Close the door* or *Stand up*. In TPR, there is a primary emphasis on comprehending the L2. It is also argued that the kinaesthetic nature of the responses is helpful in the L2 learning process. Although TPR is still promoted by Asher, there is not much current SLA research investigating this method.

Asher, J. (1977) *Learning Another Language through Actions: The Complete Teachers' Guidebook* (Los Gatos, CA: Sky Oaks Publications).
www.tpr-world.com.

Transfer

At its most basic, transfer refers to the **cross-linguistic influences** that occur in L2 learning. Generally in SLA, transfer is viewed as the influence of the L1 on the L2. An early perspective on transfer, beginning in the 1960s, was expressed in the **contrastive analysis hypothesis**, which examined the structures of various languages in order to determine the cross-linguistic influences they might have on learners learning a second language. The contrastive analysis hypothesis argued that features that were present in the L1 would be easy to learn in the L2; however, features that were not present in the L1 would be difficult to learn in the L2. This explanatory theory of SLA fell out of favour, however, as research showed that the presence or absence of a feature in the L1 did not necessarily correspond with the respective ease or difficulty of learning a feature in the L2. For example, some L2 features that are present in a learner's L1 may still be difficult to learn; conversely, some L2 features that are not present in the L1 may be easy to learn in the L2. It is generally acknowledged nowadays that transfer or cross-linguistic influences do occur, but such influences are not viewed as deterministically as in the contrastive analysis hypothesis.

It is common to refer to several types of transfer. Positive transfer occurs when features of the L1 help facilitate L2 learning. Thus for example, the fact that both English and Spanish mark plurality with /s/ can facilitate the learning of this feature when learners of one language learn the other. In contrast, negative transfer occurs when the presence or absence of a feature in the L1 hinders the development of a feature in the L2. An example of negative transfer can be seen in the difficulty with which L1 speakers of Japanese or Korean may have in learning the English article system, given that their languages do not use such a system.

While transfer is usually considered to occur from the L1 to the L2, it may also be bi-directional, meaning that is possible for the L2 to influence learners' use of their L1. For example, one study found that Dutch speaking immigrants who had lived for a long time in New Zealand directly translated English words back into Dutch. For instance, they would refer to a *pineapple* as a *pijnappel*, which literally means *pain apple*, instead of using the Dutch word *ananas*. In addition to transfer occurring from the L2 to the L1, transfer from the L2 may occur when additional languages are learned. This phenomenon has been related to **language distance** with learners more likely to transfer from their L2 to their L3 if they feel that the L2 is more closely related to the L3 than is the L1. For example, Cenoz (2001) found that Basque/Spanish bilinguals were more likely to transfer features from Spanish, rather than Basque, when learning English, given the relatively close linguistic relationship between English and Spanish.

Other factors that may influence transfer include age, with older learners more likely to transfer than younger learners, and linguistic feature, with content words more likely to be transferred than function words.

Cenoz, J. (2001) 'The effect of linguistic distance, L2 status and age on cross-linguistic influence in third language acquisition', in J. Cenoz, B. Hufeisen and U. Jessner (eds) *Cross-linguistic Influence in Third Language Acquisition: Psycholinguistic Perspectives* (Clevedon: Multilingual Matters), 8–20.
Montrul, S. (2010) 'Dominant language transfer in adult second language learners and heritage speakers', *Second Language Research*, 26, 293–327.

Transfer error

Errors which are based on learners assuming that the L2 functions in a similar way to their L1. Transfer errors can be assumed to be made by speakers of a specific L1 learning a specific L2. These errors differ from **developmental errors** which are expected to occur in the process of L2 learning regardless of a learner's L1. Transfer errors can be lexical in which a learner may assume that a word or phrase in one language can be directly translated into another. For example, a Dutch learner of English might say *that does not go up*, which is a direct translation of a verbal phrase *opgaan* meaning *that doesn't apply.* Transfer errors can also be grammatical if a learner assumes that a grammatical rule applies similarly in both languages. For example, a French learner of English might say: *He kissed passionately his girlfriend* because French allows an adverb to come between the verb and the direct object; however, English does not.

T-unit

The commonly used term for 'terminable unit', which refers to a main clause with all its attached subordinate clauses. T-units have been used to measure grammatical **accuracy** (number of errors per T-unit), syntactic **complexity** (number of clauses per T-unit) and a range of other aspects of written and spoken discourse. The examples below show various T-units.

1. *He was happy. (One T-unit)*
2. *He came back from the concert, and he was happy. (Two t-units)*
3. *After he came back from the concert, he was happy. (One t-unit)*

Bardovi-Harlig, K. (1992) 'A second look at t-unit analysis: reconsidering the sentence', *TESOL Quarterly*, 26, 390–5.

Turn-taking

Turn-taking occurs when language production changes from one person to another. The concept is important in **interactionist approaches** to SLA as well as in **conversation analysis** in which turns are viewed as a basic unit of analysis. It is through turn-taking that interlocutors demonstrate their understanding of the current interaction as they respond to previous turns and produce additional utterances. In the example below, the learner makes a mistake in her use of the word *depression*. The teacher's response identifies that there is a problem in the learner's utterance by drawing attention to the word class of the problematic word. However, analysis of the learner's subsequent turn shows that she did not treat the teacher's question as a request for information regarding the word class of *depression*, but rather as an indication that she should provide the correct form of the word. Thus, by analysing the turn-taking involved, researchers can get an understanding of how participants make sense of their interaction. Other aspects of analysis in turn-taking involve the length of turn and how they are transferred from one person to another. In addition, the similarities and differences between turn-taking in face-to-face and **computer-mediated communication** has been investigated.

L: he was depression in prison
T: oo what part of speech is depression
L: oh, depressed
(Loewen 2005: 372)

Loewen, S. (2005) 'Incidental focus on form and second language learning', *Studies in Second Language Acquisition*, 27, 361–86.
Seedhouse, P. (2004) 'The interactional architecture of the language classroom: a conversation analysis perspective', *Language Learning*, 54, supplement 1, x–300.

Turn-tracking

The monitoring by interlocutors of messages in **computer-mediated communication** to determine the origin and intended audience of a message. Turn-tracking is used to facilitate **turn-taking**. Turn-tracking has been investigated to determine the extent to which interlocutors comprehend and are able to manage the online interaction.

Typological universals

Typological universals are linguistic features that are common to a large number of languages. In identifying typological universals, linguists attempt to determine which kinds of structures are **unmarked** or **prototypical** in languages. One example of a typological universal is word order. Some languages, such as English, have the following word order: subject, verb, object (SVO). However, other languages, such as Japanese, have the verb at the end of the sentence, SOV. These patterns of word order are found across the world's languages. Furthermore, it has also been found that languages such as English with SVO word order, generally have prepositional phrases in which the preposition comes before the noun, such as *in the house*; in contrast, SOV languages typically have prepositional phrases in which the preposition comes after the noun. In fact, such words are often called postpositions, rather than prepositions. When it comes to learning a second language, it is argued that learners will have an easier time learning features that are more common to the world's languages.

In addition, the study of typological universals often draws on implicational hierarchies, which state that if a language has feature X, then it will also have feature Y. For example, the **accessibility hierarchy** proposes an order of difficulty for relative clauses, beginning with subject relative clauses and advancing to comparative object relative clauses. Languages vary in the types of relative clauses they possess; however, each language contains all of the relative clause types leading up to the most advanced one in the language. These typological hierarchies have been found to influence L2 learning, with learners progressing through the various stages in order.

Comrie, B. (2007) 'The acquisition of relative clauses in relation to language typology', *Studies in Second Language Acquisition*, 29, 301–9.
Ramat, A. (2003) *Typology and Second Language Acquisition* (Berlin: Mouton de Gruyter).

T

Universal grammar (UG)

A theory of language learning first proposed by Noam Chomsky in 1957. It proposes that humans possess an innate, genetic ability for language: consequently, it is a theory that is specific to language learning and does not account for other types of learning. Chomsky argued that L1 acquisition is not primarily the result of external, environmental factors. In other words, L1 learning does not occur simply as a result of learners receiving **input** and then mimicking that input in production. One reason for this belief is that L1 speakers develop a complete linguistic system and are able to generate an infinite number of sentences; however, they are only exposed to a limited amount of input. This **poverty of the stimulus** argument also questions how language learners can learn something that is absent in the language, because learners know that certain grammatical constructions are not possible, even though they have not been explicitly told that this is the case. For example, L1 speakers of English know that the first three sentences below are grammatical. In addition, they know that the last sentence is not grammatical, even though it is most likely that no one has explicitly told them so. If learners rely solely on input, they should not be able to determine whether or not the last sentence is grammatical because they cannot be sure that the reason they have not heard such a sentence is simply a matter of chance and that such a sentence actually is possible, or they have not heard the sentence because it is not grammatical.

Mary told John a story.
Mary told a story to John.
Mary explained the problem to John.
*Mary explained John the problem.

Therefore, Chomsky suggested that the human brain contains something similar to a **language acquisition device** that is present from birth. Thus, even before babies are exposed to language, their brains contain a set of linguistic principles that will guide them in learning their L1. UG contends that all languages share similar abstract qualities; however, these abstract qualities are realized differently in different languages. A simple example is that all languages contain subjects, verbs and objects, but the order in which they occur in sentences differs in different languages. English is a subject/verb/object language, while Japanese is a subject/object/verb language.

Another aspect of UG that should be mentioned is that it is concerned with the abstract mental representations of language that speakers have, referred to as **competence**, rather than with speakers' use of the language in actual production

Table 7 Alternative positions regarding access to UG in L2 acquisition

Position	Description	Main assumptions
Complete access	L1 provides learners with a 'quick' setting for the L2 parameter if the value is the same, otherwise the L2 learner proceeds in the same way as the L1 learner. L2 learners have full access to UG principles.	L2 learners will be able to attain full linguistic competence: there is no critical period blocking L2 acquisition.
No access (the fundamental difference hypothesis)	L2 learners no longer have access to the principles and parameters of UG; general learning strategies replace UG.	L2 is not equal to L1 acquisition; adults fail to achieve full linguistic competence; 'wild grammars' can occur.
Partial access (i.e. via L1)	L2 learners have full access to UG principles but can only access those parameters operative in their L1; they may be able to reset L1 parameters by means of general learning strategies.	L2 and L1 acquisition are the same in part; adults fail to achieve full linguistic competence; no 'wild grammars' are evident.
Dual access (the competition model)	L2 learners have access to UG but this is partly blocked by the use of general learning strategies.	L2 is equal to L1 acquisition in part; adults fail to achieve full linguistic competence; adults manifest similar and different linguistic behaviour from children.

Source: Ellis (2008: 625).

or **performance**. Thus, UG proposes that even though L1 speakers may make mistakes in their production, their underlying competence does not change.

The specific details of the theory of UG have changed over time, for example from a government/binding paradigm to a minimalist programme. Nevertheless, the general claim of an inherent, innate language ability remains, and UG is still the predominant theory of L1 learning. However, the role of UG for L2 learning is less clear. Is UG available for L2 learning just like it is for L1 learning? A related question is: if L1 learners start with UG, what do L2 learners start with? A series of options have been put forward to answer these questions (Table 7). One of the issues related to the accessibility of UG relates to age effects, with the suggestion being that UG is not available for L2 learning after children reach puberty. This notion is referred to as the **critical period hypothesis**.

Cook, V. and Newson, M. (2007) *Chomsky's Universal Grammar: An Introduction* (Malden, MA: Blackwell).

White, L. (2003) *Second Language Acquisition and Universal Grammar* (Cambridge: Cambridge University Press).

Unmarked

See **markedness**.

Uptake

(a) In general terms, uptake can refer to what learners learn or report having learned. One way that this type of uptake has been measured is by giving learners uptake charts at the end of a lesson and asking them to write down everything they remember learning from the lesson.

Slimani, A. (1989) 'The role of topicalization in classroom language learning', *System*, 17, 223–34.

(b)   A more technical and more common definition of uptake refers to learners' optional responses specifically to the **feedback** that is provided to them in response to the **errors** that they make during oral **interaction** (Lyster and Ranta, 1997). Uptake is considered successful when learners repair their initially incorrect utterance; however, uptake may be unsuccessful if learners fail to repair their original error. The importance of uptake for L2 learning is debated. Some argue that, as a type of **pushed output**, uptake benefits learners because it encourages them to stretch their **interlanguage** system. In addition, uptake has been argued to be an indication of **noticing**; however, it is acknowledged that the absence of uptake does not necessarily indicate a lack of noticing. On the other hand, some argue that uptake is often mere mimicking of teachers' feedback and therefore does not involve the cognitive processes needed for L2 learning. Additionally, because uptake is optional, it cannot be essential for learning.

An example of uptake is shown below. The teacher and student are involved in an **information gap** activity. The student's use of the wrong tense, in line 1, is corrected by the teacher in line 2. The uptake occurs in line 3, and it is successful because the learner produces the correct form of the verb.

1   S: so he is in prison for six years
2   T: he has=
3   S: =has been in prison for six years
4   T: yes
(Loewen, 2004: 164–5)

Lyster, R., and Ranta, L. (1997)' Corrective feedback and learner uptake: negotiation of form in communicative classrooms', *Studies in Second Language Acquisition*, 19, 37–66.

Loewen, S. (2004) 'Uptake in incidental focus on form in meaning-focused ESL lessons', *Language Learning*, 54, 153–87.

Reinders, H. (2009) 'Learner uptake and acquisition in three grammar-oriented production activities', *Language Teaching Research*, 13, 201–22.

Usage-based theories

Theories of SLA that consider the role of **input** as fundamental to acquiring the language. Learning, in this view, is input-driven and the result of massive exposure to the language. Learners match new examples of words or syntactic structures to previously encountered examples, rather than relying principally on abstract grammar rules. Usage-based theories differ from **nativist** theories of language acquisition in that they see learning primarily as **exemplar**-based and as subject to **frequency effects**, rather than relying on some form of innate linguistic ability.

Barlow, M. and Kemmer, S. (2000) *Usage-Based Models of Language* (Stanford, CA: Center for the Study of Language and Information).

Eskildsen, S. (2009) 'Constructing another language-usage-based linguistics in second language acquisition', *Applied Linguistics*, 30, 335–57.

U-shaped development

The acquisition of a linguistic structure through a progression of stages, going from correct to incorrect and back to correct usage. For example, L2 learners of English first use the irregular past tense accurately (e.g. *he went*). As they begin to understand the rules of regular past tense formation, they tend to apply the *-ed* suffix to all verbs. In other words, they **over-generalise** and produce incorrect forms like *he goed*. Subsequently, when learners learn to distinguish between regular and irregular past tense verbs, they revert to using correct forms like *he went*. This progression reflects the **developmental sequence** for English irregular past tense. The phenomenon of U-shaped development makes it difficult to use **accuracy** as a measure of language proficiency because learners may produce incorrect linguistic forms which nevertheless can represent progress towards the accurate use of the structure.

Utterance

A unit of spoken language consisting of a sequence of words. The boundaries of utterances may be identified in several ways. In interaction, utterances are often separated by turn-taking, with a short turn comprising a single utterance. However, longer turns and monologues may be divided into separate utterances by the use of intonational contours and pauses. Utterances do not necessarily coincide with written sentences. Utterances are often a unit of analysis in SLA research on oral language.

See also **AS-unit.**

Validity

The degree to which a test or research instrument reliably measures what it is intended to measure. If an instrument is valid, then its results can be considered to be an accurate representation of what is being measured. For example, if a teacher or researcher wishes to assess the oral proficiency of L2 learners, then a valid type of test might be a spontaneous oral production task. However, a 20-minute writing test would not be a valid measure of oral proficiency. In addition to general validity, several specific types of validity are recognized. Construct validity refers to how closely a test relates to the theoretical concept that is being investigated. For example, does a test designed to measure speaking ability really do so? Concurrent validity refers to how well learners' performance on one test correlates with their performance on similar tests. For instance, learners' scores on one type of writing test should be similar to their scores on other types of writing tests. Face validity refers to how test takers and other non-testing experts feel about the test's ability to measure what it is supposed to. Ecological validity refers to the degree to which a test mimics a real-life task. As an example, a grammaticality judgement test does not have high ecological validity because it is not a type of activity that people normally engage in outside of language teaching or research. Finally, it should be noted that validity is closely related to test reliability, meaning that a testing instrument consistently measures the construct under investigation.

See also **assessment.**

Wigglesworth, G. and Elder, C. (2010) 'An investigation of the effectiveness and validity of planning time in speaking test tasks', *Language Assessment Quarterly*, 7, 1–24.

Variability

See **variation.**

Variation

The degree to which learners differ in their production of the target language. Interspeaker variation occurs when learners studying the same target language vary from each other in their production. Although such variation may be due to proficiency differences, it is also possible for learners of similar levels to differ from each other. In contrast, intraspeaker variation occurs when a learner uses different linguistic structures in different contexts. Intraspeaker variation can be systematic, in which a learner regularly uses one linguistic form in one context, but another linguistic form in another context. However, learners do not always use one form in one context and another form in another context; rather, the use of different forms is probabilistic, meaning that a given form might be more or less likely to occur in a given context. In contrast to systematic variation, free variation refers to a learner's random use of various linguistic forms in a variety of contexts. Variation can also refer to the differences in how L1 speakers and L2 learners use the target language.

The study of L2 speaker variation has been formalized in variationist perspectives of SLA. Dennis Preston, an early proponent of variation research, has identified several factors which may influence linguistic variation. Sociocultural factors may encourage learners to choose different forms in different social contexts. For example, learners may use non-contracted forms such as *I will* or *does not* in more formal contexts, and they may use contracted forms such as *I'll* and *doesn't* in more informal contexts. Another factor which may influence variation is linguistic context. One study by Young (1991) found that Chinese learners of English varied in their use of the plural marker *-s*, depending on the types of sounds that both preceded and followed the place where the *-s* should be. In addition, the plural marker was more likely to be present when there was already an indicator of plurality, such as *two* or *three*, than when there was not.

In addition to concurrent variability, variationist approaches are concerned with change over time. While it is acknowledged that the way L1 speakers use language changes over time (as is evidenced by the difference between the English that Shakespeare used in his writing as compared to the language that we use today), in L2 learning the change in language happens much more quickly as learners continue to develop their interlanguage systems.

Preston, D. (2002) 'A variationist perspective on second language acquisition: psycholinguistic concerns', in R. Kaplan (ed.) *The Oxford Handbook of Applied Linguistics* (Oxford: Oxford University Press), 141–59.

Tarone, E. (2002) 'Frequency effects, noticing, and creativity: factors in a variationist interlanguage framework', *Studies in Second Language Acquisition*, 24, 287–96.

Young, R. (1991) *Variation in Interlanguage Morphology* (New York: Peter Lang).

Verbal report

V

A research method that involves learners verbalizing their thoughts, either while (concurrently) or after (retrospectively) performing a task. For example, learners might be asked to say what they are thinking while they are revising an essay based on corrective feedback supplied by the teacher. Alternatively, learners might be shown a video of a previous class and asked to report what they were thinking at specific moments during the classroom interaction. Verbal reports are argued to provide insight into cognitive processes, such as **noticing**, that learners use during L2 production, comprehension and learning. Types of verbal reports include **immediate recalls**, **immediate reports**, **stimulated recalls**, **talk-alouds** and **think-alouds**.

See also **introspective research methods**.

Bowles, M. (2010) 'Concurrent verbal reports in second language acquisition research', *Annual Review of Applied Linguistics*, 30, 111–27.

Sachs, R. and Polio, C. (2007) 'Learners' uses of two types of written feedback on a L2 writing revision task', *Studies in Second Language Acquisition*, 29, 67–100.

Veridicality

The extent to which learners' comments provided during a retrospective **verbal report** are an accurate reflection of the learners' actual cognitive processes at an earlier point in time. For example, while watching a video of their interaction during a previous class, a learner might report noticing that one of his or her errors was corrected. If the learner did indeed notice the error correction during the classroom interaction and reported it in a subsequent verbal report, then that report is said to be veridical. If, however, the learner noticed the error correction while watching the video, but did not notice it during the original class interaction, then the subsequent verbal report is not veridical because it does not reflect the learner's thinking at the time of the event. Ensuring that learners' verbal reports are veridical is important for accurately measuring constructs such as **noticing**.

Visuo-spatial sketchpad

See **working memory**.

Vocabulary

Quite simply, vocabulary refers to the words in a language. Historically, SLA research has been primarily concerned with grammar, particularly in the wake of Chomsky's proposal of **universal grammar** theory, which focused on how innate acquisition processes assisted in the process of acquiring linguistic rules. However, over the past several decades, research into vocabulary acquisition has become a major focus in SLA research. There are several areas of investigation. One issue relates to what it means to know a word. In addition to the primary meaning of a word, there may be additional meanings, **collocations** and idioms associated with the word. Another area of interest relates to the effectiveness of various methods of vocabulary leaning. As an example, several studies have found that the **keyword technique** is a successful method for learning L2 vocabulary. Related to the issue of vocabulary instruction is the issue of **incidental acquisition**. Of course, learners may directly study and learn numerous L2 words; however, there are many more words to learn than there is time in class. Therefore, researchers have been interested in the incidental acquisition of vocabulary that may occur during extensive reading in the L2. Finally, researchers have also used linguistic **corpora** – large collections of either written or spoken language – to identify the frequency and collocation patterns in both L1 and L2 speakers' discourse. Such information can help learners and teachers decide which vocabulary items might be of most benefit to learners.

V

See also **Lexicon**.

Laufer, B. (2009) 'Research timeline: second language vocabulary acquisition from language input and from form-focused activities', *Language Teaching*, 42, 341–54.

Nation, I.S.P. (2001) *Learning Vocabulary in Another Language* (Cambridge: Cambridge University Press).

Willingness to communicate (WTC)

L2 learners' readiness to engage in L2 interaction, either inside or outside of the L2 classroom. Willingness to communicate is related to the concept of **motivation** but refers specifically to learners' inclination to initiate or participate in L2 communication. WTC has been shown to be dynamic and to be subject to change as a result of environmental factors such as the context, the interlocutor and the type of interaction. In addition, individual learner differences such as personality, perceived proficiency and communicative anxiety can also influence a learner's willingness to communicate. Figure 8 illustrates numerous layers and constructs, such as motivation and contextual factors, that can be seen as influencing WTC. In addition, the figure shows that WTC influences L2 use. It has been argued that language teachers should encourage learners' willingness to communicate to increase opportunities for L2 input and output.

MacIntyre, P. (2007) 'Willingness to communicate in the second language: understanding the decision to speak as a volitional process', *The Modern Language Journal*, 91, 564–76.

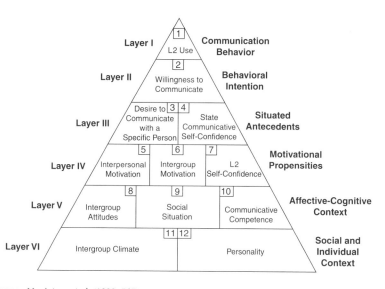

Source: MacIntyre et al. (1998: 547).

Figure 8 Heuristic model of variables influencing WTC

MacIntyre, P., Clément, R., Dörnyei, Z. and Noels, K. (1998) 'Conceptualizing willingness to communicate in a L2: a situational model of L2 confidence and affiliation', *Modern Language Journal*, 82, 545–62.

Within-task planning

The type of planning that occurs while learners are engaged in either written or spoken L2 production tasks. Within-task planning can be either pressured (i.e. timed) or unpressured (i.e. untimed), depending on the amount of time learners are allowed to complete the task. Unpressured within-task planning, which allows learners unlimited planning time, may help learners to formulate their production more accurately because they are able to monitor their production more closely. Within-task planning has also been called **on-line planning**, and it contrasts with **pre-task planning**.

See also **planning.**

Manchon, R. and Larios, J. de (2007) 'On the temporal nature of planning in L1 and L2 Composing', *Language Learning*, 57, 549–93.

Working memory

A construct that refers to a temporary memory storage system used to process and rehearse linguistic **input** and language information retrieved from **long-term memory**. Working memory is conceptually similar to short-term memory; however, the latter term has fallen into disuse in SLA and psycholinguistic research. Working memory is limited in its capacity, both in terms of the amount of information it can hold (which is thought to be around seven items for most individuals) and the amount of processing it can do. Information in working memory decays rapidly and disappears unless it is processed and committed to long-term memory. The capacity of working memory and the speed of information decay within it vary among individuals. An example of working memory in everyday life is when an individual looks up a telephone number and remembers it, often by repeating it mentally, until the number is dialled, after which the number generally exits working memory rather than being committed to long-term memory. Working memory is thought to be controlled by a central executive system which regulates processing between different tasks. Additional components of working memory include a visuo-spatial sketchpad where non-verbal material is maintained and a phonological loop where verbal material is maintained.

Some studies of working memory in SLA have investigated the effects of input rehearsal and have found that preventing such rehearsal impairs L2 acquisition. Other studies have found a significant relationship between individual differences in working memory capacity and L2 learning, with larger working memories aiding learning by enabling learners to notice more corrective feedback or to notice relationships between related elements in a sentence that are separated by intervening words or morphemes (e.g. subject–verb agreement). Working memory can be measured in several ways. For example, a reading span test can be administered in which participants are presented with multiple sets of sentences. Participants must judge the plausibility of the sentences as well as remember the last word of each sentence. After each set of sentences, participants are asked to recall the final word of each sentence. The difficulty of the task is increased by adding additional sentences to each set. Thus, the initial set may consist of only two sentences, while the maximum number of sentences is generally six. The more words a participant is able to recall, the greater is his or her working memory. One issue related to measuring working memory for L2 learners is the language in which the test is administered. It may be the case that using L2 stimuli may not accurately measure learners' working memory, particularly if they are lower proficiency learners. However, while tests of working memory may be available in some languages, they are not available in all languages.

Baddeley, A.D. (2003) 'Working memory and language: an overview', *Journal of Communication Disorders*, 36, 189–208.

Ellis, N. and Sinclair, B. (1996) 'Working memory in the acquisition of vocabulary and syntax: putting language in good order', *The Quarterly Journal of Experimental Psychology*, 49a, 234–49.

Mackey, A., Adams, R., Stafford, C. and Winke, P. (2010) 'Exploring the relationship between modified output and working memory capacity', *Language Learning*, 60, 501–33.

WTC

See **willingness to communicate.**

Z z

Zone of proximal development (ZPD)

A metaphorical construct in Vygotsky's **sociocultural theory** that represents the distance between what individuals can do on their own and what they can do with assistance from another individual. In its original formulation from developmental psychology, the ZPD was viewed as consisting of the relationship between a novice (generally a child) and an expert (usually an adult). In SLA theory, the relationship between the novice learner and expert teacher is also viewed as important in enabling the learner to do more on his or her own. However, SLA theory has also shown that learners can assist each other in the ZPD, with the result that they may be able to produce language together that is more advanced than either one could produce individually.

See also **scaffolding.**

Guerrero, M. and Villamil, O. (2000) 'Activating the ZPD: mutual scaffolding in L2 peer revision', *The Modern Language Journal*, 84, 51–68.

Nassaji, H. and Swain, M. (2000) 'A Vygotskian perspective on corrective feedback in L2: the effect of random versus negotiated help on the learning of English articles', *Language Awareness*, 9, 34–51.

Key References

Doughty, C. and Long, M. (2003) *The Handbook of Second Language Acquisition* (Malden, MA: Blackwell).

Ellis, R. (2008) *The Study of SLA*, 2nd edn (Oxford: Oxford University Press).

Gass, S. and Selinker, L. (2008) *Second Language Acquisition: An Introductory Course*, 3rd edn (New York: Routledge).

Hinkel, E. (2005) *Handbook of Research in Second Language Teaching and Learning* (Mahwah, NJ: Lawrence Erlbaum).

Lightbown, P. and Spada, N. (2006) *How Languages Are Learned*, 3rd edn (Oxford: Oxford University Press).

Ortega, L. (2009) *Understanding Second Language Acquisition* (London: Hodder Arnold).

Saville-Troike, M. (2006) *Introducing Second Language Acquisition* (Cambridge: Cambridge University Press).

VanPatten, B. and Williams, J. (2007) *Theories in Second Language Acquisition: An Introduction* (Mahwah, NJ: Lawrence Erlbaum).

Index